the GRAYAREA™

ALL OF THIS CAN BE YOURS

i®

IMAGE COMICS, INC.
Erik Larsen - *Publisher*
Todd McFarlane - *President*
Marc Silvestri - *CEO*
Jim Valentino - *Vice-President*
Eric Stephenson - *Executive Director*
Missie Miranda - *Controller*
Brett Evans - *Production Manager*
B. Clay Moore - *PR & Marketing Coordinator*
Allen Hui - *Production Artist*
Joe Keatinge - *Traffic Manager*
Mia MacHatton - *Administrative Assistant*
www.imagecomics.com

THE GRAY AREA, VOL. 1: ALL OF THIS CAN BE YOURS, 2005. Published by Image Comics, Inc., Office publication: 1942 University Avenue, Suite 305, Berkeley, California 94704. Copyright © 2005 John Romita and Glen Brunswick. All rights reserved. The Gray Area™ (including all prominent characters featured in issue), The Gray Area™ logo and all The Gray Area™ character likenesses are trademarks of John Romita, Jr. Glen Brunswick, unless otherwise noted. Image Comics® is a trademark of Image Comics, Inc. All rights reser No part of this publication may be reproduced or transmitted, in any form or by any means (except for for sh excerpts for review purposes) without the express written permission of Image Comics, Inc. All nam characters, events and locales in this publication are entirely fictional. Any resemblance to actual pers (living or dead), events or places, without satiric intent, is coincidental. PRINTED IN CANADA

written by
GLEN BRUNSWICK

pencils by
JOHN ROMITA, JR.

inks by
KLAUS JANSON

letters by
JOHN WORKMAN

colors by
BILL CRABTREE

created by
JOHN ROMITA, JR.
& GLEN BRUNSWICK

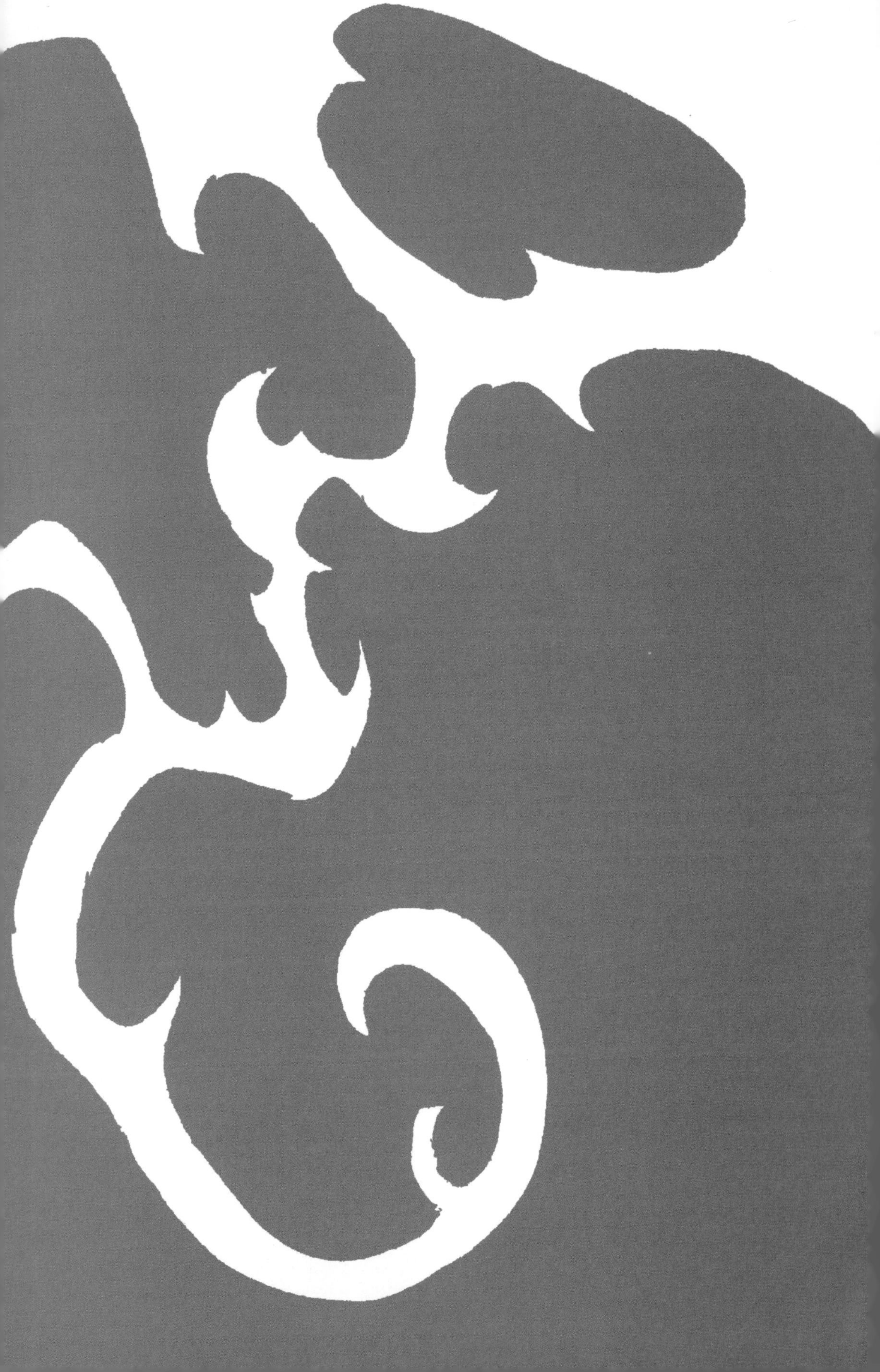

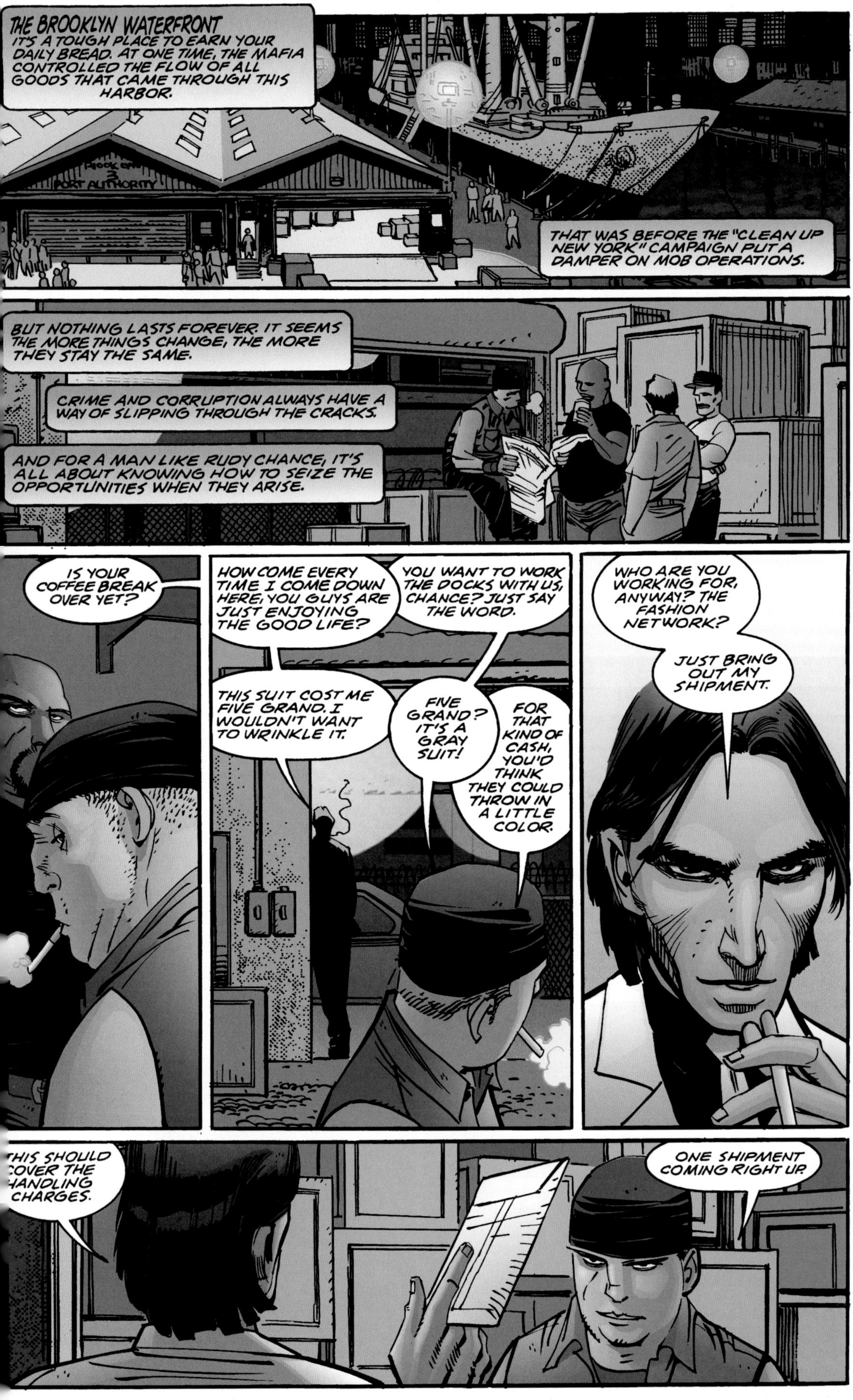
THE BROOKLYN WATERFRONT
IT'S A TOUGH PLACE TO EARN YOUR DAILY BREAD. AT ONE TIME, THE MAFIA CONTROLLED THE FLOW OF ALL GOODS THAT CAME THROUGH THIS HARBOR.
PORT AUTHORITY
THAT WAS BEFORE THE "CLEAN UP NEW YORK" CAMPAIGN PUT A DAMPER ON MOB OPERATIONS.
BUT NOTHING LASTS FOREVER. IT SEEMS THE MORE THINGS CHANGE, THE MORE THEY STAY THE SAME.
CRIME AND CORRUPTION ALWAYS HAVE A WAY OF SLIPPING THROUGH THE CRACKS.
AND FOR A MAN LIKE RUDY CHANCE, IT'S ALL ABOUT KNOWING HOW TO SEIZE THE OPPORTUNITIES WHEN THEY ARISE.
IS YOUR COFFEE BREAK OVER YET?
HOW COME EVERY TIME I COME DOWN HERE, YOU GUYS ARE JUST ENJOYING THE GOOD LIFE?
YOU WANT TO WORK THE DOCKS WITH US, CHANCE? JUST SAY THE WORD.
THIS SUIT COST ME FIVE GRAND. I WOULDN'T WANT TO WRINKLE IT.
FIVE GRAND? IT'S A GRAY SUIT!
FOR THAT KIND OF CASH, YOU'D THINK THEY COULD THROW IN A LITTLE COLOR.
WHO ARE YOU WORKING FOR, ANYWAY? THE FASHION NETWORK?
JUST BRING OUT MY SHIPMENT.
THIS SHOULD COVER THE HANDLING CHARGES.
ONE SHIPMENT COMING RIGHT UP.

MAKE SURE YOU SEND KARL MY REGARDS.

I DIDN'T KNOW KARL HAD ANY FRIENDS.

HE DOESN'T. THE BASTARD.

HE WAS KGB. HE BEAT ME PRETTY BADLY ONCE. FRACTURED MY SKULL.

BUT WHEN I CAME TO THE U.S., HE GOT ME THIS JOB.

I'LL SEND HIM YOUR LOVE.

YEAH, YOU DO THAT.

THE WESTSIDE HIGHWAY! WHAT A JOKE! HOW THEY CAN CALL THIS TWO-LANE OVERCROWDED STREET A "HIGHWAY" IS BEYOND ME.

A PIT STOP IN MANHATTAN SHOULDN'T TAKE TOO MUCH TIME.

I'VE GOT TO DEPOSIT ONE OF THESE BOXES INTO THE RUDY CHANCE RETIREMENT FUND. AFTER ALL, A MAN'S GOT TO TAKE CARE OF HIMSELF.

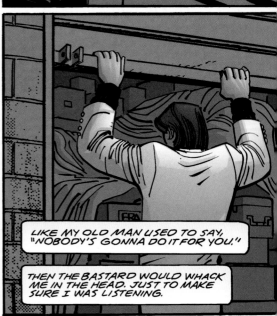

LIKE MY OLD MAN USED TO SAY, "NOBODY'S GONNA DO IT FOR YOU."

THEN THE BASTARD WOULD WHACK ME IN THE HEAD. JUST TO MAKE SURE I WAS LISTENING.

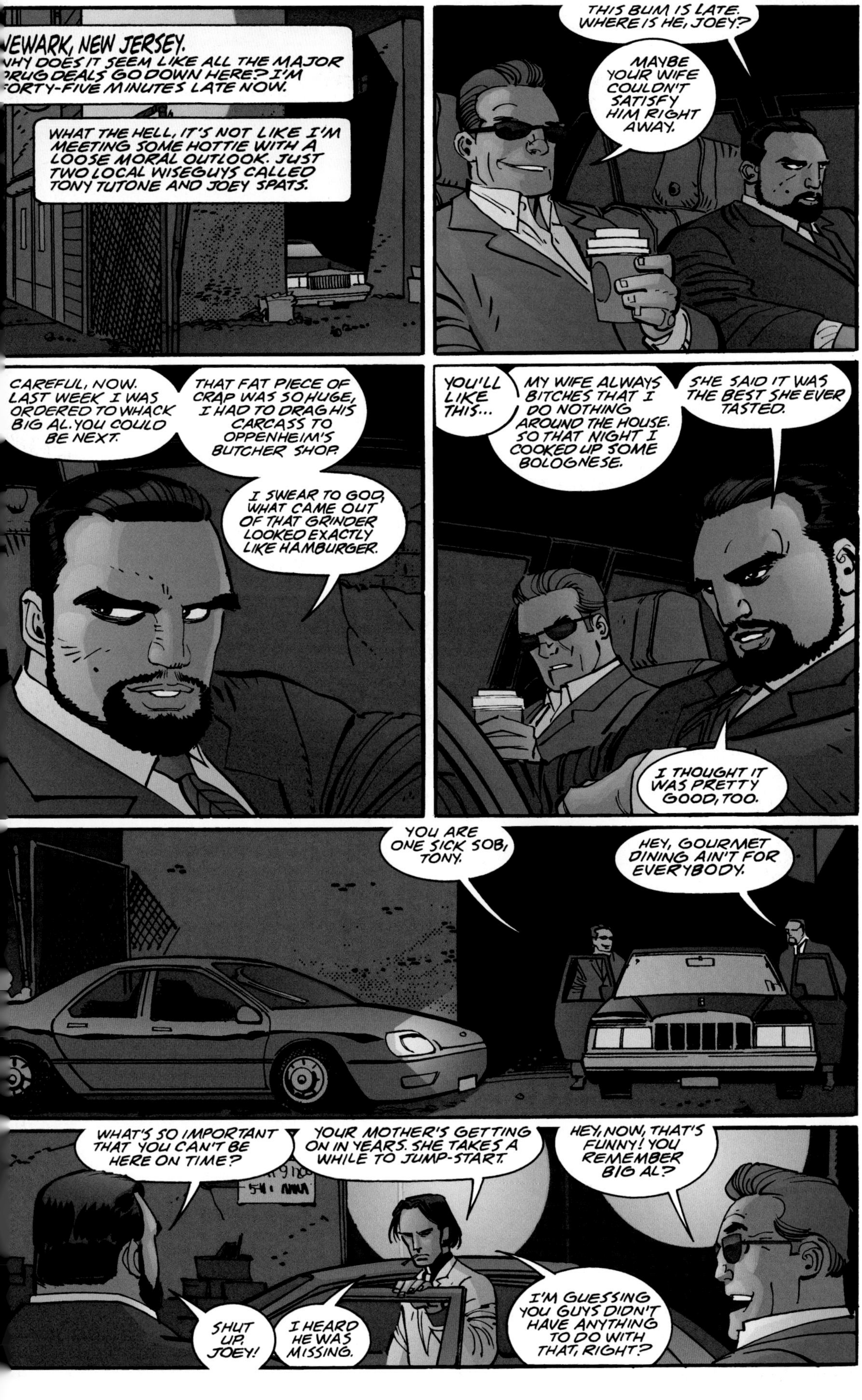
NEWARK, NEW JERSEY.
WHY DOES IT SEEM LIKE ALL THE MAJOR DRUG DEALS GO DOWN HERE? I'M FORTY-FIVE MINUTES LATE NOW.
WHAT THE HELL, IT'S NOT LIKE I'M MEETING SOME HOTTIE WITH A LOOSE MORAL OUTLOOK. JUST TWO LOCAL WISEGUYS CALLED TONY TUTONE AND JOEY SPATS.
THIS BUM IS LATE. WHERE IS HE, JOEY?
MAYBE YOUR WIFE COULDN'T SATISFY HIM RIGHT AWAY.
CAREFUL, NOW. LAST WEEK I WAS ORDERED TO WHACK BIG AL. YOU COULD BE NEXT.
THAT FAT PIECE OF CRAP WAS SO HUGE, I HAD TO DRAG HIS CARCASS TO OPPENHEIM'S BUTCHER SHOP.
I SWEAR TO GOD, WHAT CAME OUT OF THAT GRINDER LOOKED EXACTLY LIKE HAMBURGER.
YOU'LL LIKE THIS...
MY WIFE ALWAYS BITCHES THAT I DO NOTHING AROUND THE HOUSE. SO THAT NIGHT I COOKED UP SOME BOLOGNESE.
SHE SAID IT WAS THE BEST SHE EVER TASTED.
I THOUGHT IT WAS PRETTY GOOD, TOO.
YOU ARE ONE SICK SOB, TONY.
HEY, GOURMET DINING AIN'T FOR EVERYBODY.
WHAT'S SO IMPORTANT THAT YOU CAN'T BE HERE ON TIME?
YOUR MOTHER'S GETTING ON IN YEARS. SHE TAKES A WHILE TO JUMP-START.
HEY, NOW, THAT'S FUNNY! YOU REMEMBER BIG AL?
SHUT UP, JOEY!
I HEARD HE WAS MISSING.
I'M GUESSING YOU GUYS DIDN'T HAVE ANYTHING TO DO WITH THAT, RIGHT?

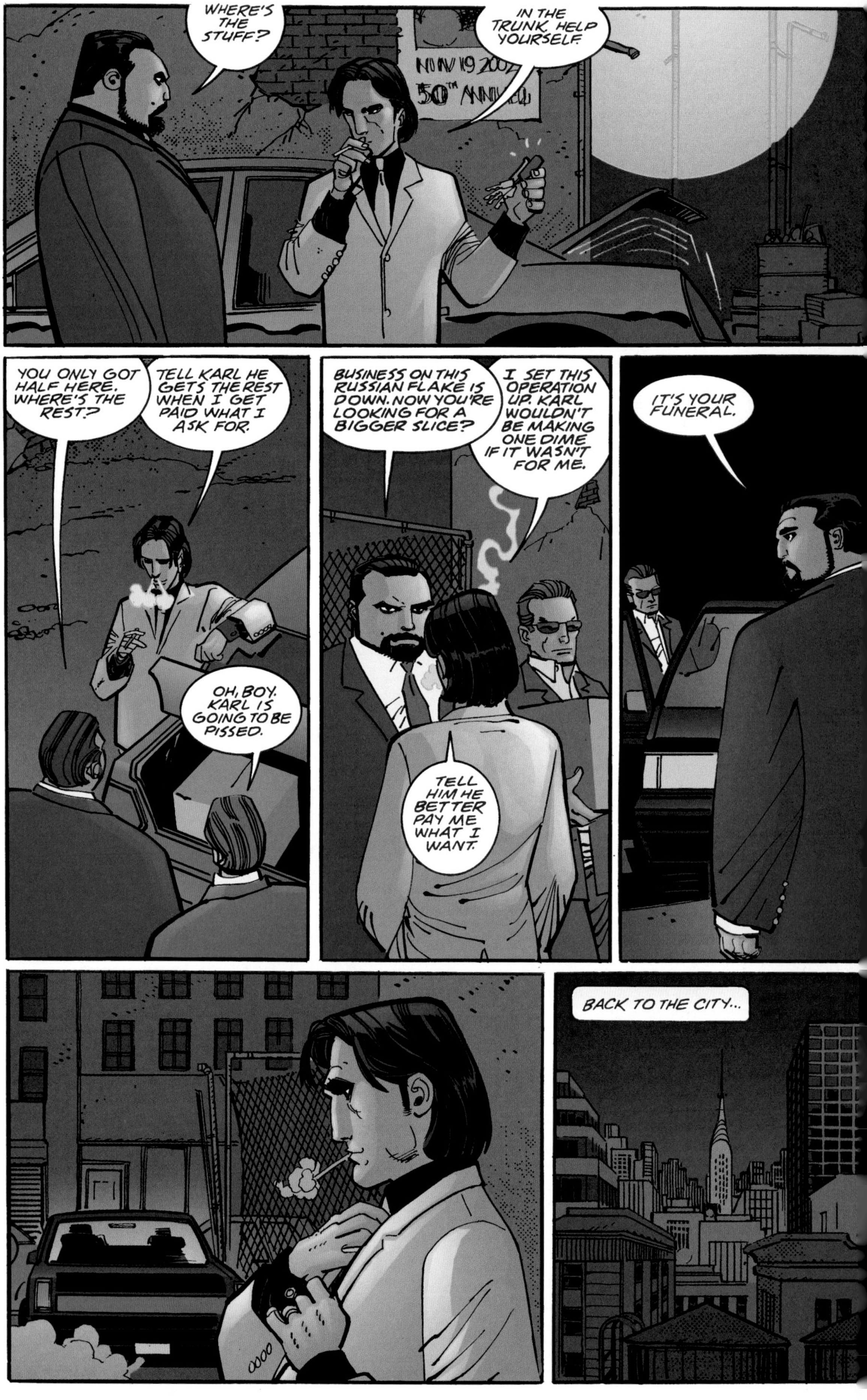
WHERE'S THE STUFF?
IN THE TRUNK. HELP YOURSELF.
NOV 19 2002 50TH ANNIV
YOU ONLY GOT HALF HERE. WHERE'S THE REST?
TELL KARL HE GETS THE REST WHEN I GET PAID WHAT I ASK FOR.
OH, BOY. KARL IS GOING TO BE PISSED.
BUSINESS ON THIS RUSSIAN FLAKE IS DOWN. NOW YOU'RE LOOKING FOR A BIGGER SLICE?
I SET THIS OPERATION UP. KARL WOULDN'T BE MAKING ONE DIME IF IT WASN'T FOR ME.
TELL HIM HE BETTER PAY ME WHAT I WANT.
IT'S YOUR FUNERAL.
BACK TO THE CITY...

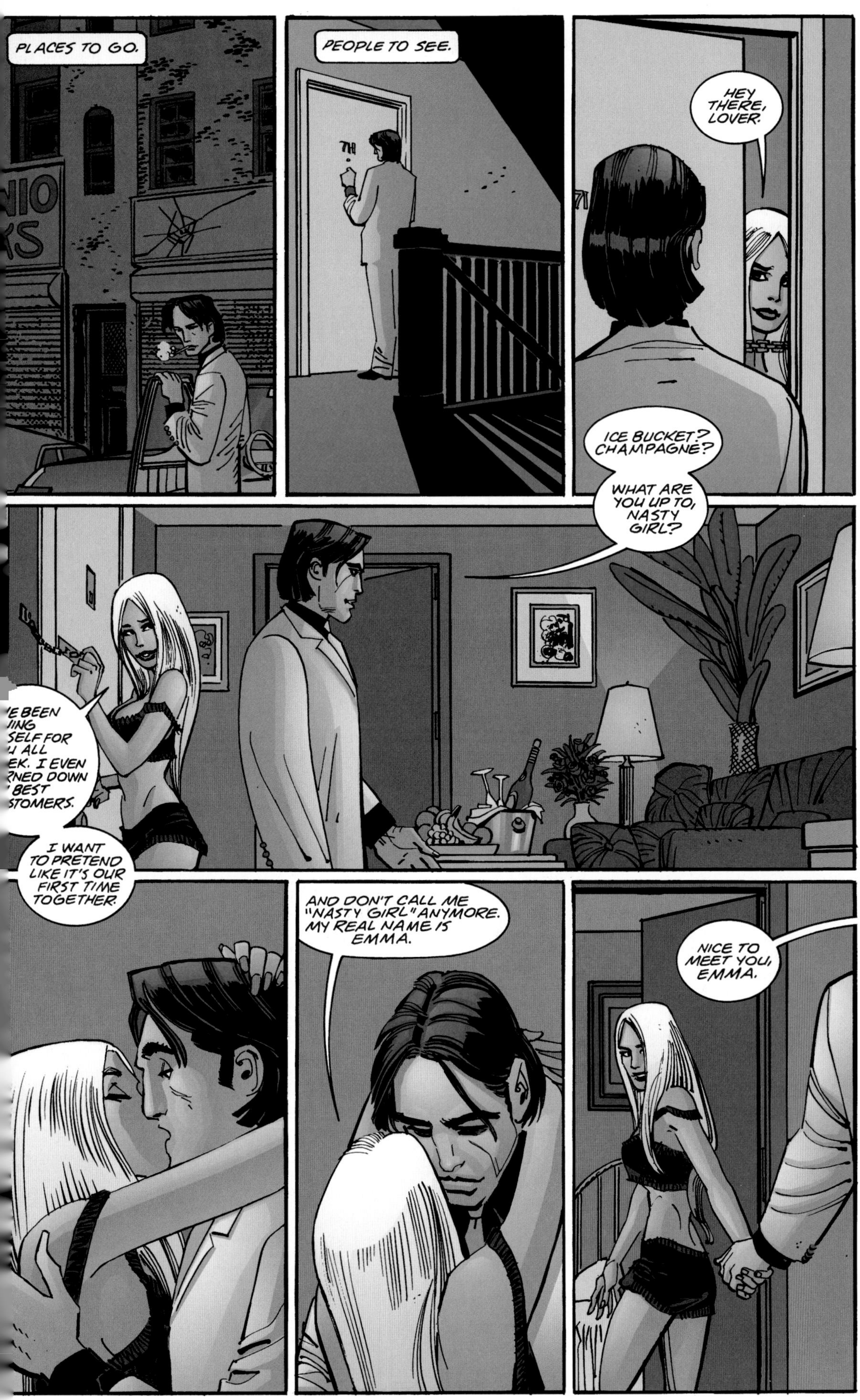
PLACES TO GO.
PEOPLE TO SEE.
HEY THERE, LOVER.
ICE BUCKET? CHAMPAGNE?
WHAT ARE YOU UP TO, NASTY GIRL?
'VE BEEN ING SELF FOR U ALL EK. I EVEN RNED DOWN BEST STOMERS.
I WANT TO PRETEND LIKE IT'S OUR FIRST TIME TOGETHER.
AND DON'T CALL ME "NASTY GIRL" ANYMORE. MY REAL NAME IS EMMA.
NICE TO MEET YOU, EMMA.

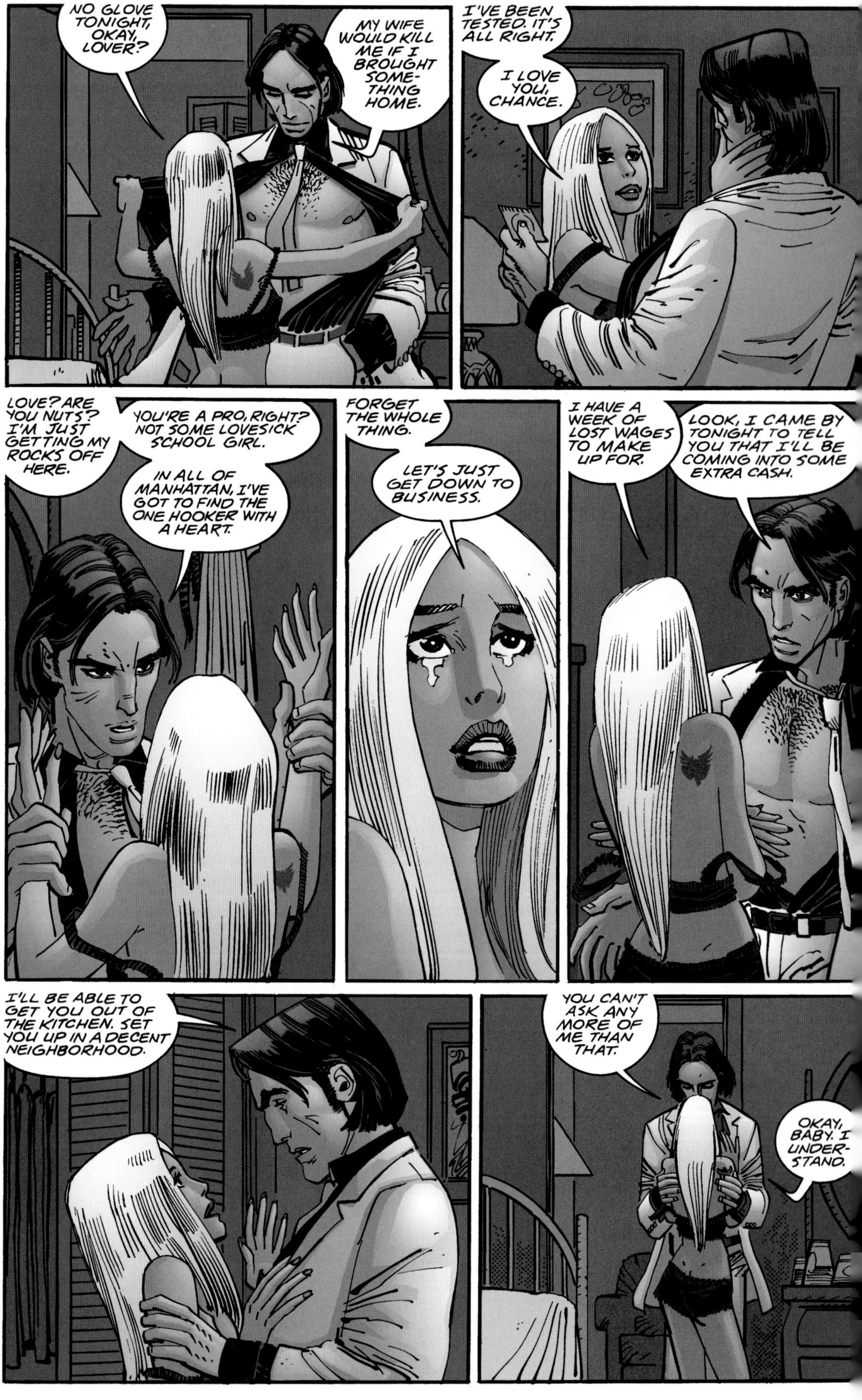
NO GLOVE TONIGHT, OKAY, LOVER?
MY WIFE WOULD KILL ME IF I BROUGHT SOME-THING HOME.
I'VE BEEN TESTED. IT'S ALL RIGHT.
I LOVE YOU, CHANCE.
LOVE? ARE YOU NUTS? I'M JUST GETTING MY ROCKS OFF HERE.
YOU'RE A PRO, RIGHT? NOT SOME LOVESICK SCHOOL GIRL.
IN ALL OF MANHATTAN, I'VE GOT TO FIND THE ONE HOOKER WITH A HEART.
FORGET THE WHOLE THING.
LET'S JUST GET DOWN TO BUSINESS.
I HAVE A WEEK OF LOST WAGES TO MAKE UP FOR.
LOOK, I CAME BY TONIGHT TO TELL YOU THAT I'LL BE COMING INTO SOME EXTRA CASH.
I'LL BE ABLE TO GET YOU OUT OF THE KITCHEN. SET YOU UP IN A DECENT NEIGHBORHOOD.
YOU CAN'T ASK ANY MORE OF ME THAN THAT.
OKAY, BABY. I UNDER-STAND.

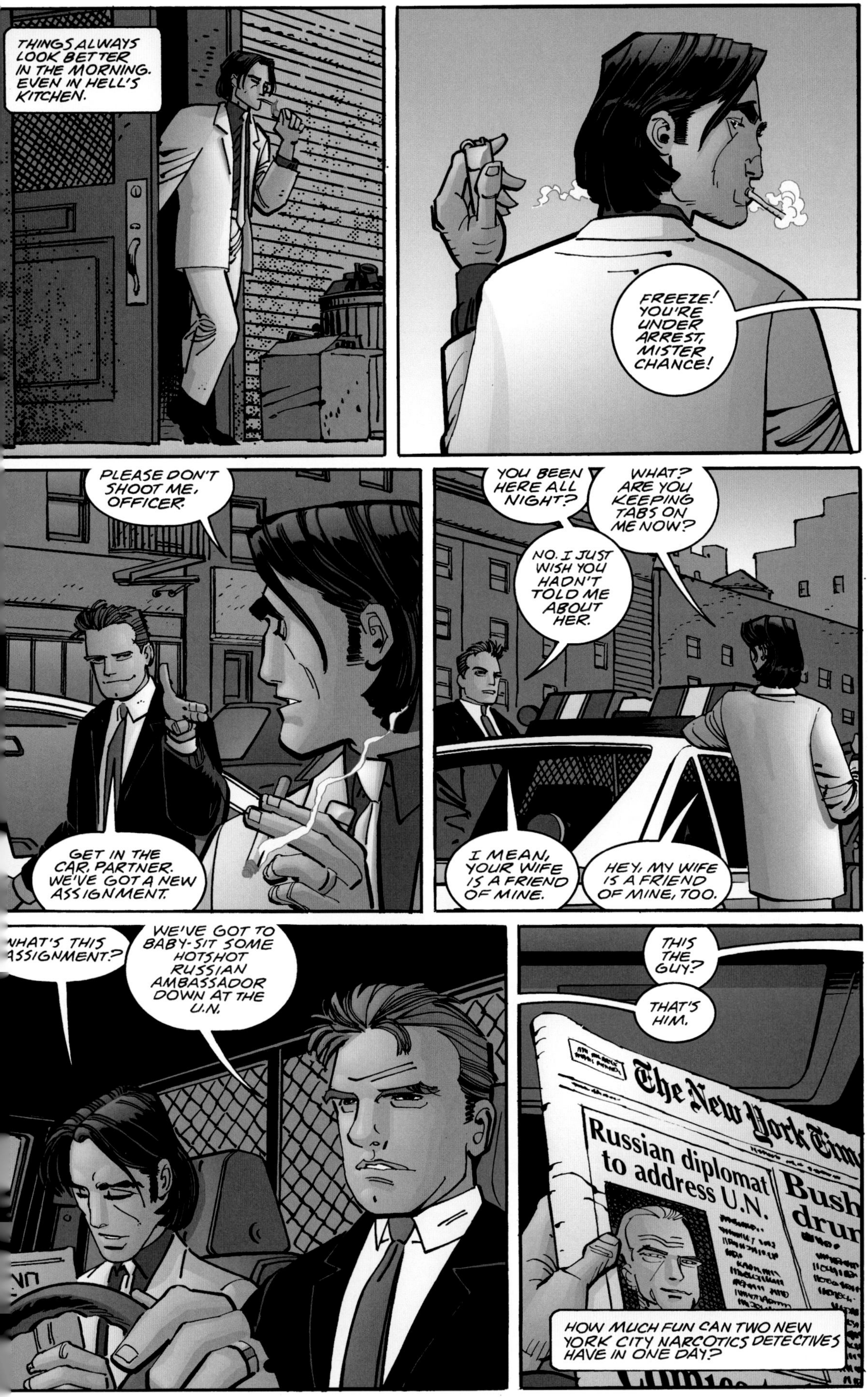
THINGS ALWAYS LOOK BETTER IN THE MORNING. EVEN IN HELL'S KITCHEN.
FREEZE! YOU'RE UNDER ARREST, MISTER CHANCE!
PLEASE DON'T SHOOT ME, OFFICER.
GET IN THE CAR, PARTNER. WE'VE GOT A NEW ASSIGNMENT.
YOU BEEN HERE ALL NIGHT?
WHAT? ARE YOU KEEPING TABS ON ME NOW?
NO. I JUST WISH YOU HADN'T TOLD ME ABOUT HER.
I MEAN, YOUR WIFE IS A FRIEND OF MINE.
HEY, MY WIFE IS A FRIEND OF MINE, TOO.
WHAT'S THIS ASSIGNMENT?
WE'VE GOT TO BABY-SIT SOME HOTSHOT RUSSIAN AMBASSADOR DOWN AT THE U.N.
THIS THE GUY?
THAT'S HIM.
The New York Times
Russian diplomat to address U.N.
Bush
HOW MUCH FUN CAN TWO NEW YORK CITY NARCOTICS DETECTIVES HAVE IN ONE DAY?

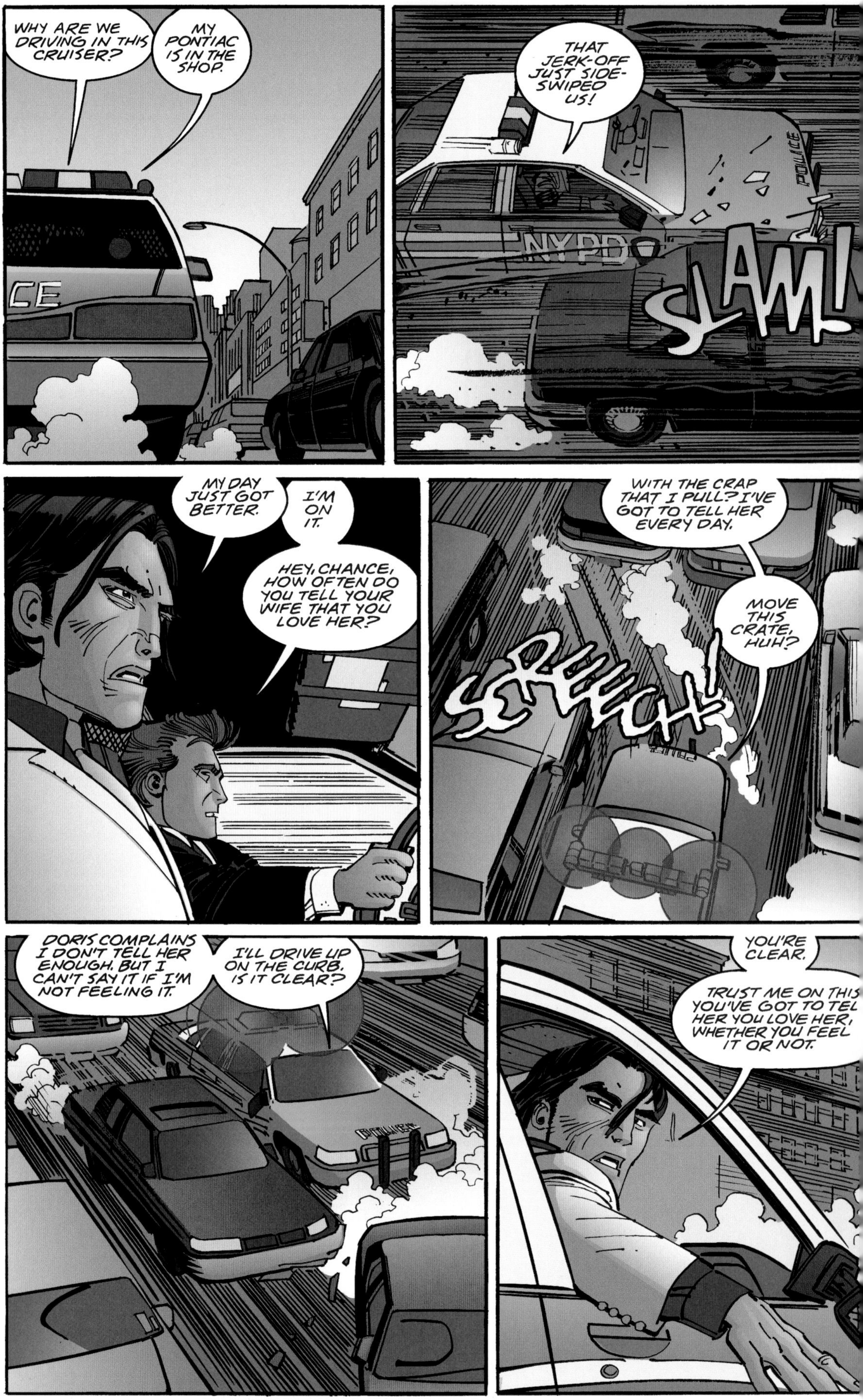

WHY ARE WE DRIVING IN THIS CRUISER?
MY PONTIAC IS IN THE SHOP.
THAT JERK-OFF JUST SIDE-SWIPED US!
SLAM!
MY DAY JUST GOT BETTER.
I'M ON IT.
HEY, CHANCE, HOW OFTEN DO YOU TELL YOUR WIFE THAT YOU LOVE HER?
WITH THE CRAP THAT I PULL? I'VE GOT TO TELL HER EVERY DAY.
MOVE THIS CRATE, HUH?
SCREEECH!
DORIS COMPLAINS I DON'T TELL HER ENOUGH. BUT I CAN'T SAY IT IF I'M NOT FEELING IT.
I'LL DRIVE UP ON THE CURB. IS IT CLEAR?
YOU'RE CLEAR.
TRUST ME ON THIS YOU'VE GOT TO TEL HER YOU LOVE HER, WHETHER YOU FEEL IT OR NOT.

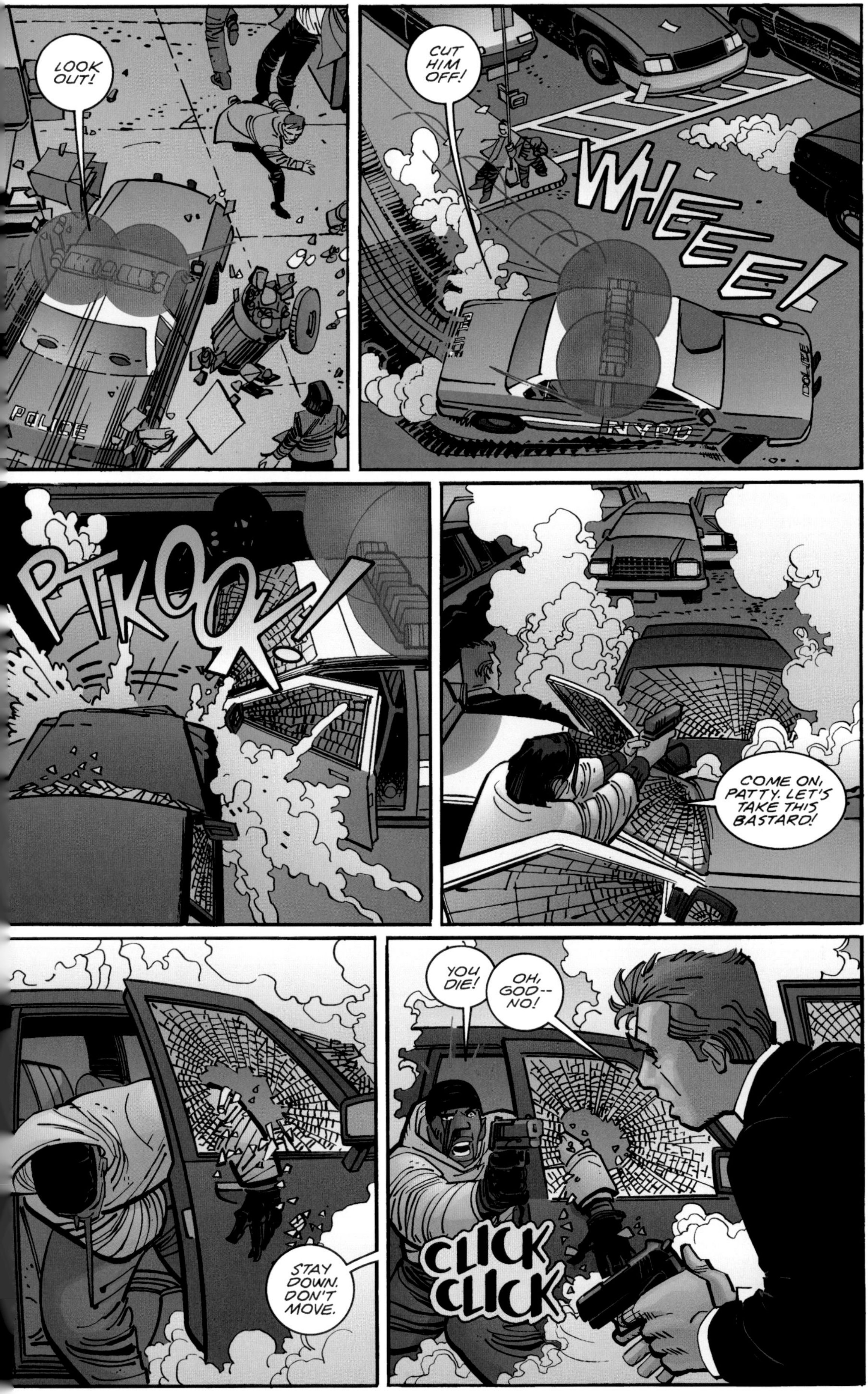
LOOK OUT!
CUT HIM OFF!
WHEEEE!
POLICE
NYPD
PTKOOW!
COME ON, PATTY. LET'S TAKE THIS BASTARD!
STAY DOWN. DON'T MOVE.
YOU DIE!
OH, GOD-- NO!
CLICK CLICK

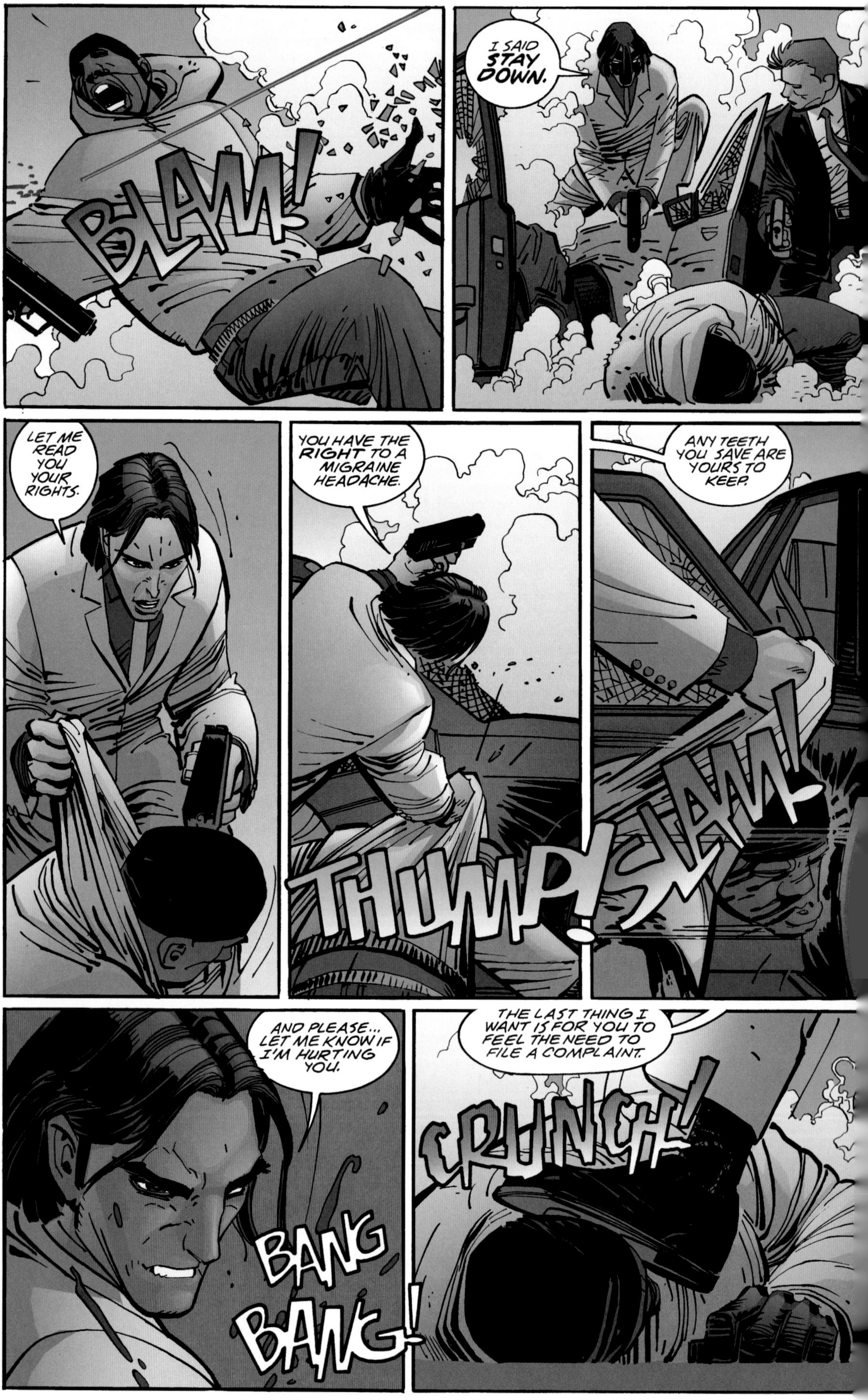
BLAM!
I SAID STAY DOWN.
LET ME READ YOU YOUR RIGHTS.
YOU HAVE THE RIGHT TO A MIGRAINE HEADACHE.
ANY TEETH YOU SAVE ARE YOURS TO KEEP.
THUMP!
SLAM!
AND PLEASE... LET ME KNOW IF I'M HURTING YOU.
BANG BANG!
THE LAST THING I WANT IS FOR YOU TO FEEL THE NEED TO FILE A COMPLAINT.
CRUNCH!

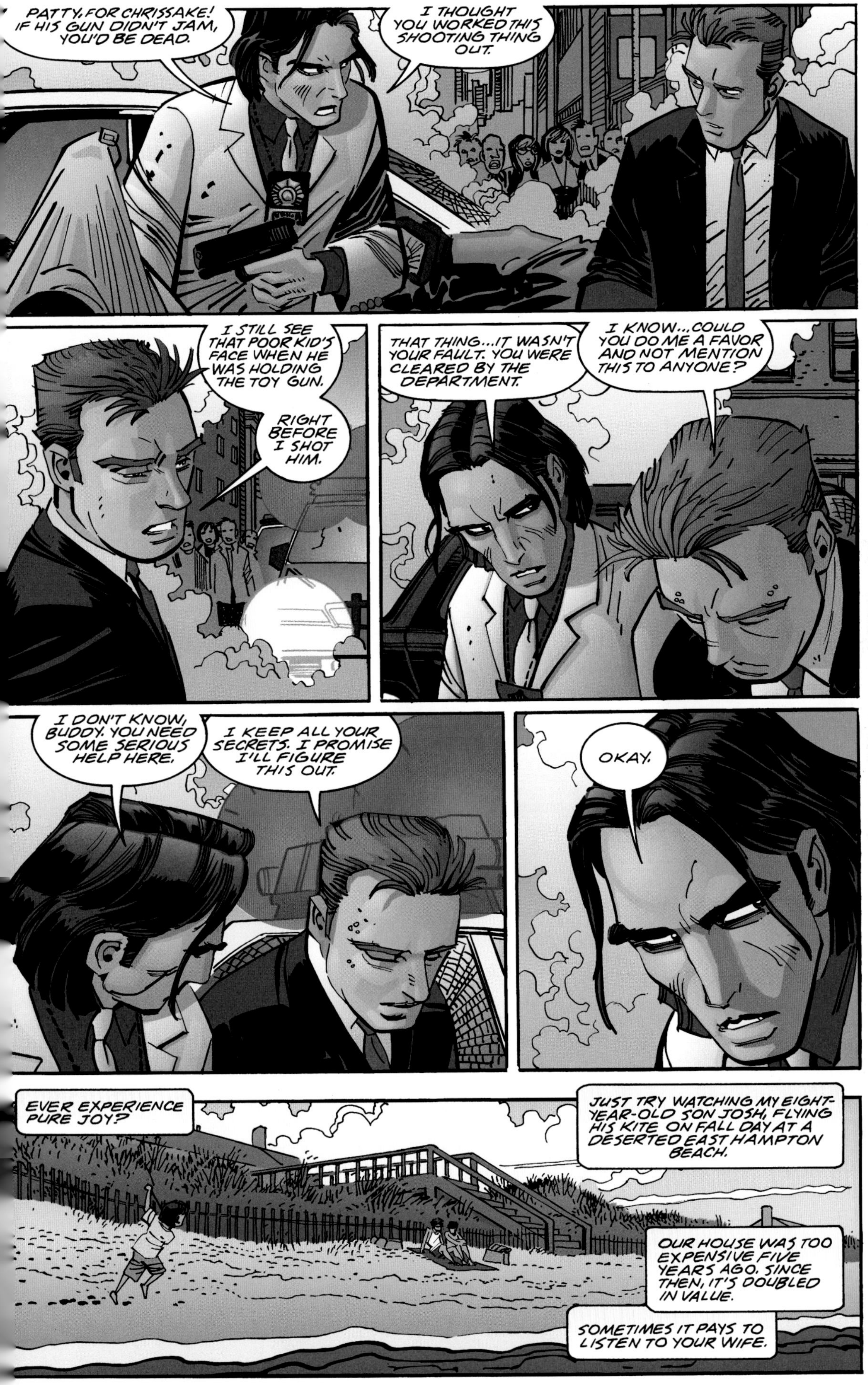
PATTY, FOR CHRISSAKE! IF HIS GUN DIDN'T JAM, YOU'D BE DEAD.
I THOUGHT YOU WORKED THIS SHOOTING THING OUT.
I STILL SEE THAT POOR KID'S FACE WHEN HE WAS HOLDING THE TOY GUN.
RIGHT BEFORE I SHOT HIM.
THAT THING...IT WASN'T YOUR FAULT. YOU WERE CLEARED BY THE DEPARTMENT.
I KNOW...COULD YOU DO ME A FAVOR AND NOT MENTION THIS TO ANYONE?
I DON'T KNOW, BUDDY. YOU NEED SOME SERIOUS HELP HERE.
I KEEP ALL YOUR SECRETS. I PROMISE I'LL FIGURE THIS OUT.
OKAY.
EVER EXPERIENCE PURE JOY?
JUST TRY WATCHING MY EIGHT-YEAR-OLD SON JOSH, FLYING HIS KITE ON FALL DAY AT A DESERTED EAST HAMPTON BEACH.
OUR HOUSE WAS TOO EXPENSIVE FIVE YEARS AGO. SINCE THEN, IT'S DOUBLED IN VALUE.
SOMETIMES IT PAYS TO LISTEN TO YOUR WIFE.

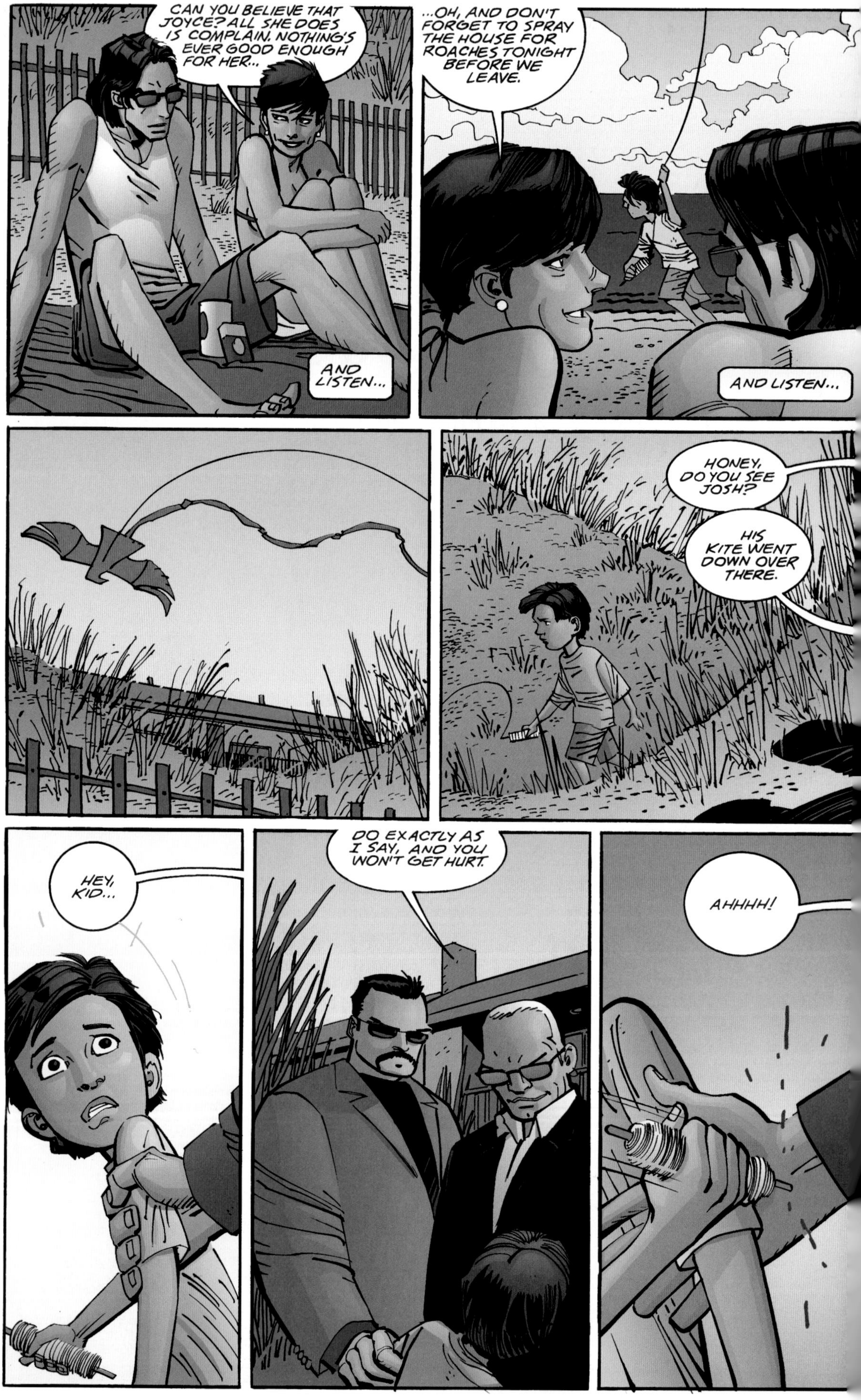
CAN YOU BELIEVE THAT JOYCE? ALL SHE DOES IS COMPLAIN. NOTHING'S EVER GOOD ENOUGH FOR HER...
AND LISTEN...
...OH, AND DON'T FORGET TO SPRAY THE HOUSE FOR ROACHES TONIGHT BEFORE WE LEAVE.
AND LISTEN...
HONEY, DO YOU SEE JOSH?
HIS KITE WENT DOWN OVER THERE.
HEY, KID...
DO EXACTLY AS I SAY, AND YOU WON'T GET HURT.
AHHHH!

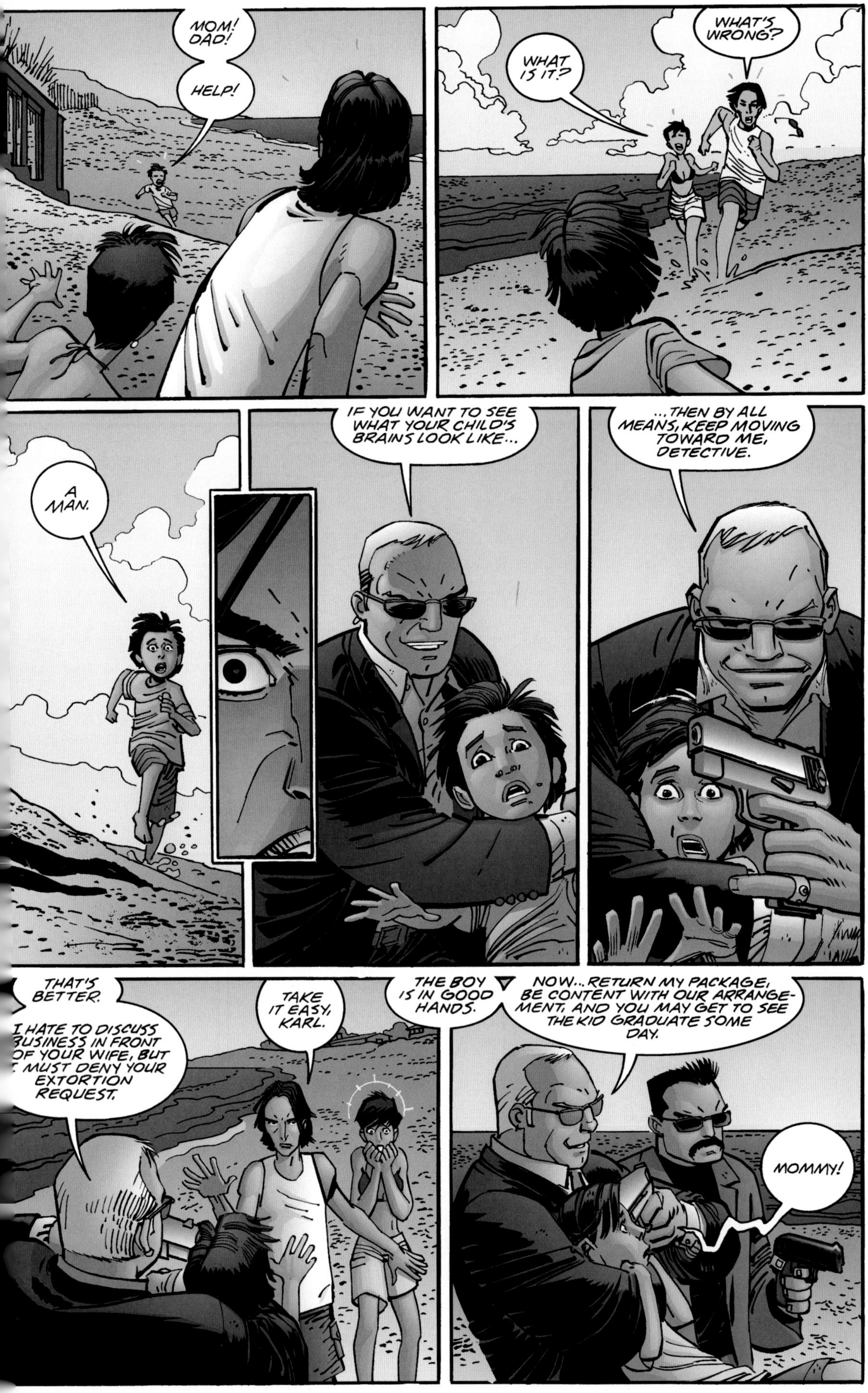
MOM! DAD!
HELP!
WHAT IS IT?
WHAT'S WRONG?
A MAN.
IF YOU WANT TO SEE WHAT YOUR CHILD'S BRAINS LOOK LIKE...
...THEN BY ALL MEANS, KEEP MOVING TOWARD ME, DETECTIVE.
THAT'S BETTER.
I HATE TO DISCUSS BUSINESS IN FRONT OF YOUR WIFE, BUT I MUST DENY YOUR EXTORTION REQUEST.
TAKE IT EASY, KARL.
THE BOY IS IN GOOD HANDS.
NOW...RETURN MY PACKAGE, BE CONTENT WITH OUR ARRANGEMENT, AND YOU MAY GET TO SEE THE KID GRADUATE SOME DAY.
MOMMY!

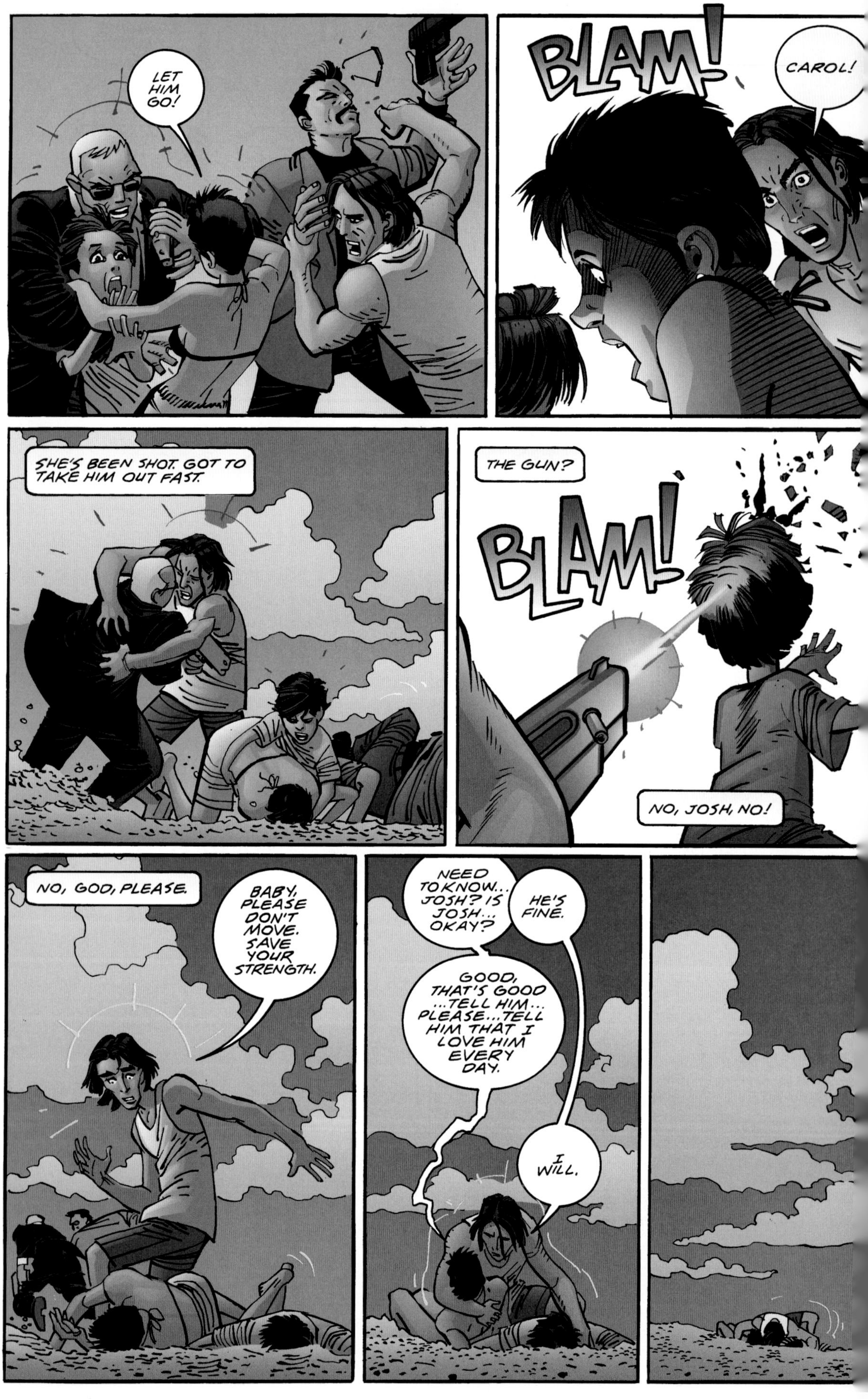
LET HIM GO!
BLAM!
CAROL!
SHE'S BEEN SHOT. GOT TO TAKE HIM OUT FAST.
THE GUN?
BLAM!
NO, JOSH, NO!
NO, GOD, PLEASE.
BABY, PLEASE DON'T MOVE. SAVE YOUR STRENGTH.
NEED TO KNOW... JOSH? IS JOSH... OKAY?
HE'S FINE.
GOOD, THAT'S GOOD ...TELL HIM... PLEASE...TELL HIM THAT I LOVE HIM EVERY DAY.
I WILL.

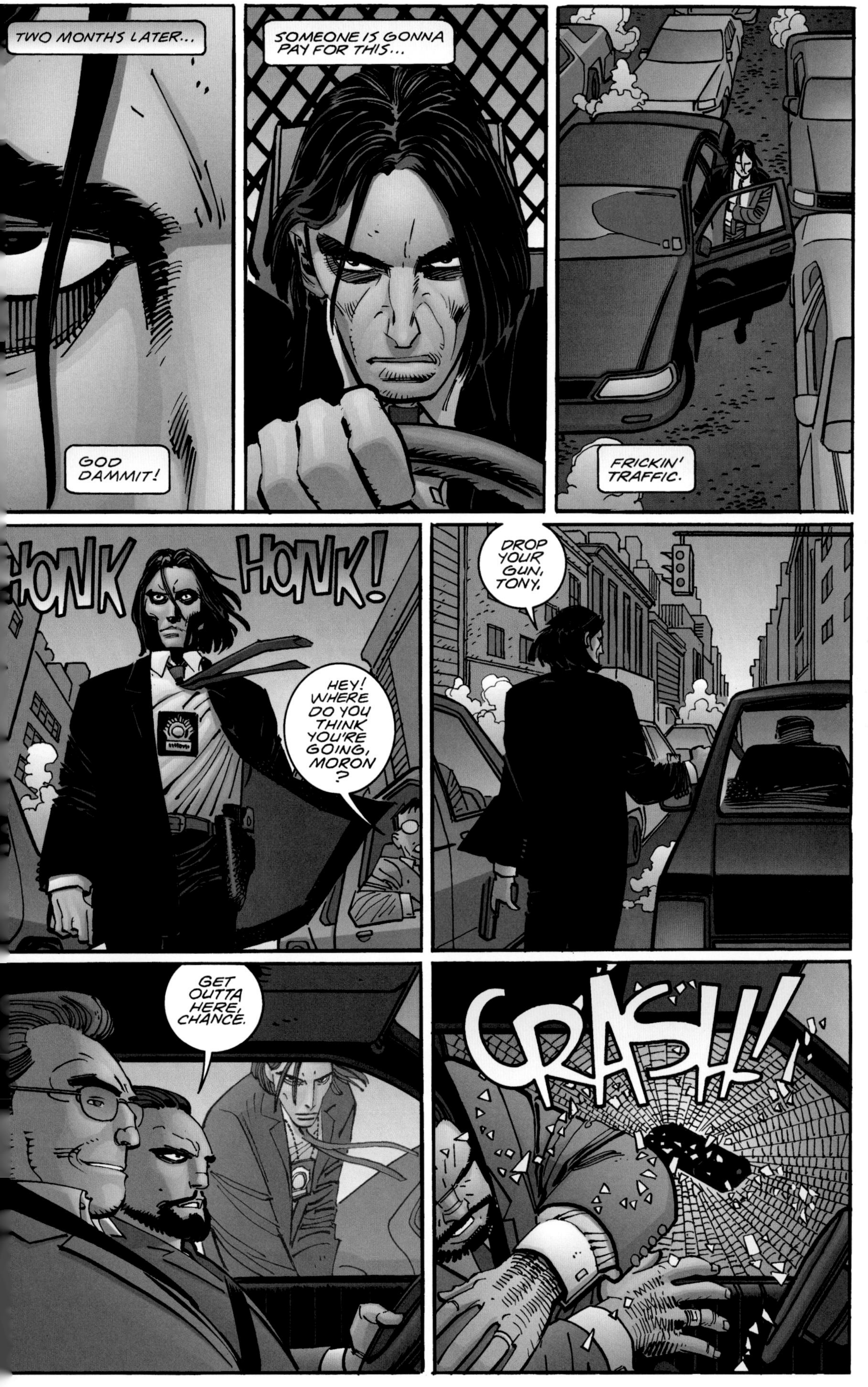
TWO MONTHS LATER...
GOD DAMMIT!
SOMEONE IS GONNA PAY FOR THIS...
FRICKIN' TRAFFIC.
HONK HONK!
HEY! WHERE DO YOU THINK YOU'RE GOING, MORON?
DROP YOUR GUN, TONY.
GET OUTTA HERE, CHANCE.
CRASH!!

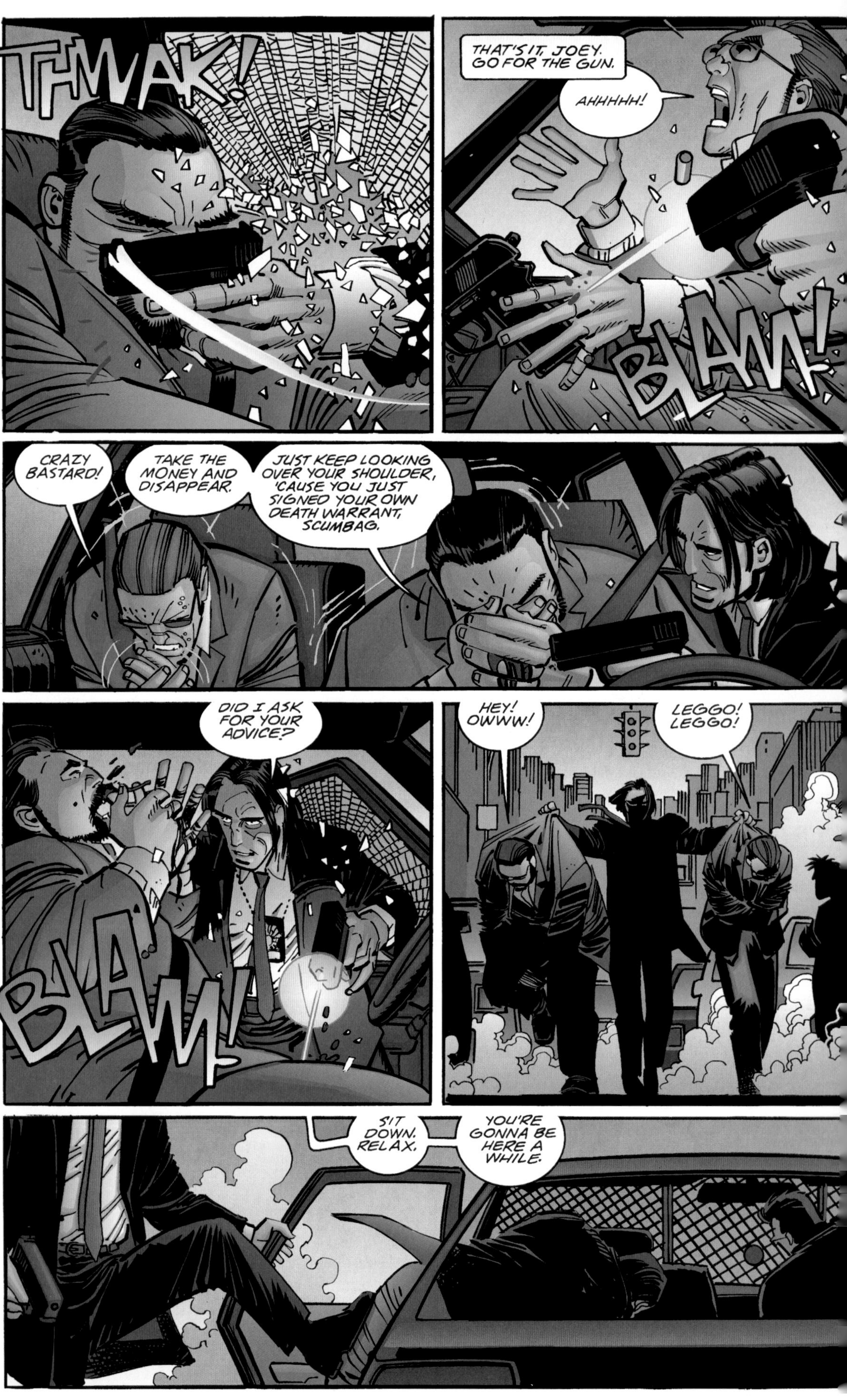
THWAK!
THAT'S IT, JOEY. GO FOR THE GUN.
AHHHHH!
BLAM!
CRAZY BASTARD!
TAKE THE MONEY AND DISAPPEAR.
JUST KEEP LOOKING OVER YOUR SHOULDER, 'CAUSE YOU JUST SIGNED YOUR OWN DEATH WARRANT, SCUMBAG.
DID I ASK FOR YOUR ADVICE?
BLAM!
HEY! OWWW!
LEGGO! LEGGO!
SIT DOWN. RELAX.
YOU'RE GONNA BE HERE A WHILE.

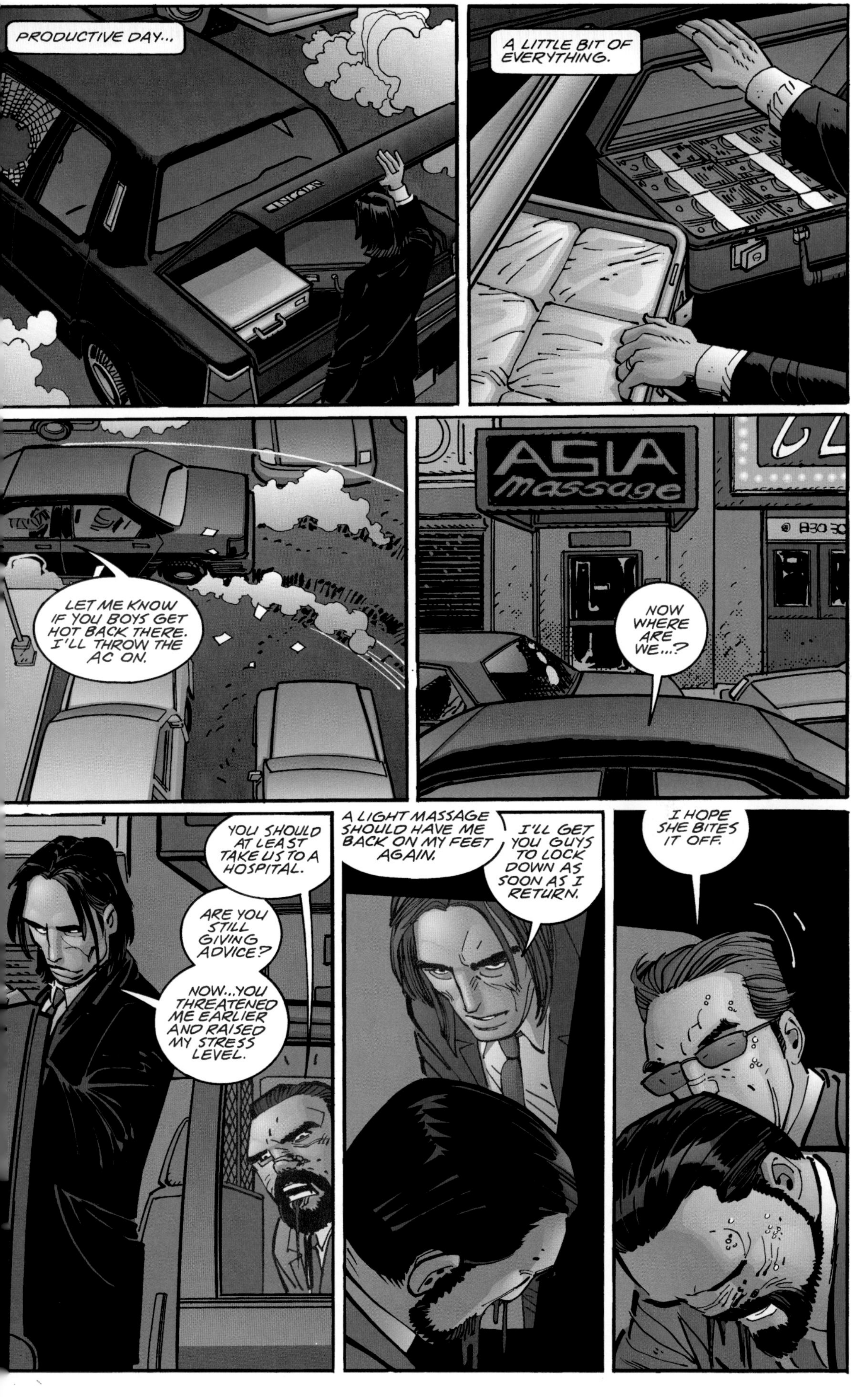
PRODUCTIVE DAY...
A LITTLE BIT OF EVERYTHING.
LET ME KNOW IF YOU BOYS GET HOT BACK THERE. I'LL THROW THE AC ON.
ASIA massage
NOW WHERE ARE WE...?
YOU SHOULD AT LEAST TAKE US TO A HOSPITAL.
ARE YOU STILL GIVING ADVICE?
NOW...YOU THREATENED ME EARLIER AND RAISED MY STRESS LEVEL.
A LIGHT MASSAGE SHOULD HAVE ME BACK ON MY FEET AGAIN.
I'LL GET YOU GUYS TO LOCK DOWN AS SOON AS I RETURN.
I HOPE SHE BITES IT OFF.

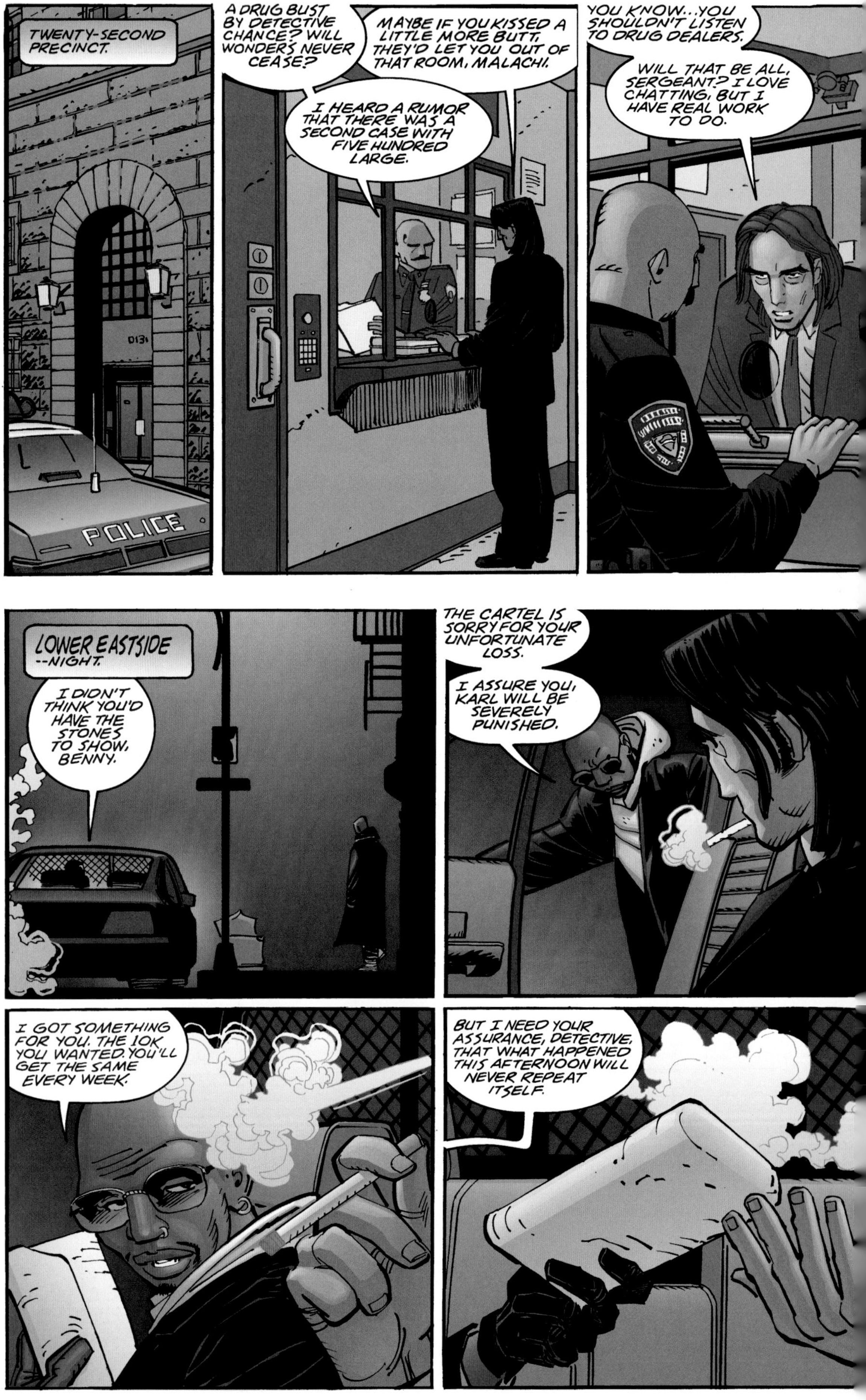
TWENTY-SECOND PRECINCT.
POLICE
A DRUG BUST BY DETECTIVE CHANCE? WILL WONDERS NEVER CEASE?
MAYBE IF YOU KISSED A LITTLE MORE BUTT, THEY'D LET YOU OUT OF THAT ROOM, MALACHI.
I HEARD A RUMOR THAT THERE WAS A SECOND CASE WITH FIVE HUNDRED LARGE.
YOU KNOW...YOU SHOULDN'T LISTEN TO DRUG DEALERS.
WILL THAT BE ALL, SERGEANT? I LOVE CHATTING, BUT I HAVE REAL WORK TO DO.
LOWER EASTSIDE --NIGHT.
I DIDN'T THINK YOU'D HAVE THE STONES TO SHOW, BENNY.
THE CARTEL IS SORRY FOR YOUR UNFORTUNATE LOSS.
I ASSURE YOU, KARL WILL BE SEVERELY PUNISHED.
I GOT SOMETHING FOR YOU. THE 10K YOU WANTED. YOU'LL GET THE SAME EVERY WEEK.
BUT I NEED YOUR ASSURANCE, DETECTIVE, THAT WHAT HAPPENED THIS AFTERNOON WILL NEVER REPEAT ITSELF.

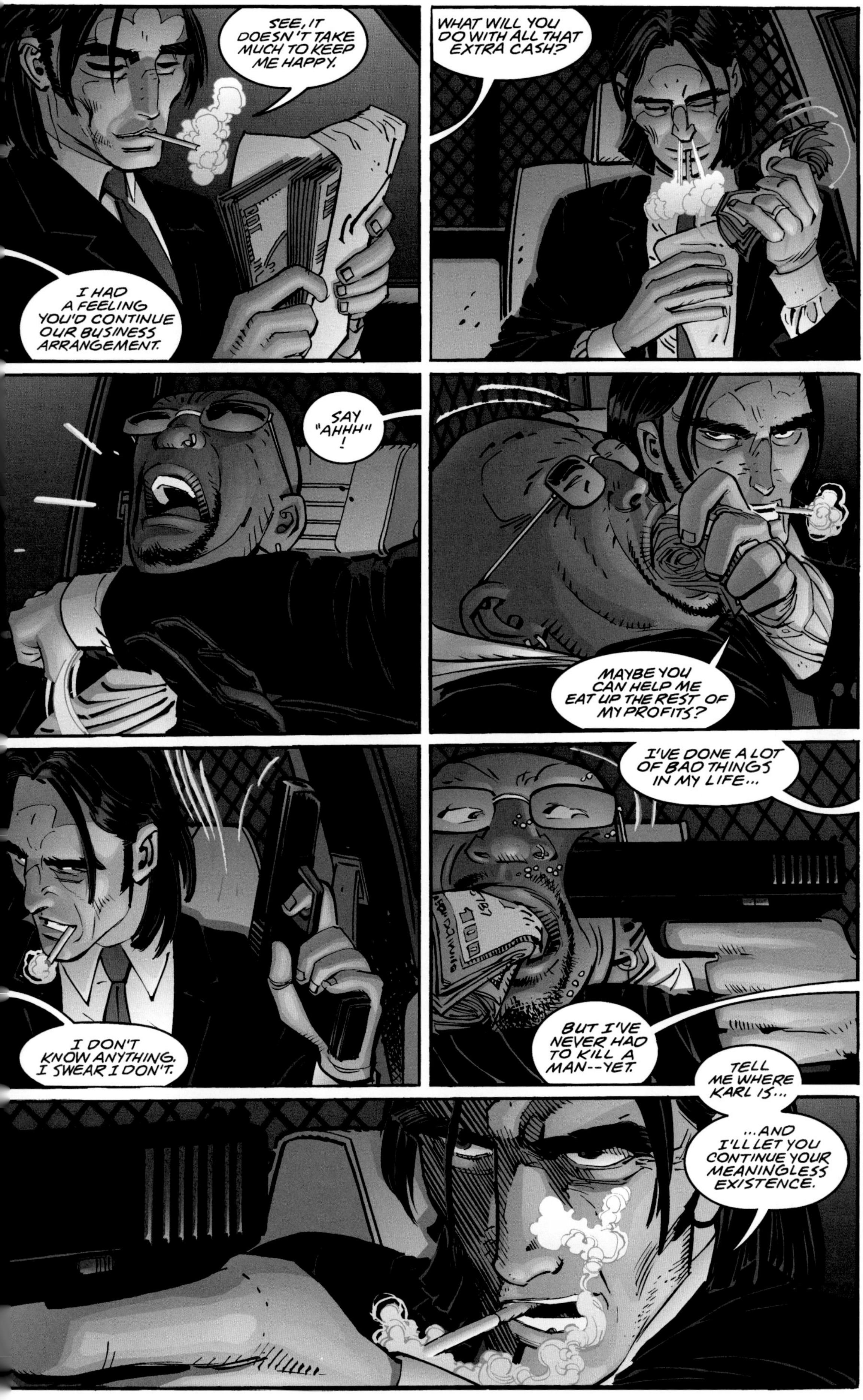
SEE, IT DOESN'T TAKE MUCH TO KEEP ME HAPPY.
I HAD A FEELING YOU'D CONTINUE OUR BUSINESS ARRANGEMENT.
WHAT WILL YOU DO WITH ALL THAT EXTRA CASH?
SAY "AHHH"!
MAYBE YOU CAN HELP ME EAT UP THE REST OF MY PROFITS?
I DON'T KNOW ANYTHING. I SWEAR I DON'T.
I'VE DONE A LOT OF BAD THINGS IN MY LIFE...
BUT I'VE NEVER HAD TO KILL A MAN--YET.
TELL ME WHERE KARL IS...
...AND I'LL LET YOU CONTINUE YOUR MEANINGLESS EXISTENCE.

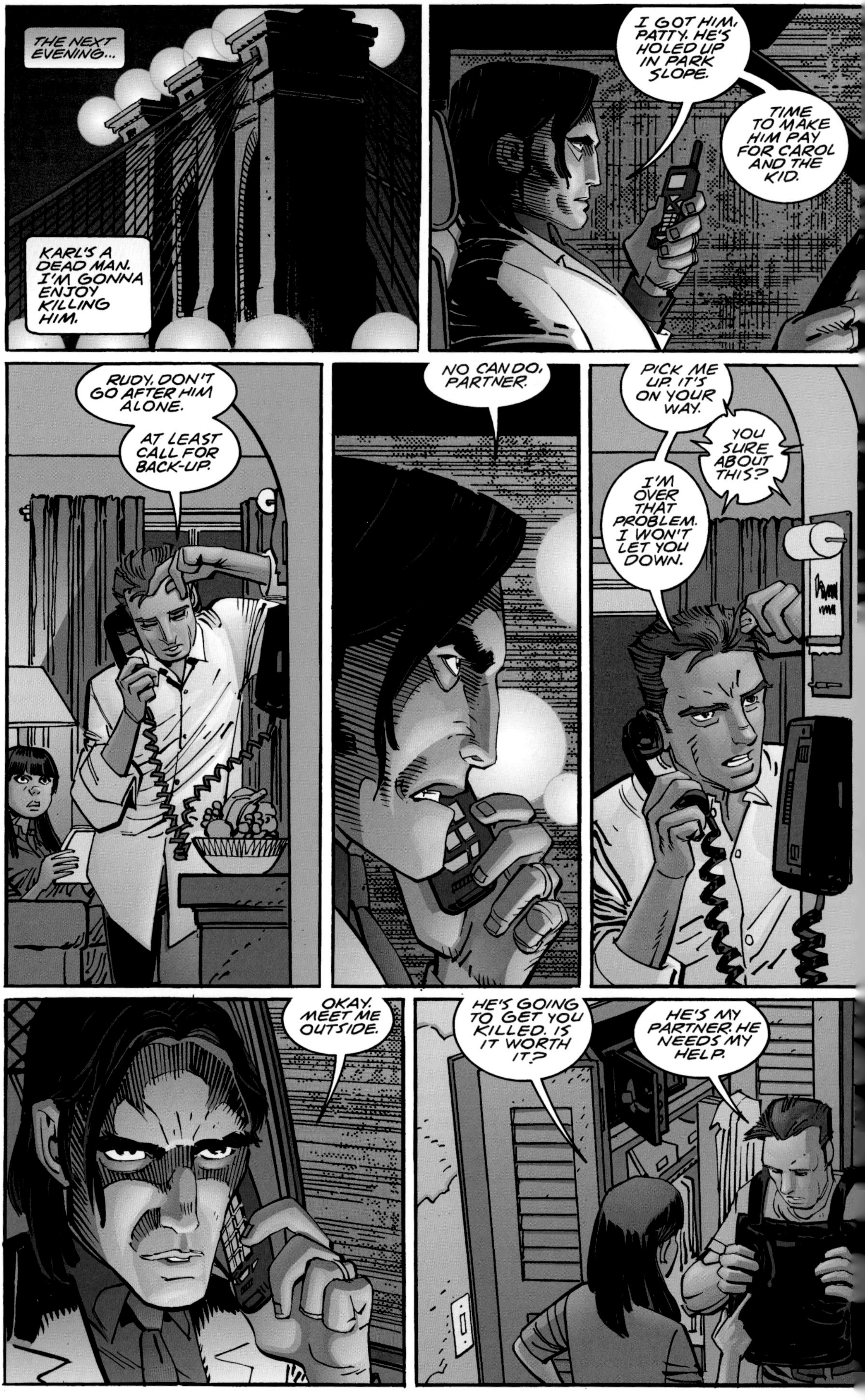
THE NEXT EVENING...
KARL'S A DEAD MAN. I'M GONNA ENJOY KILLING HIM.
I GOT HIM, PATTY. HE'S HOLED UP IN PARK SLOPE.
TIME TO MAKE HIM PAY FOR CAROL AND THE KID.
RUDY, DON'T GO AFTER HIM ALONE.
AT LEAST CALL FOR BACK-UP.
NO CAN DO, PARTNER.
PICK ME UP. IT'S ON YOUR WAY.
YOU SURE ABOUT THIS?
I'M OVER THAT PROBLEM. I WON'T LET YOU DOWN.
OKAY. MEET ME OUTSIDE.
HE'S GOING TO GET YOU KILLED. IS IT WORTH IT?
HE'S MY PARTNER. HE NEEDS MY HELP.

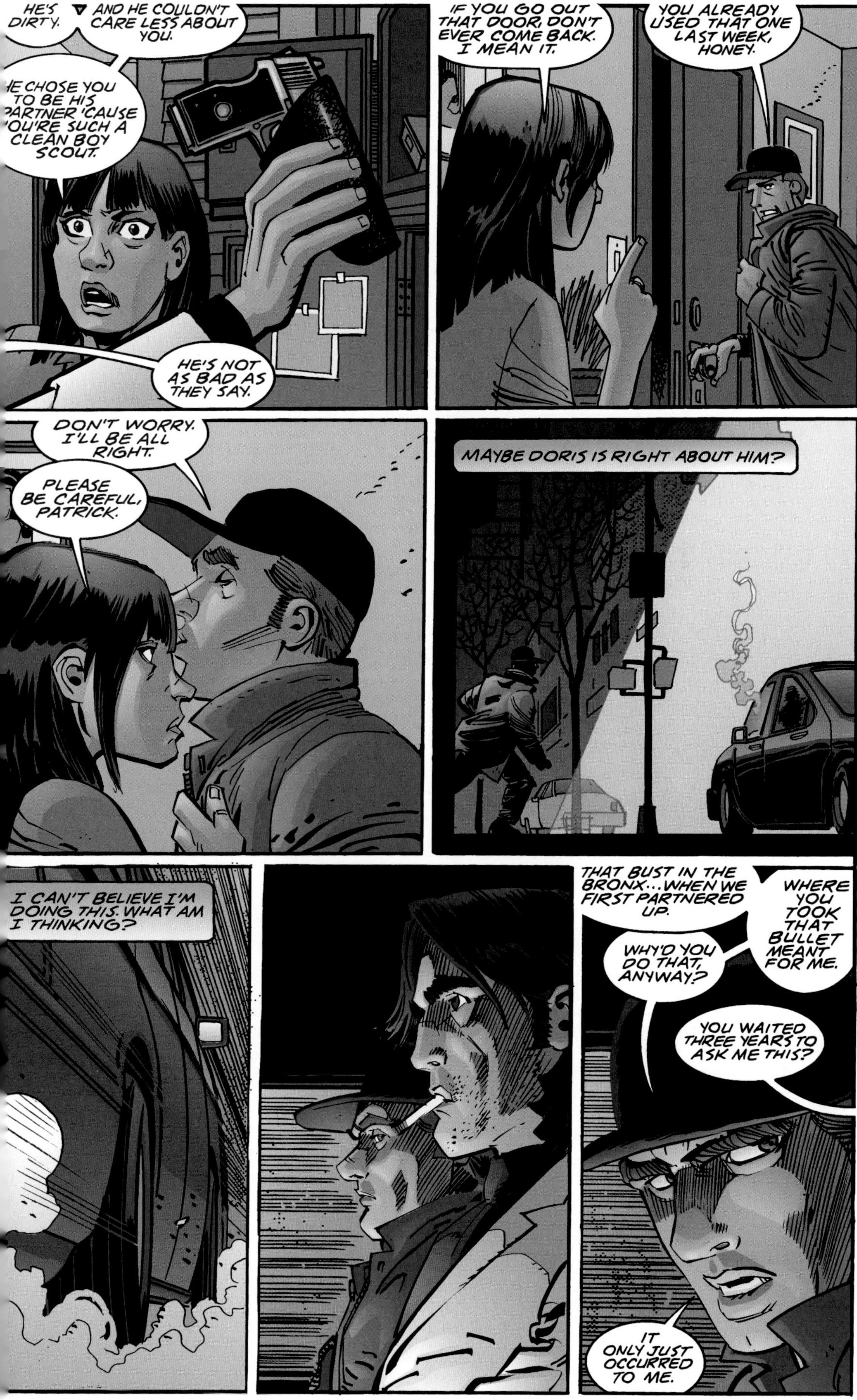
HE'S DIRTY.
AND HE COULDN'T CARE LESS ABOUT YOU.
HE CHOSE YOU TO BE HIS PARTNER 'CAUSE YOU'RE SUCH A CLEAN BOY SCOUT.
HE'S NOT AS BAD AS THEY SAY.
IF YOU GO OUT THAT DOOR, DON'T EVER COME BACK. I MEAN IT.
YOU ALREADY USED THAT ONE LAST WEEK, HONEY.
DON'T WORRY. I'LL BE ALL RIGHT.
PLEASE BE CAREFUL, PATRICK.
MAYBE DORIS IS RIGHT ABOUT HIM?
I CAN'T BELIEVE I'M DOING THIS. WHAT AM I THINKING?
THAT BUST IN THE BRONX...WHEN WE FIRST PARTNERED UP.
WHERE YOU TOOK THAT BULLET MEANT FOR ME.
WHY'D YOU DO THAT, ANYWAY?
YOU WAITED THREE YEARS TO ASK ME THIS?
IT ONLY JUST OCCURRED TO ME.

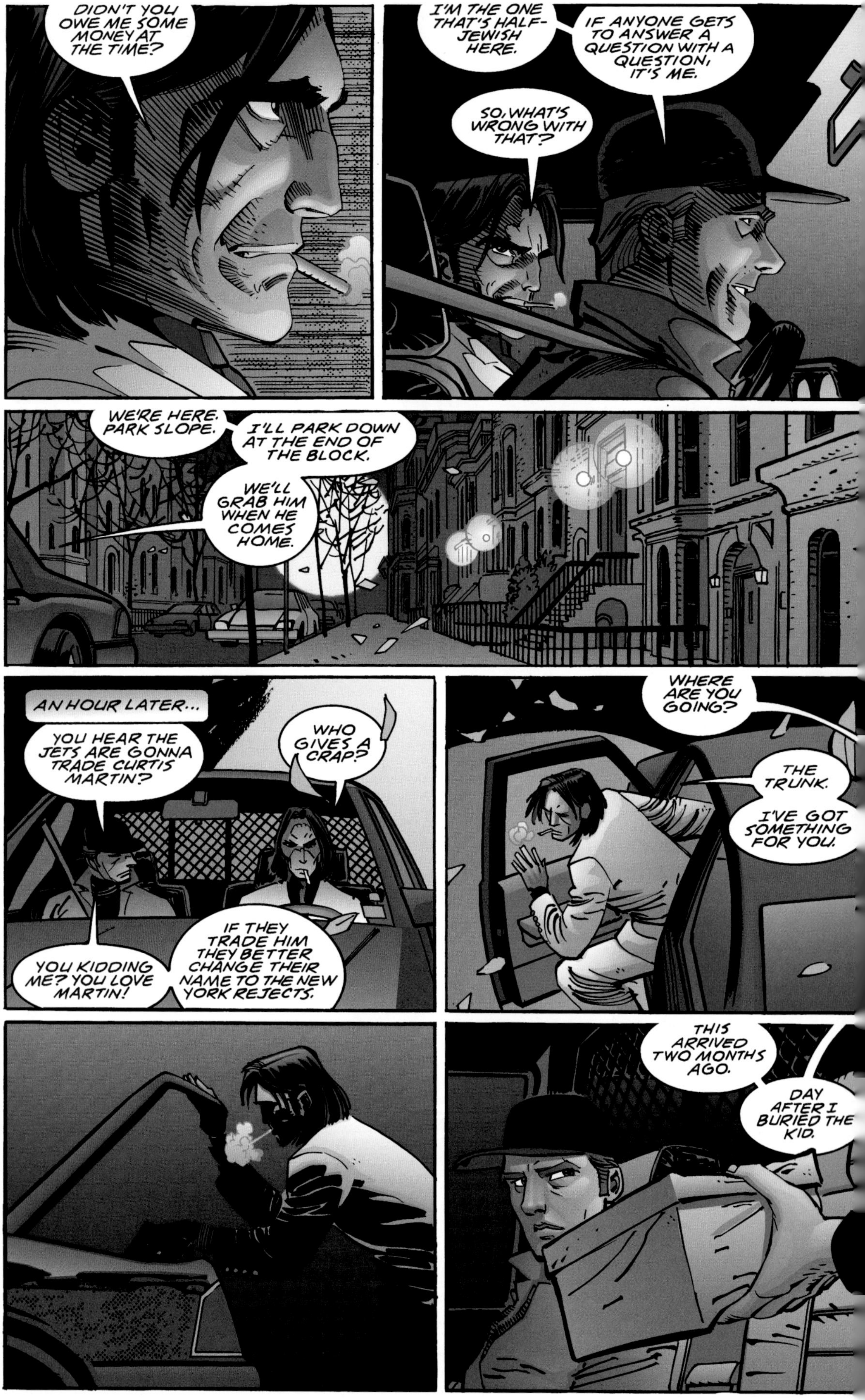
DIDN'T YOU OWE ME SOME MONEY AT THE TIME?
I'M THE ONE THAT'S HALF-JEWISH HERE.
IF ANYONE GETS TO ANSWER A QUESTION WITH A QUESTION, IT'S ME.
SO, WHAT'S WRONG WITH THAT?
WE'RE HERE. PARK SLOPE.
I'LL PARK DOWN AT THE END OF THE BLOCK.
WE'LL GRAB HIM WHEN HE COMES HOME.
AN HOUR LATER...
YOU HEAR THE JETS ARE GONNA TRADE CURTIS MARTIN?
WHO GIVES A CRAP?
YOU KIDDING ME? YOU LOVE MARTIN!
IF THEY TRADE HIM THEY BETTER CHANGE THEIR NAME TO THE NEW YORK REJECTS.
WHERE ARE YOU GOING?
THE TRUNK.
I'VE GOT SOMETHING FOR YOU.
THIS ARRIVED TWO MONTHS AGO.
DAY AFTER I BURIED THE KID.

YOU KEEP IT.

NO! THIS WAS FOR THE KID'S BIRTHDAY, HUH?

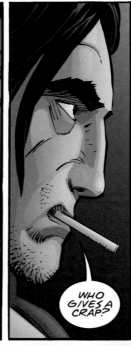

WHO GIVES A CRAP?

SO TIRED...

CAN'T OPEN MY EYES...

I STILL SEE JOSH...

HE'S JUST INCHES AWAY.

PLEASE, GIVE ME ONE MORE SECOND...

I CAN STILL SAVE HIM.

NO! NO!

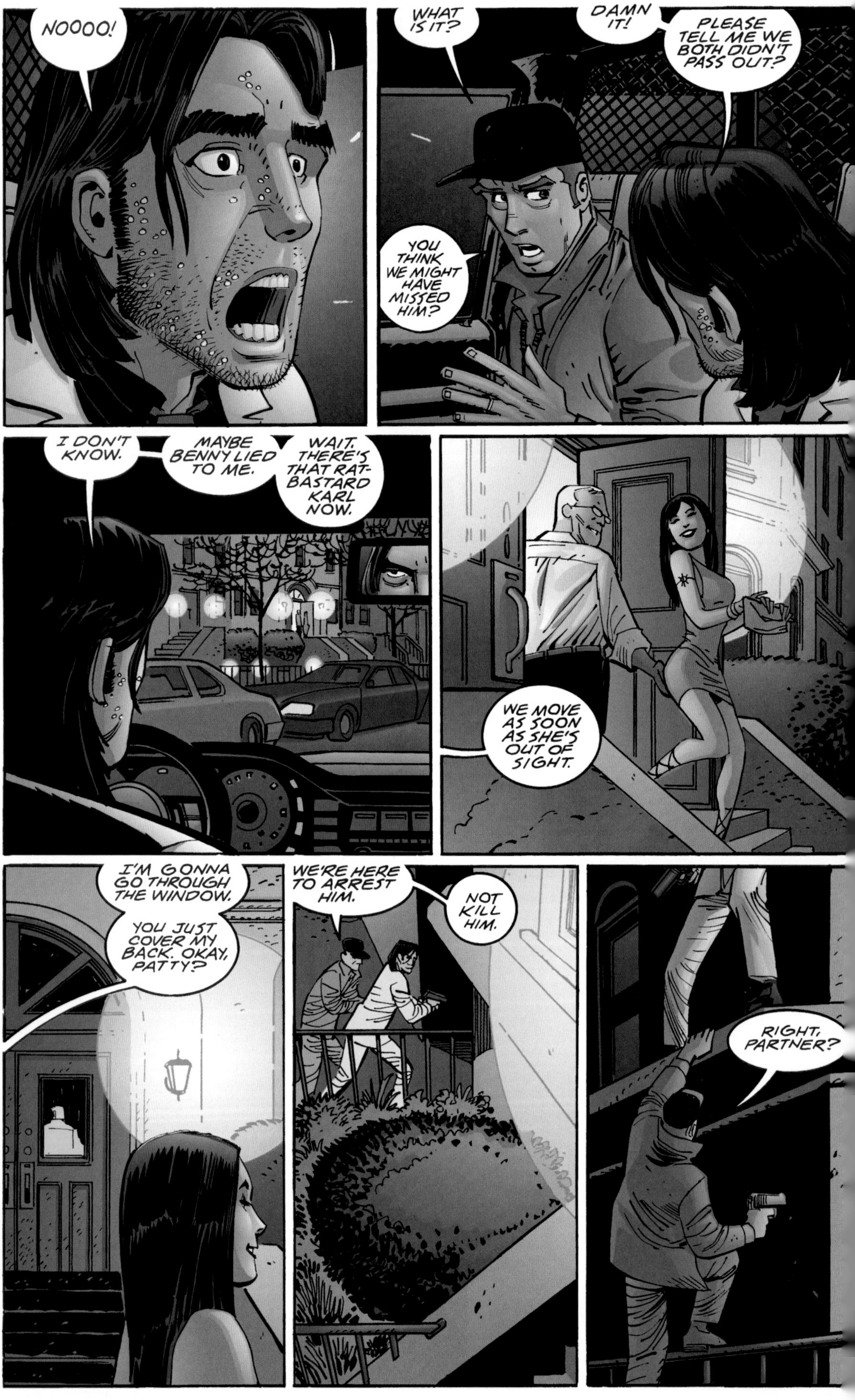
NOOOO!
WHAT IS IT?
DAMN IT!
PLEASE TELL ME WE BOTH DIDN'T PASS OUT?
YOU THINK WE MIGHT HAVE MISSED HIM?
I DON'T KNOW.
MAYBE BENNY LIED TO ME.
WAIT. THERE'S THAT RAT-BASTARD KARL NOW.
WE MOVE AS SOON AS SHE'S OUT OF SIGHT.
I'M GONNA GO THROUGH THE WINDOW.
YOU JUST COVER MY BACK. OKAY, PATTY?
WE'RE HERE TO ARREST HIM.
NOT KILL HIM.
RIGHT, PARTNER?

CREECH!

CLICK!

WAIT TILL YOUR EYES ADJUST TO THE DARK.

...HTS SNAP ON...

SORRY, DETECTIVE. BUT TRESPASSING IN THIS NEIGHBORHOOD IS PUNISHABLE BY DEATH.

TIME TO PRAY.

YOU SCUMBAG!

NO, PLEASE, NO!

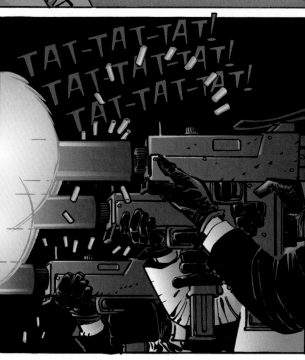

TAT-TAT-TAT!
TAT-TAT-TAT!
TAT-TAT-TAT!

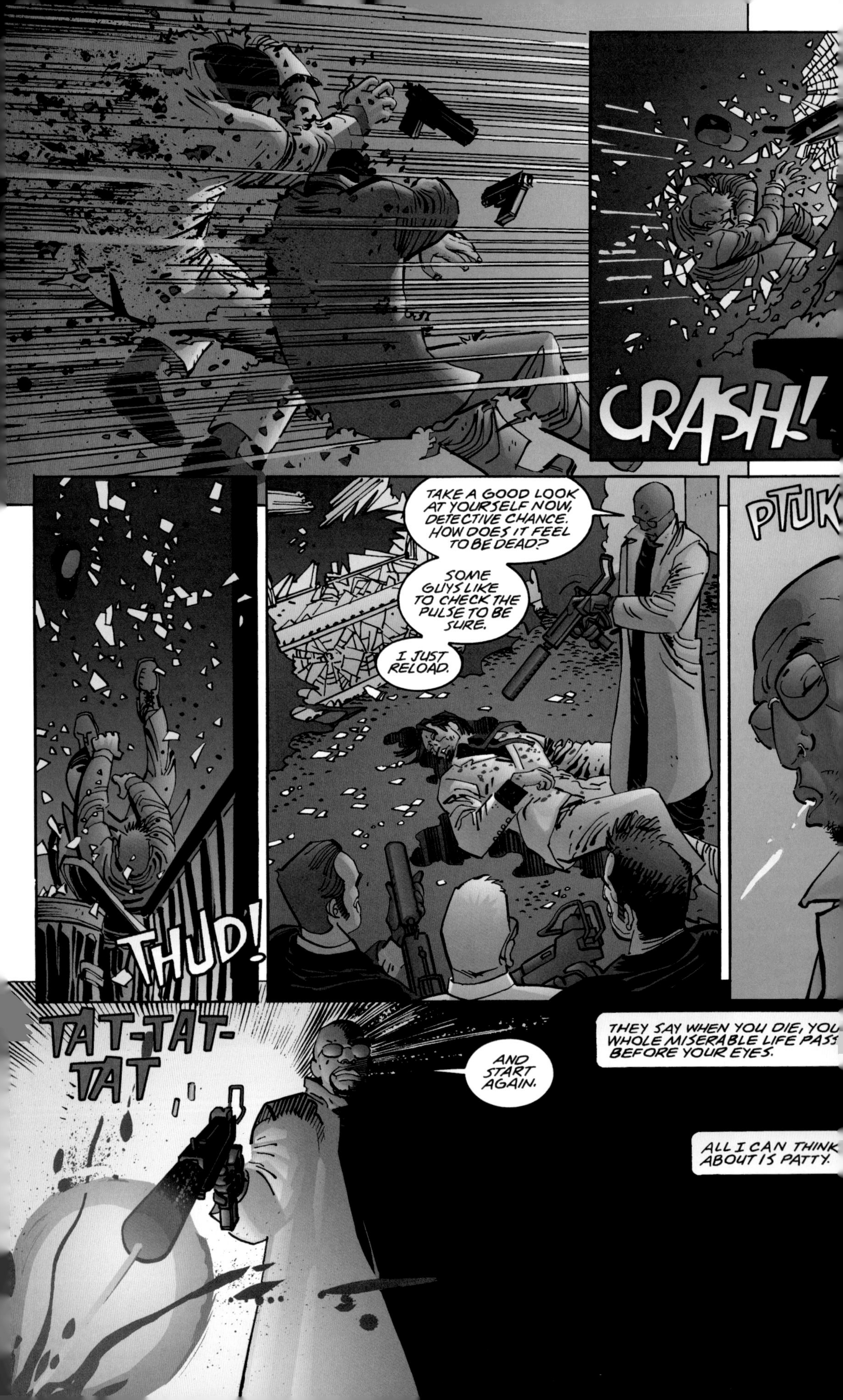
CRASH!
THUD!
TAKE A GOOD LOOK AT YOURSELF NOW, DETECTIVE CHANCE. HOW DOES IT FEEL TO BE DEAD?
SOME GUYS LIKE TO CHECK THE PULSE TO BE SURE.
I JUST RELOAD.
PTUK
TAT-TAT-TAT
AND START AGAIN.
THEY SAY WHEN YOU DIE, YOU WHOLE MISERABLE LIFE PASS BEFORE YOUR EYES.
ALL I CAN THINK ABOUT IS PATTY.

I LET YOU DOWN, BUDDY.

INTENSIVE
CARE 1-5
NEONATAL

CROWN HEIGHTS HOSPITAL, ICU.

MRS. GOODMAN, HE'S STILL IN A COMA. ALL WE CAN DO IS KEEP HIM BREATHING.

...S VEST DID PROTECT ...M, BUT HE HAS DEEP ...TERNAL INJURIES. HE MAY NEVER RECOVER. I'M SO SORRY.

DORIS, I DON'T KNOW WHAT TO SAY.

THIS IS ALL MY FAULT.

WHAT'S GOING ON...?

SHE CAN'T HEAR YOU, MR. CHANCE.

WHO SAID THAT?

OH, I GET IT. I'M DEAD, HUH?

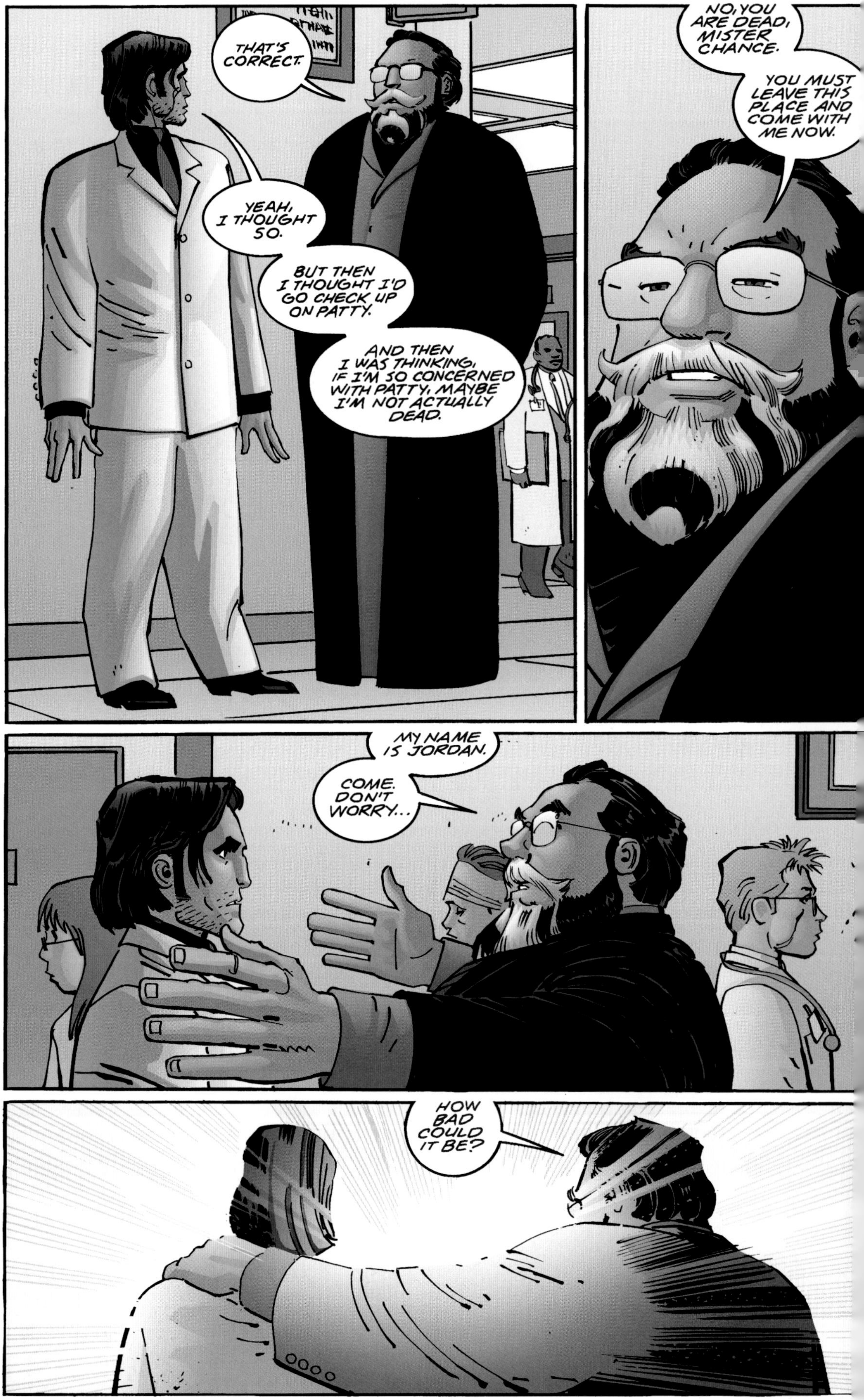
THAT'S CORRECT.
YEAH, I THOUGHT SO.
BUT THEN I THOUGHT I'D GO CHECK UP ON PATTY.
AND THEN I WAS THINKING, IF I'M SO CONCERNED WITH PATTY, MAYBE I'M NOT ACTUALLY DEAD.
NO, YOU ARE DEAD, MISTER CHANCE.
YOU MUST LEAVE THIS PLACE AND COME WITH ME NOW.
MY NAME IS JORDAN.
COME. DON'T WORRY...
HOW BAD COULD IT BE?

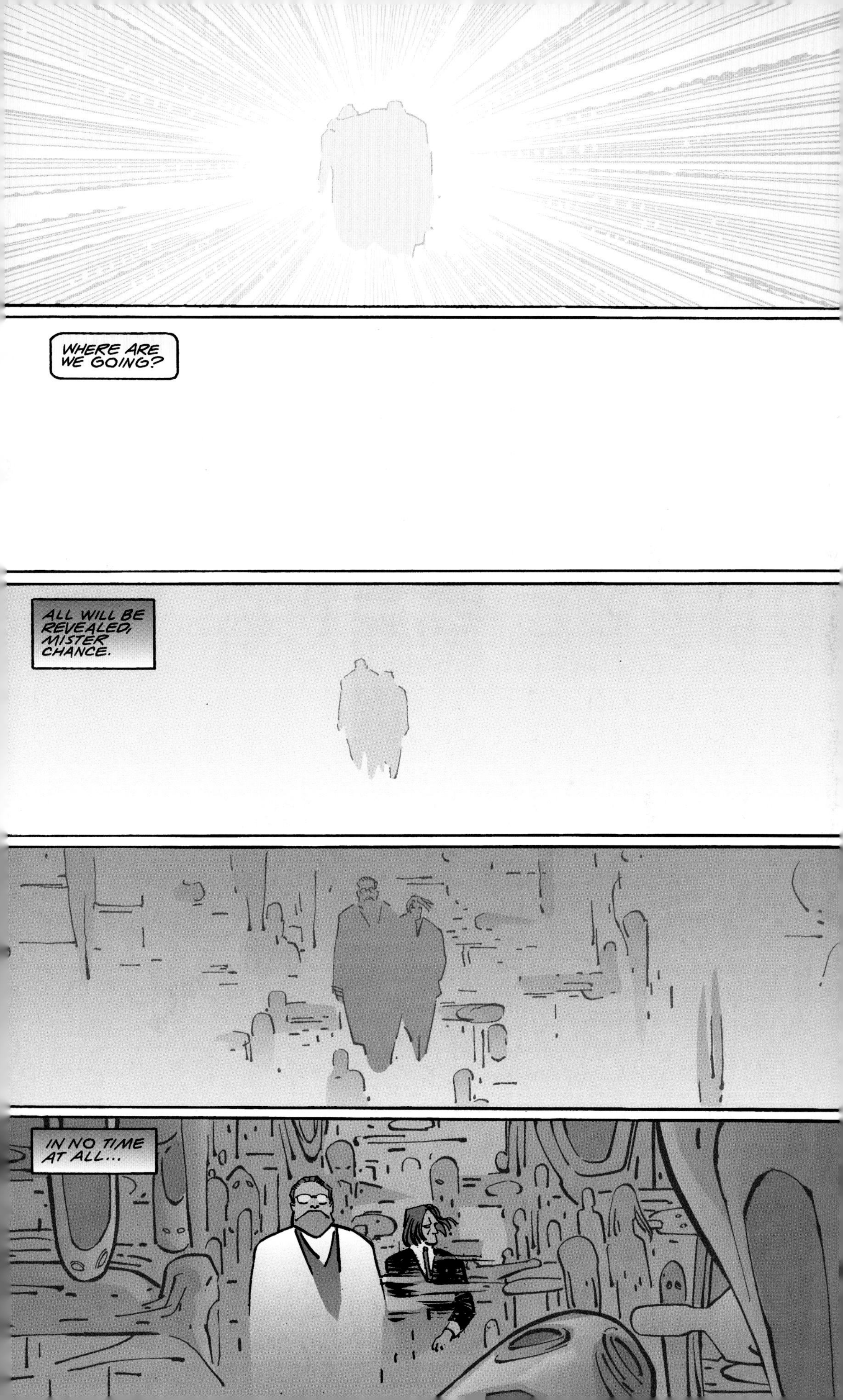
WHERE ARE WE GOING?
ALL WILL BE REVEALED, MISTER CHANCE.
IN NO TIME AT ALL...

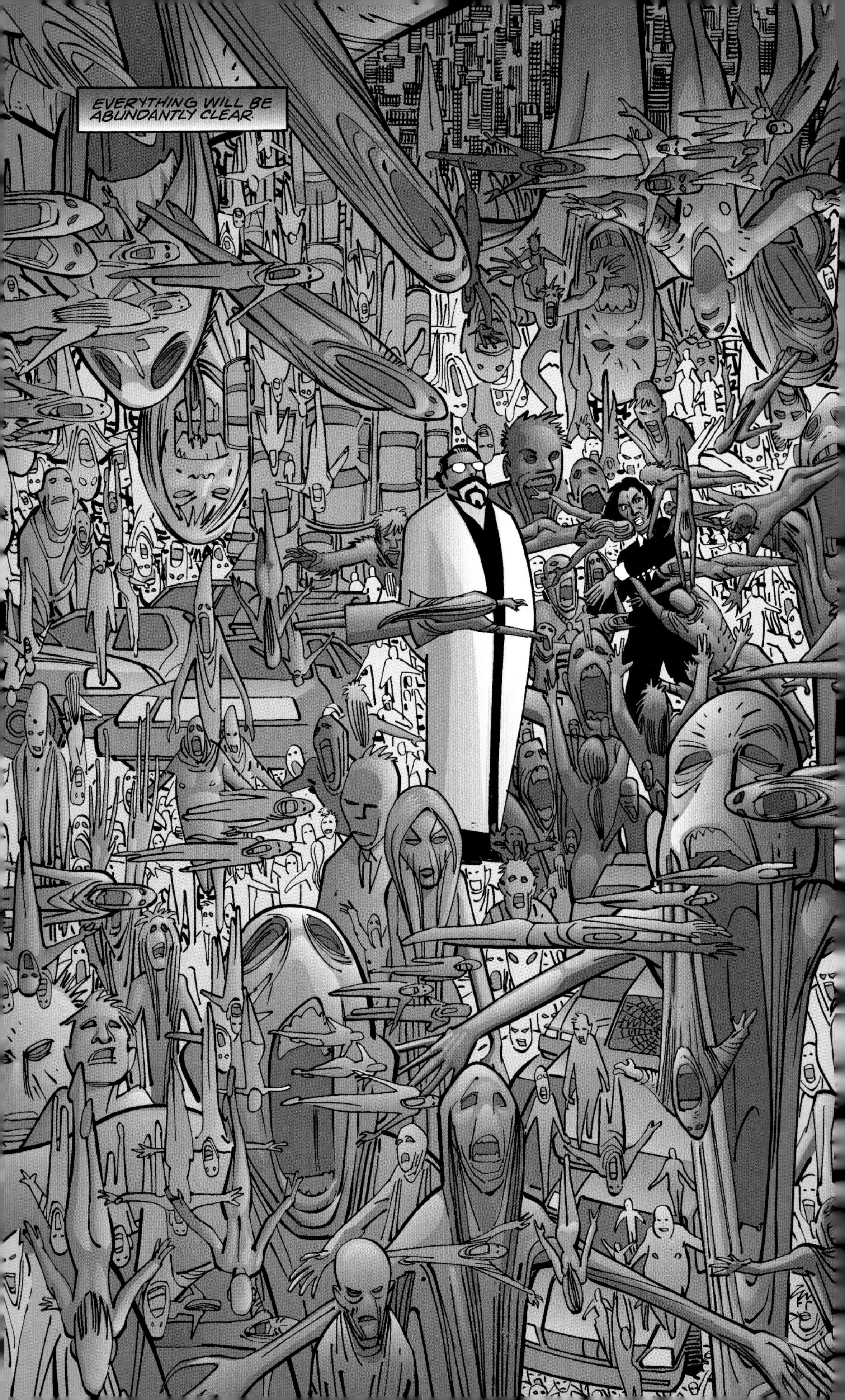
EVERYTHING WILL BE ABUNDANTLY CLEAR.

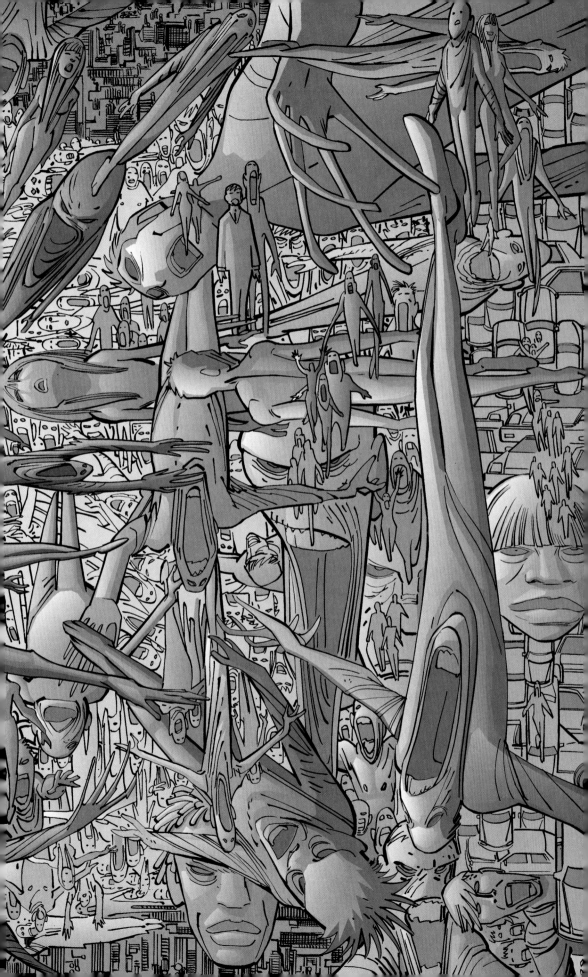

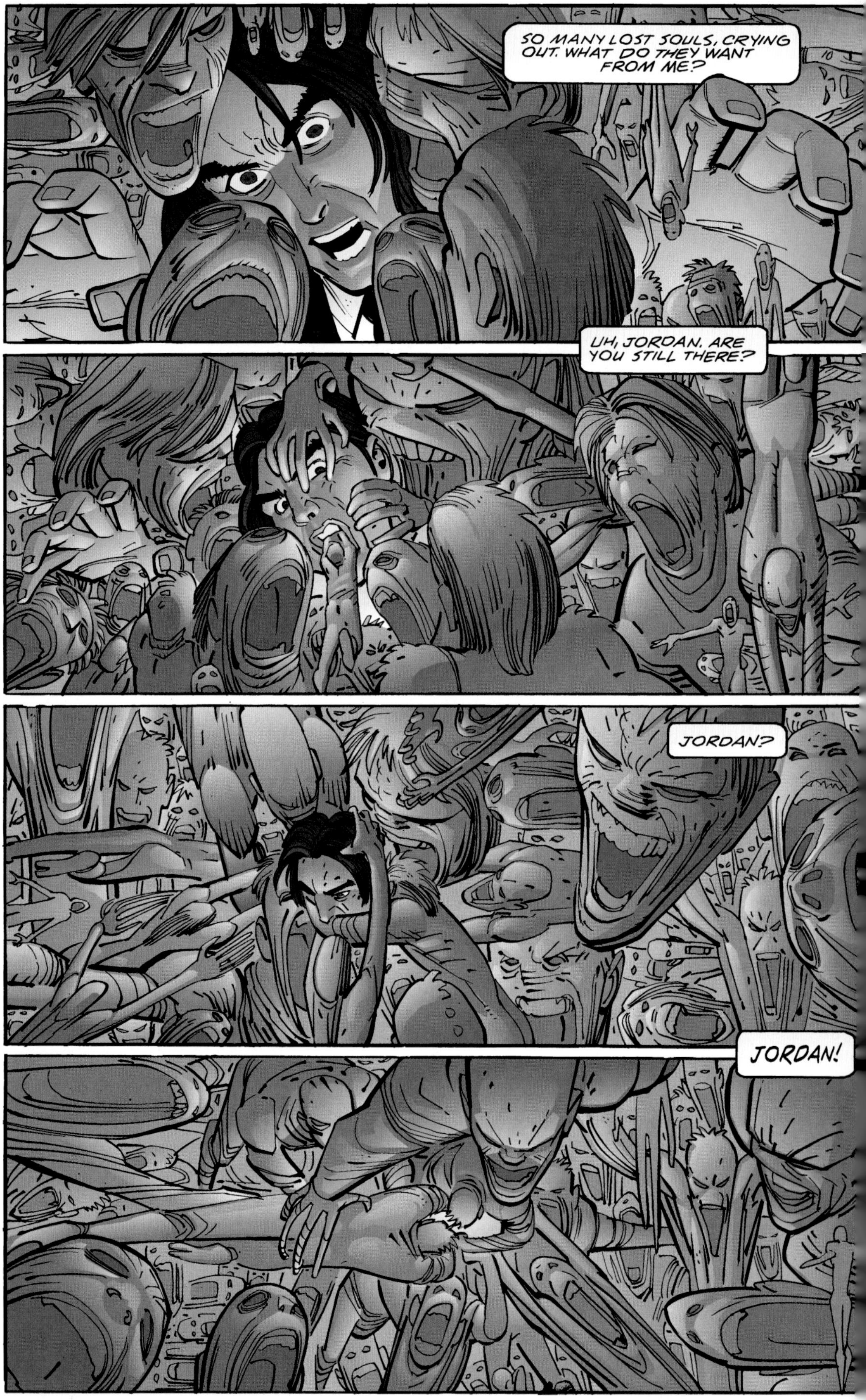
SO MANY LOST SOULS, CRYING OUT. WHAT DO THEY WANT FROM ME?
UH, JORDAN. ARE YOU STILL THERE?
JORDAN?
JORDAN!

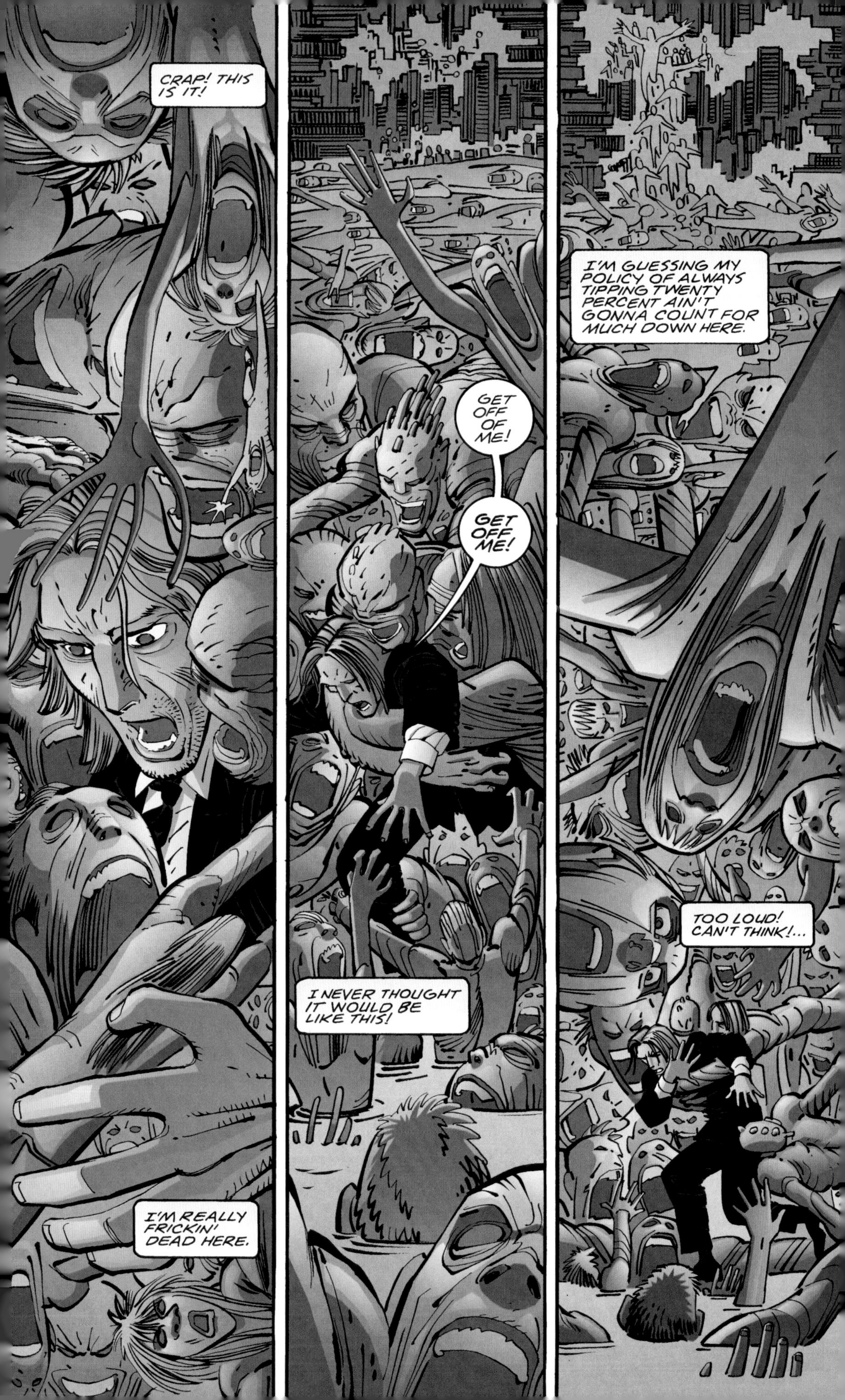
CRAP! THIS IS IT!
I'M REALLY FRICKIN' DEAD HERE.
GET OFF OF ME!
GET OFF ME!
I NEVER THOUGHT IT WOULD BE LIKE THIS!
I'M GUESSING MY POLICY OF ALWAYS TIPPING TWENTY PERCENT AIN'T GONNA COUNT FOR MUCH DOWN HERE.
TOO LOUD! CAN'T THINK!...

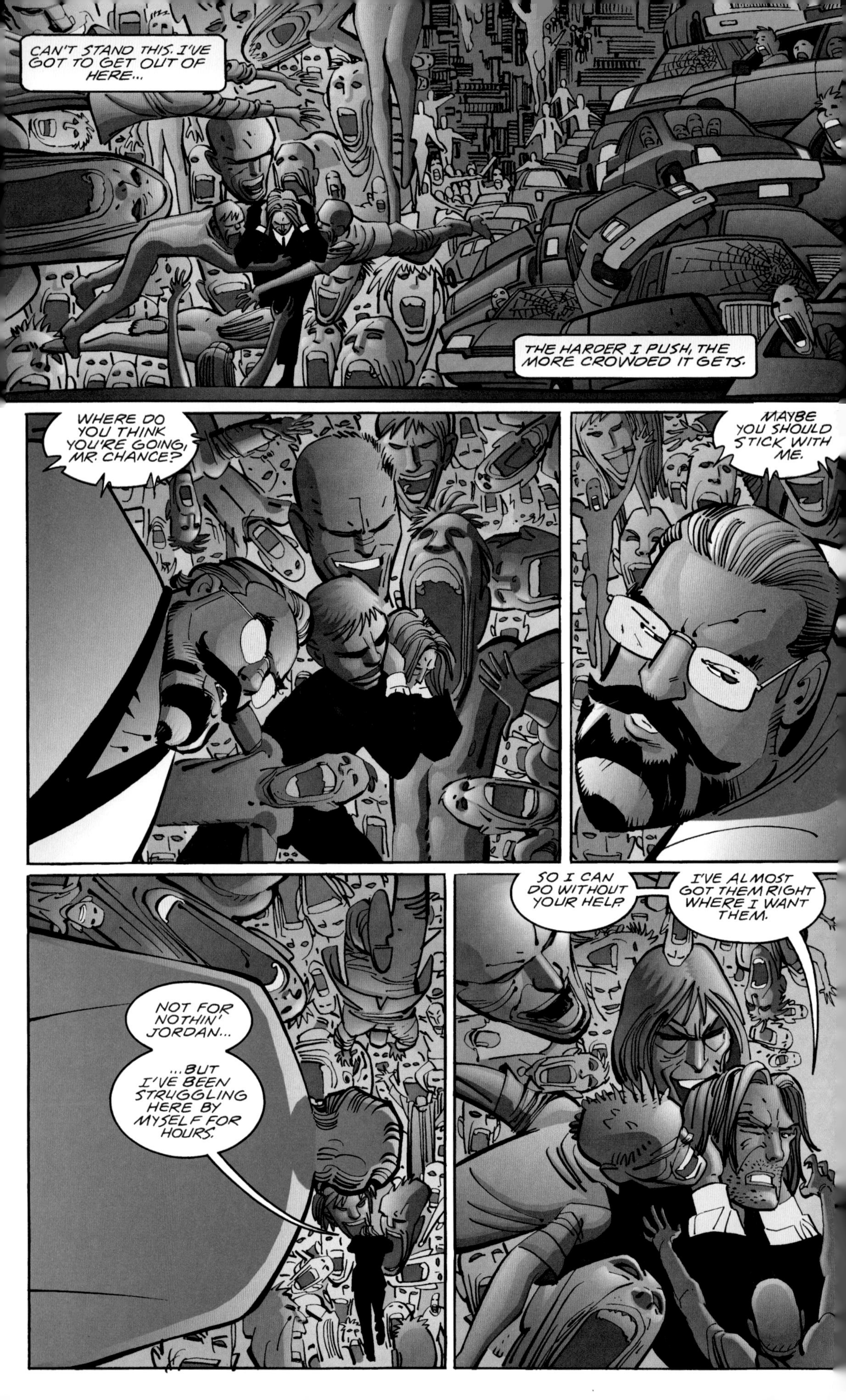
CAN'T STAND THIS. I'VE GOT TO GET OUT OF HERE...
THE HARDER I PUSH, THE MORE CROWDED IT GETS.
WHERE DO YOU THINK YOU'RE GOING, MR. CHANCE?
MAYBE YOU SHOULD STICK WITH ME.
NOT FOR NOTHIN' JORDAN...
...BUT I'VE BEEN STRUGGLING HERE BY MYSELF FOR HOURS.
SO I CAN DO WITHOUT YOUR HELP.
I'VE ALMOST GOT THEM RIGHT WHERE I WANT THEM.

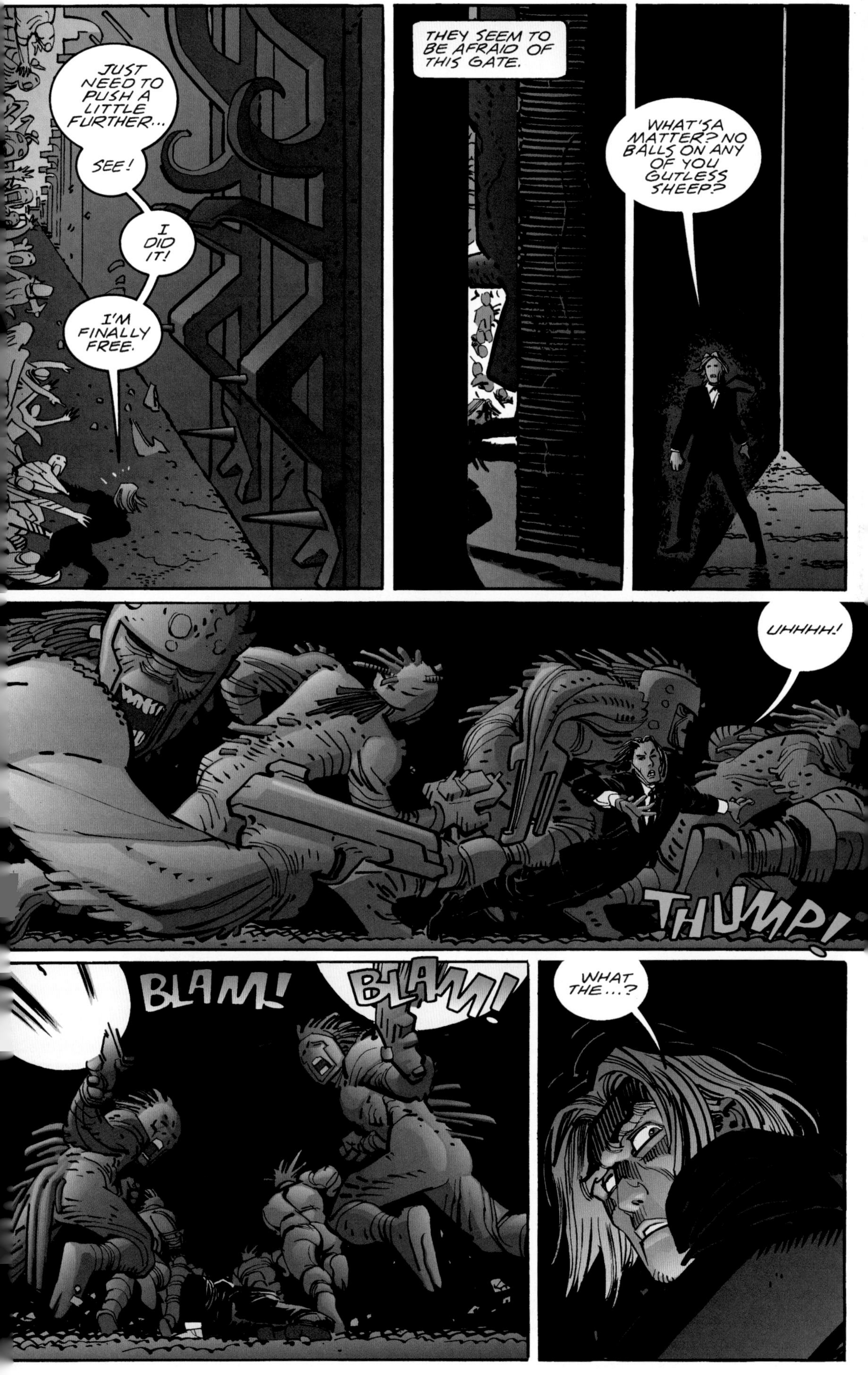
JUST NEED TO PUSH A LITTLE FURTHER...
SEE!
I DID IT!
I'M FINALLY FREE.
THEY SEEM TO BE AFRAID OF THIS GATE.
WHAT'SA MATTER? NO BALLS ON ANY OF YOU GUTLESS SHEEP?
UHHHH!
THUMP!
BLAM!
BLAM!
WHAT THE...?

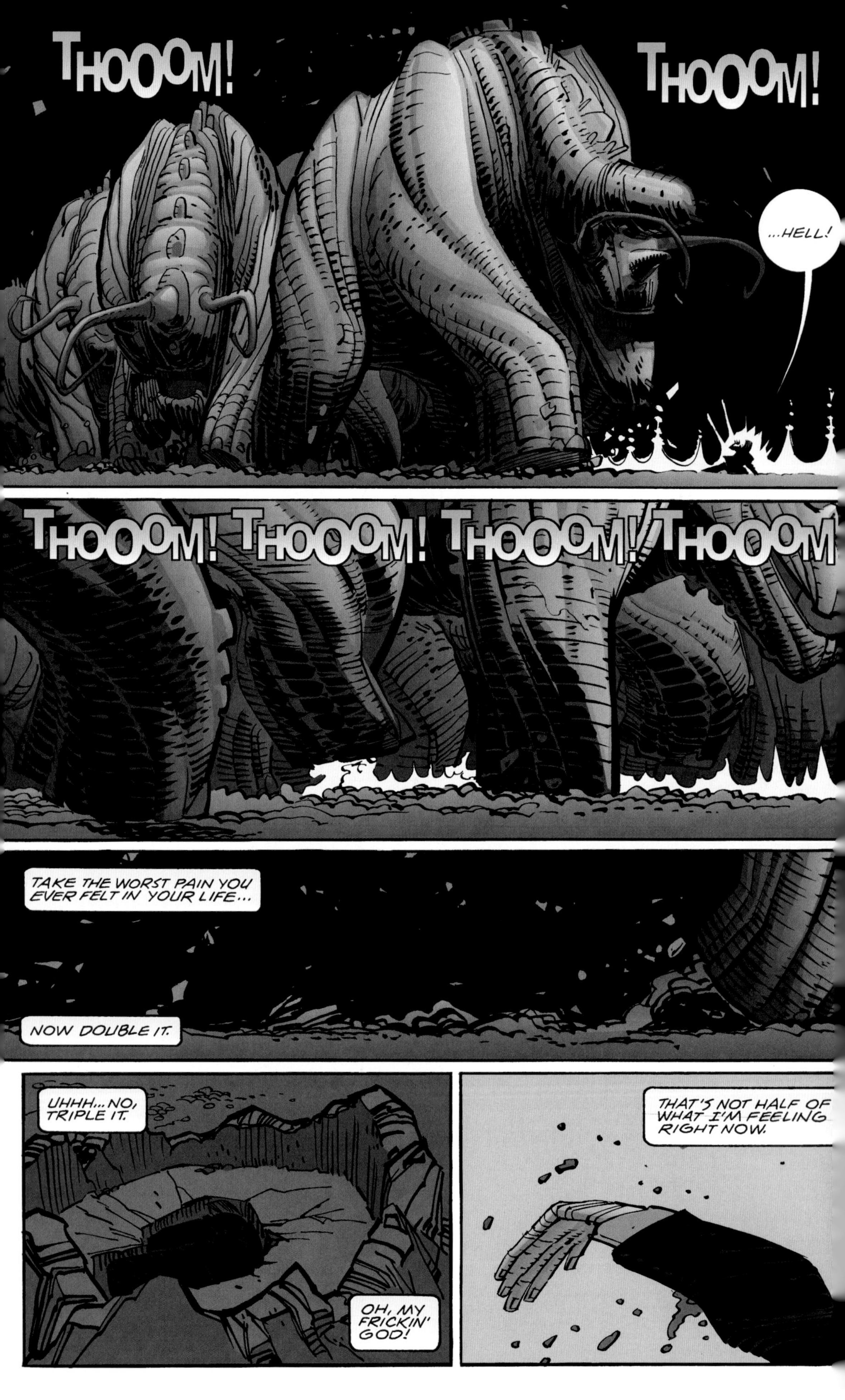
THOOOM!
THOOOM!
...HELL!
THOOOM! THOOOM! THOOOM! THOOOM
TAKE THE WORST PAIN YOU EVER FELT IN YOUR LIFE...
NOW DOUBLE IT.
UHHH... NO, TRIPLE IT.
OH, MY FRICKIN' GOD!
THAT'S NOT HALF OF WHAT I'M FEELING RIGHT NOW.

HURTS SO BAD.

BUT I GOTTA KEEP MOVING...

BABAR AND HIS BUDDIES MIGHT DECIDE TO COME BACK.

THANK GOD. I MADE IT OUT OF SAFARI-LAND.

I'M BEGINNING TO FEEL A BIT BETTER.

WHACK

E WAITED E YEARS R YOU TO E...SO I ULD GIVE OU THIS.

DIDN'T THEY TREAT YOU WELL ENOUGH IN STIR, EDDIE?

LET ME AT HIM...

THUD

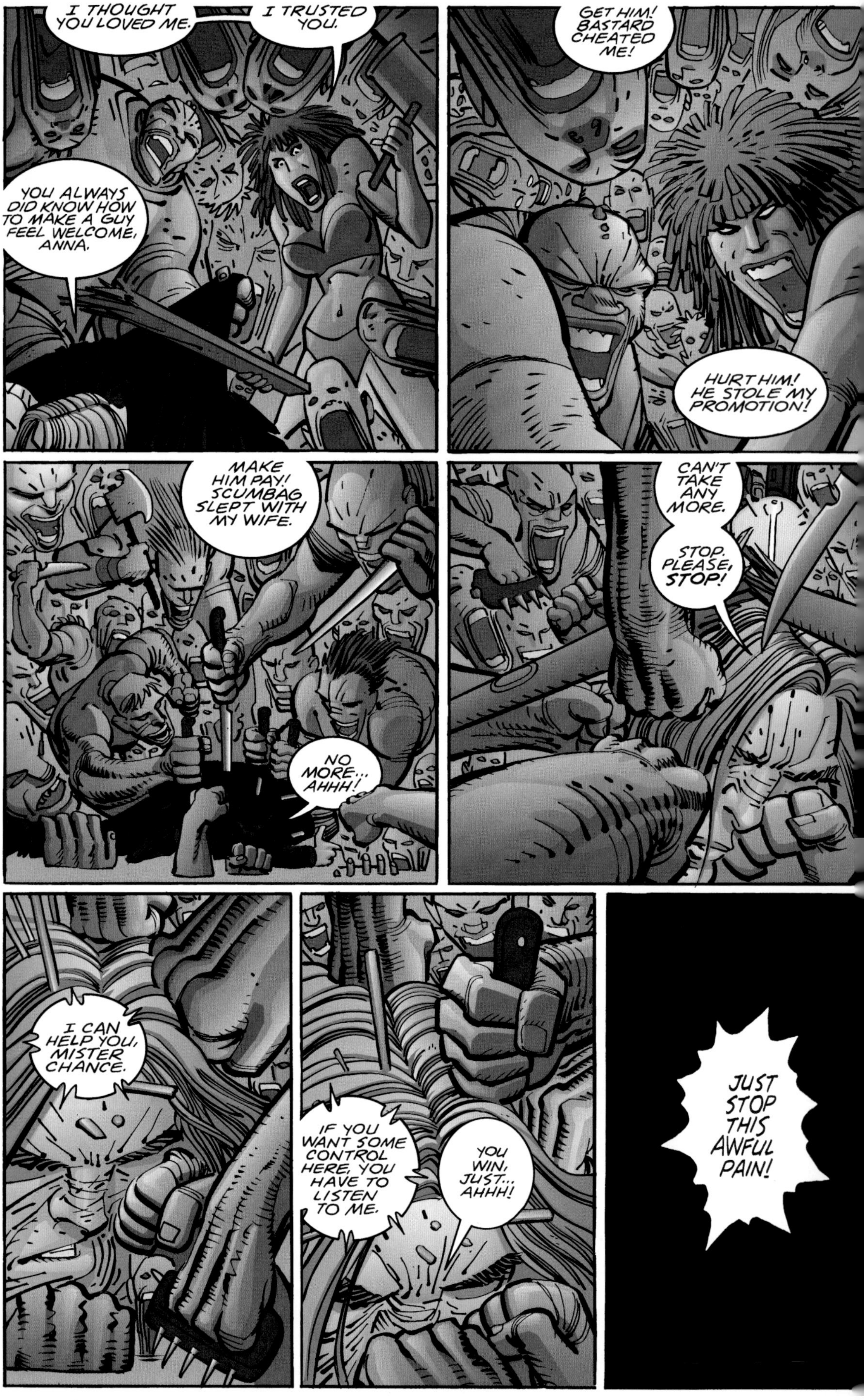
I THOUGHT YOU LOVED ME.
I TRUSTED YOU.
YOU ALWAYS DID KNOW HOW TO MAKE A GUY FEEL WELCOME, ANNA.
GET HIM! BASTARD CHEATED ME!
HURT HIM! HE STOLE MY PROMOTION!
MAKE HIM PAY! SCUMBAG SLEPT WITH MY WIFE.
NO MORE... AHHH!
CAN'T TAKE ANY MORE.
STOP. PLEASE, STOP!
I CAN HELP YOU, MISTER CHANCE.
IF YOU WANT SOME CONTROL HERE, YOU HAVE TO LISTEN TO ME.
YOU WIN, JUST... AHHH!
JUST STOP THIS AWFUL PAIN!

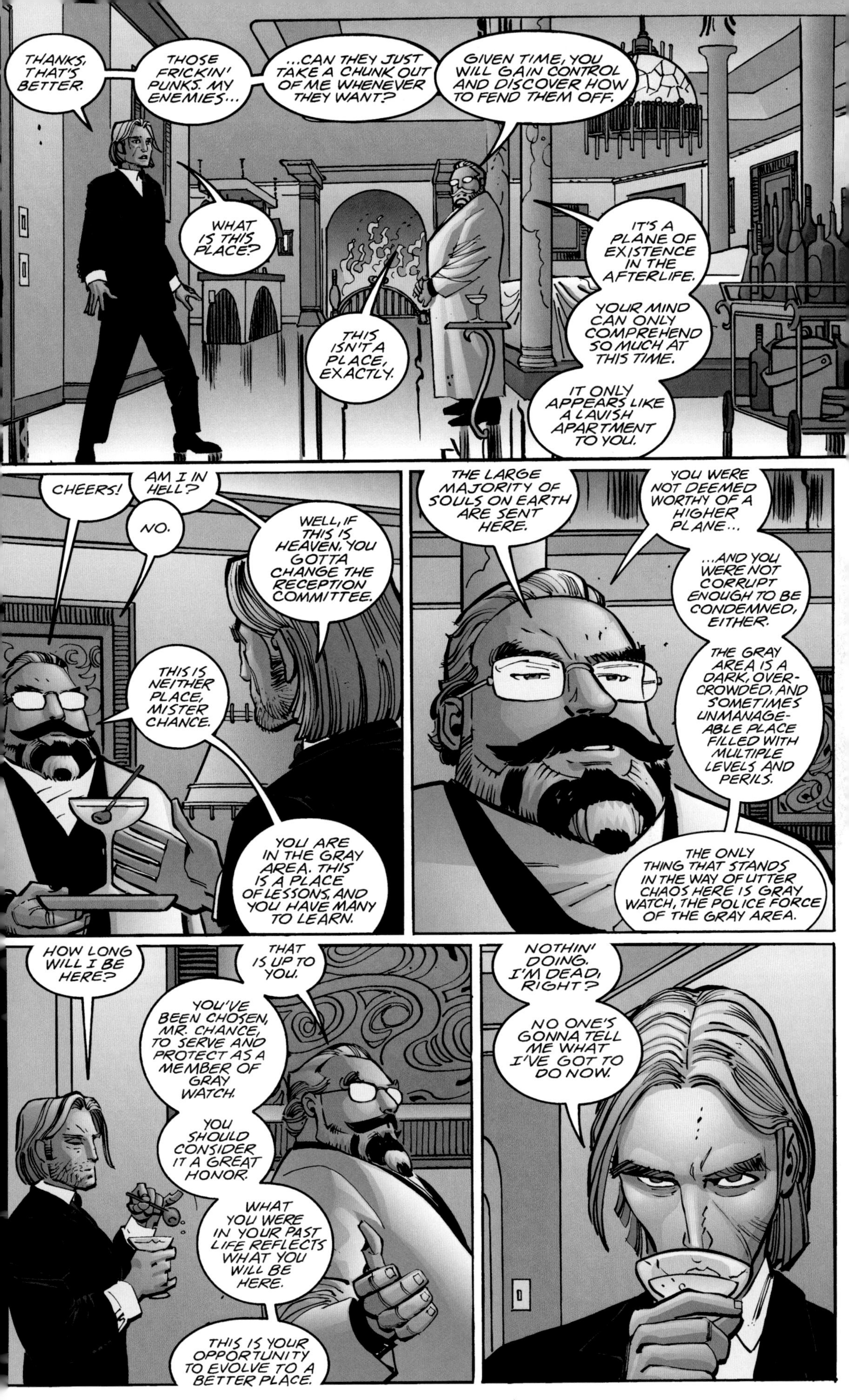

THANKS, THAT'S BETTER.
THOSE FRICKIN' PUNKS. MY ENEMIES...
...CAN THEY JUST TAKE A CHUNK OUT OF ME WHENEVER THEY WANT?
GIVEN TIME, YOU WILL GAIN CONTROL AND DISCOVER HOW TO FEND THEM OFF.
WHAT IS THIS PLACE?
THIS ISN'T A PLACE, EXACTLY.
IT'S A PLANE OF EXISTENCE IN THE AFTERLIFE.
YOUR MIND CAN ONLY COMPREHEND SO MUCH AT THIS TIME.
IT ONLY APPEARS LIKE A LAVISH APARTMENT TO YOU.
CHEERS!
AM I IN HELL?
NO.
WELL, IF THIS IS HEAVEN, YOU GOTTA CHANGE THE RECEPTION COMMITTEE.
THIS IS NEITHER PLACE, MISTER CHANCE.
YOU ARE IN THE GRAY AREA. THIS IS A PLACE OF LESSONS, AND YOU HAVE MANY TO LEARN.
THE LARGE MAJORITY OF SOULS ON EARTH ARE SENT HERE.
YOU WERE NOT DEEMED WORTHY OF A HIGHER PLANE...
...AND YOU WERE NOT CORRUPT ENOUGH TO BE CONDEMNED, EITHER.
THE GRAY AREA IS A DARK, OVER-CROWDED, AND SOMETIMES UNMANAGE-ABLE PLACE FILLED WITH MULTIPLE LEVELS AND PERILS.
THE ONLY THING THAT STANDS IN THE WAY OF UTTER CHAOS HERE IS GRAY WATCH, THE POLICE FORCE OF THE GRAY AREA.
HOW LONG WILL I BE HERE?
THAT IS UP TO YOU.
YOU'VE BEEN CHOSEN, MR. CHANCE, TO SERVE AND PROTECT AS A MEMBER OF GRAY WATCH.
YOU SHOULD CONSIDER IT A GREAT HONOR.
WHAT YOU WERE IN YOUR PAST LIFE REFLECTS WHAT YOU WILL BE HERE.
THIS IS YOUR OPPORTUNITY TO EVOLVE TO A BETTER PLACE.
NOTHIN' DOING. I'M DEAD, RIGHT?
NO ONE'S GONNA TELL ME WHAT I'VE GOT TO DO NOW.

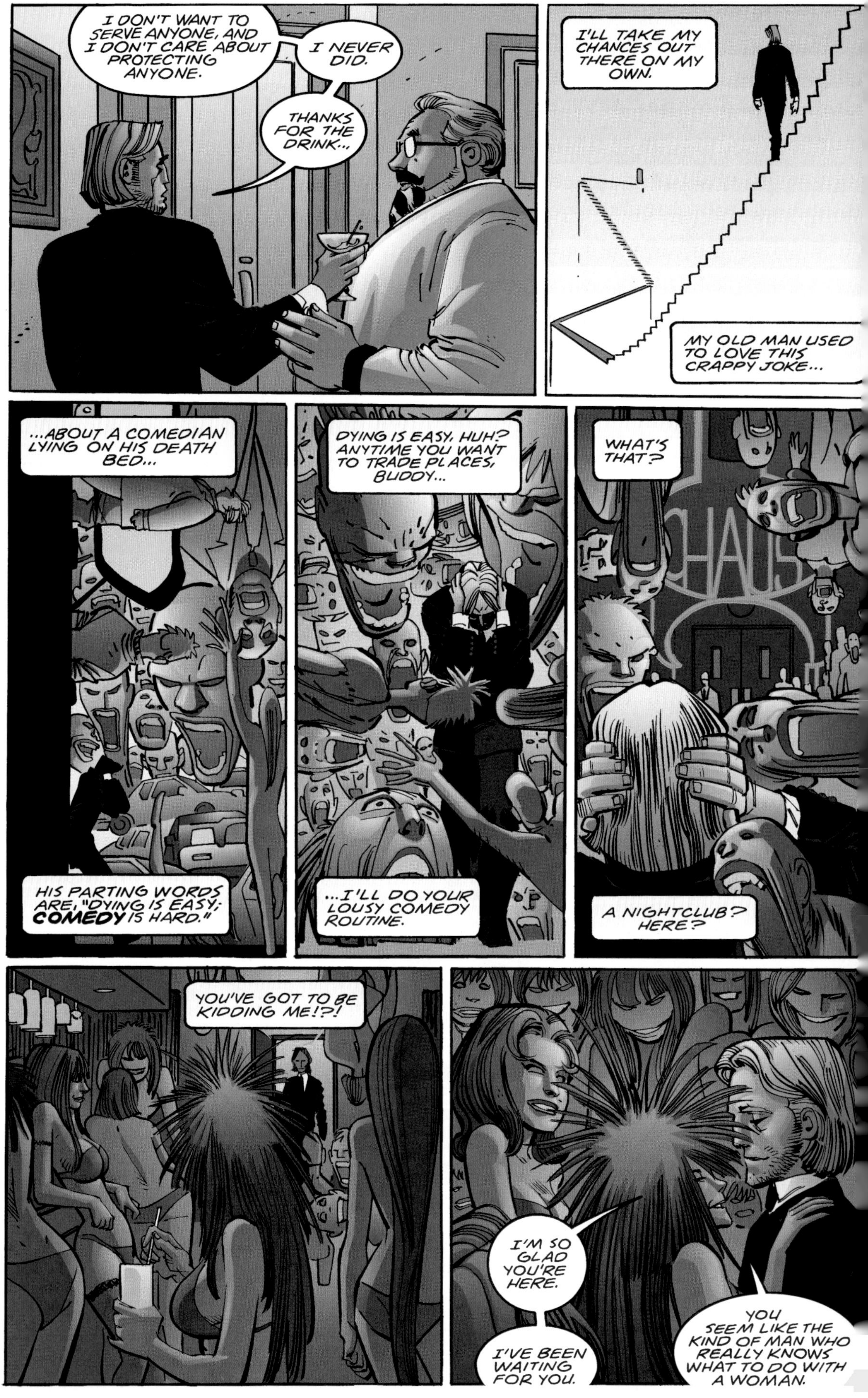
I DON'T WANT TO SERVE ANYONE, AND I DON'T CARE ABOUT PROTECTING ANYONE.
I NEVER DID.
THANKS FOR THE DRINK...
I'LL TAKE MY CHANCES OUT THERE ON MY OWN.
MY OLD MAN USED TO LOVE THIS CRAPPY JOKE...
...ABOUT A COMEDIAN LYING ON HIS DEATH BED...
HIS PARTING WORDS ARE, "DYING IS EASY; COMEDY IS HARD."
DYING IS EASY, HUH? ANYTIME YOU WANT TO TRADE PLACES, BUDDY...
...I'LL DO YOUR LOUSY COMEDY ROUTINE.
WHAT'S THAT?
CHAUS
A NIGHTCLUB? HERE?
YOU'VE GOT TO BE KIDDING ME!?!
I'M SO GLAD YOU'RE HERE.
I'VE BEEN WAITING FOR YOU.
YOU SEEM LIKE THE KIND OF MAN WHO REALLY KNOWS WHAT TO DO WITH A WOMAN.

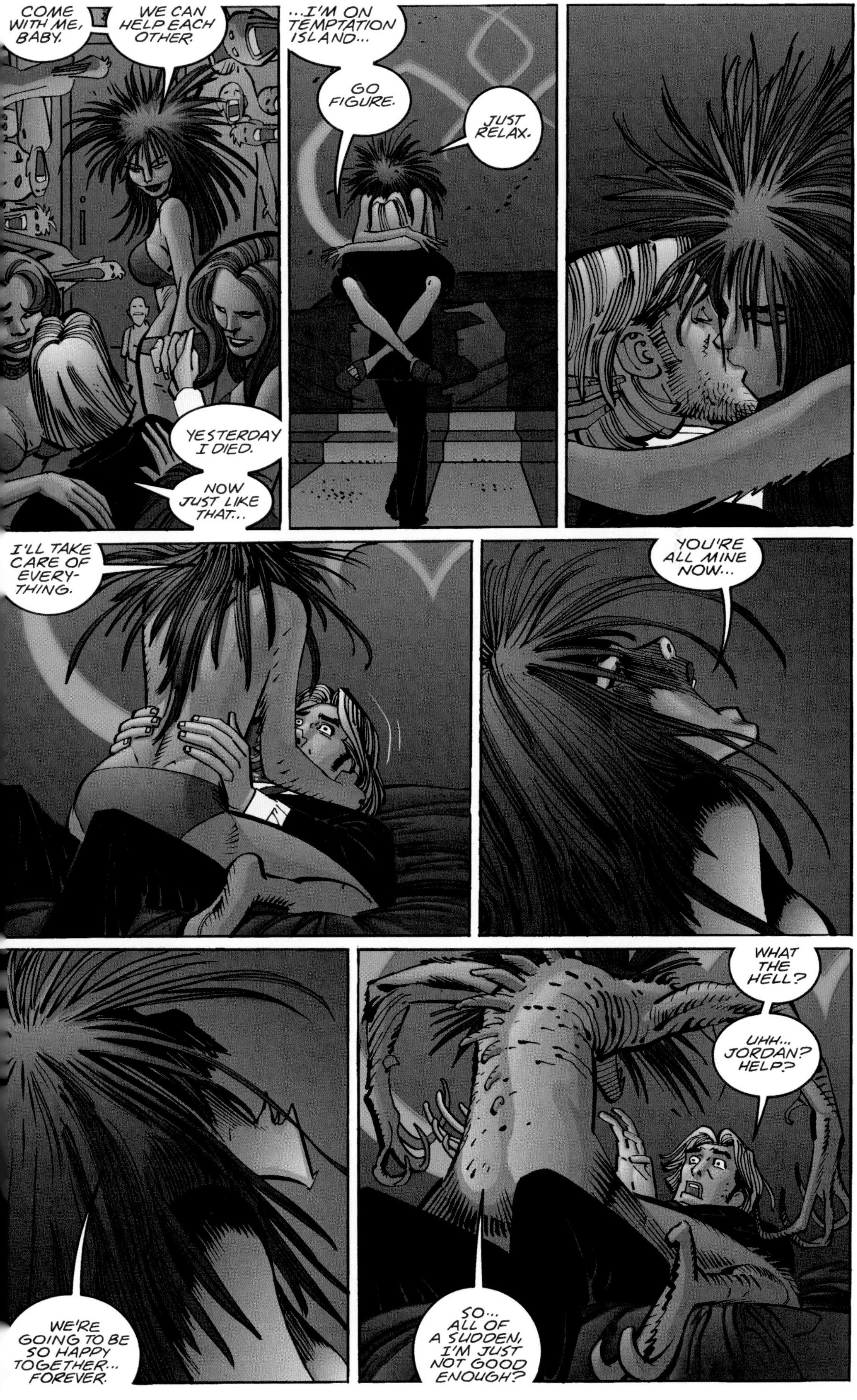
COME WITH ME, BABY.
WE CAN HELP EACH OTHER.
YESTERDAY I DIED.
NOW JUST LIKE THAT...
...I'M ON TEMPTATION ISLAND...
GO FIGURE.
JUST RELAX.
I'LL TAKE CARE OF EVERY-THING.
YOU'RE ALL MINE NOW...
WE'RE GOING TO BE SO HAPPY TOGETHER... FOREVER.
WHAT THE HELL?
UHH... JORDAN? HELP?
SO... ALL OF A SUDDEN, I'M JUST NOT GOOD ENOUGH?

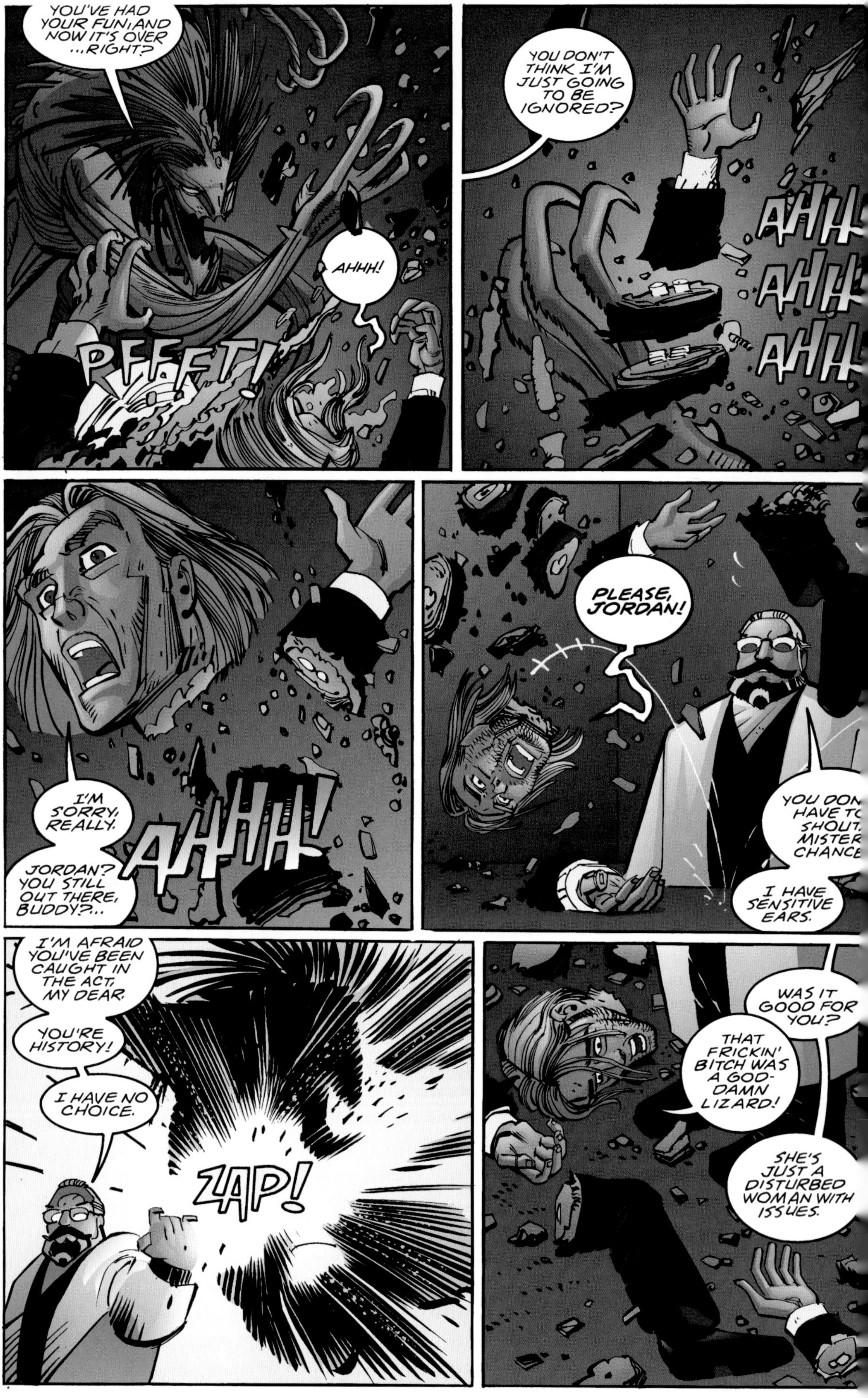
YOU'VE HAD YOUR FUN, AND NOW IT'S OVER ...RIGHT?
AHHH!
PFFFT!
YOU DON'T THINK I'M JUST GOING TO BE IGNORED?
AHH AHH AHH
I'M SORRY, REALLY.
JORDAN? YOU STILL OUT THERE, BUDDY?...
AHHH!
PLEASE, JORDAN!
YOU DON HAVE TO SHOUT, MISTER CHANCE
I HAVE SENSITIVE EARS.
I'M AFRAID YOU'VE BEEN CAUGHT IN THE ACT, MY DEAR.
YOU'RE HISTORY!
I HAVE NO CHOICE.
ZAP!
WAS IT GOOD FOR YOU?
THAT FRICKIN' BITCH WAS A GOD-DAMN LIZARD!
SHE'S JUST A DISTURBED WOMAN WITH ISSUES.

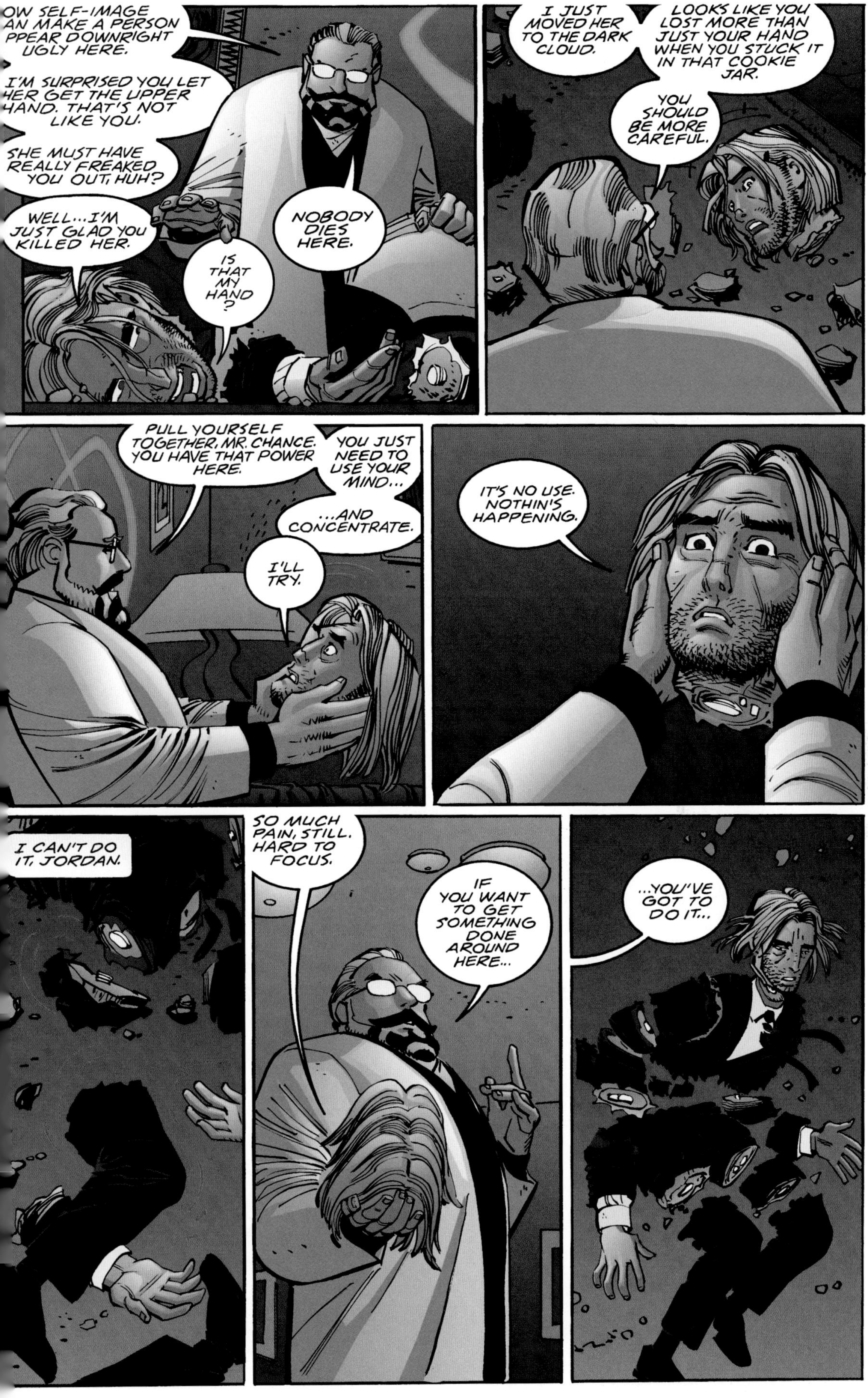
OW SELF-IMAGE
AN MAKE A PERSON
PPEAR DOWNRIGHT
UGLY HERE.
I'M SURPRISED YOU LET
HER GET THE UPPER
HAND. THAT'S NOT
LIKE YOU.
SHE MUST HAVE
REALLY FREAKED
YOU OUT, HUH?
WELL... I'M
JUST GLAD YOU
KILLED HER.
NOBODY
DIES
HERE.
IS
THAT
MY
HAND
?
I JUST
MOVED HER
TO THE DARK
CLOUD.
LOOKS LIKE YOU
LOST MORE THAN
JUST YOUR HAND
WHEN YOU STUCK IT
IN THAT COOKIE
JAR.
YOU
SHOULD
BE MORE
CAREFUL.
PULL YOURSELF
TOGETHER, MR. CHANCE.
YOU HAVE THAT POWER
HERE.
YOU JUST
NEED TO
USE YOUR
MIND...
...AND
CONCENTRATE.
I'LL
TRY.
IT'S NO USE.
NOTHIN'S
HAPPENING.
I CAN'T DO
IT, JORDAN.
SO MUCH
PAIN, STILL.
HARD TO
FOCUS.
IF
YOU WANT
TO GET
SOMETHING
DONE
AROUND
HERE...
...YOU'VE
GOT TO
DO IT...

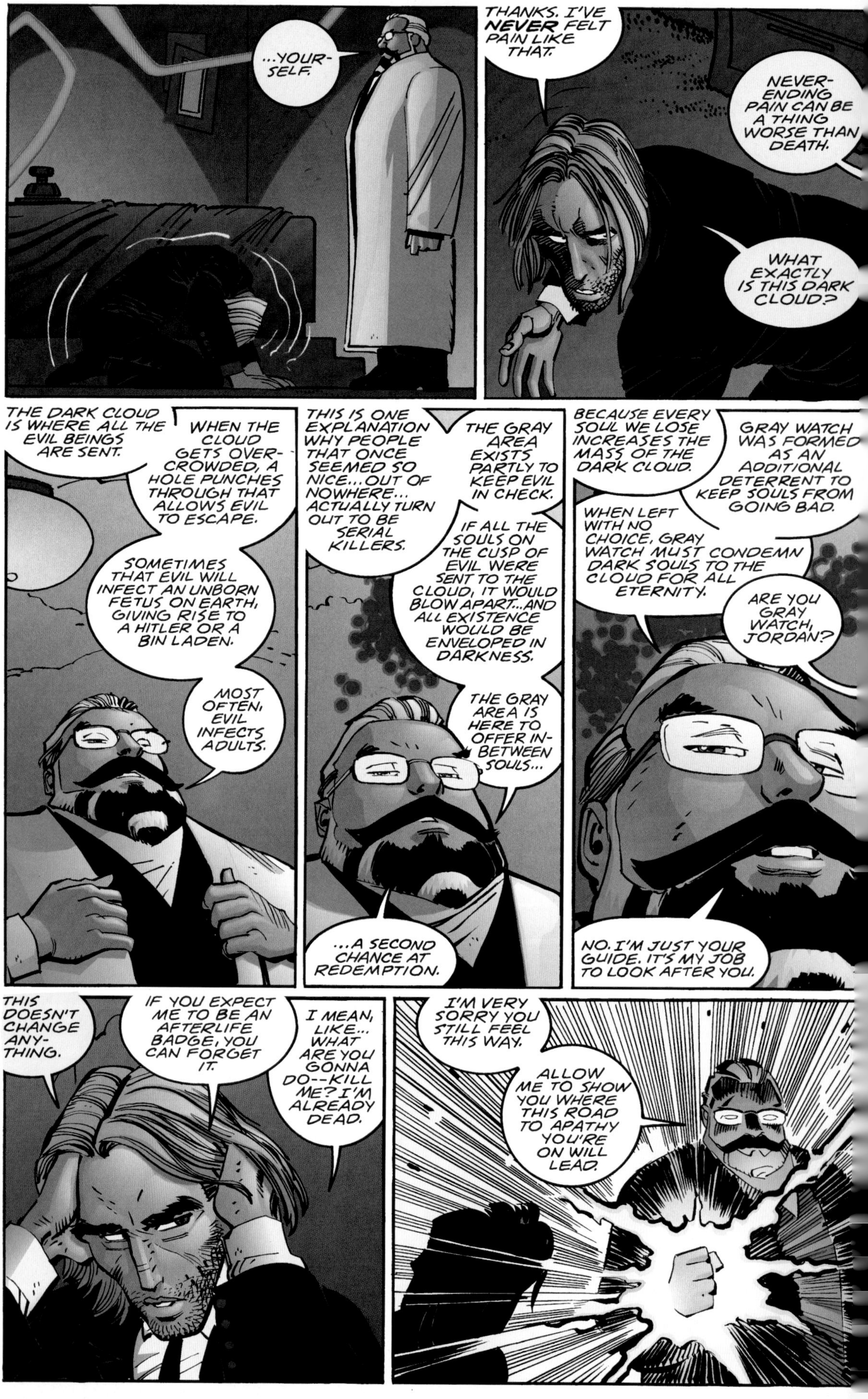

...YOURSELF.
THANKS. I'VE NEVER FELT PAIN LIKE THAT.
NEVER-ENDING PAIN CAN BE A THING WORSE THAN DEATH.
WHAT EXACTLY IS THIS DARK CLOUD?
THE DARK CLOUD IS WHERE ALL THE EVIL BEINGS ARE SENT.
WHEN THE CLOUD GETS OVER-CROWDED, A HOLE PUNCHES THROUGH THAT ALLOWS EVIL TO ESCAPE.
SOMETIMES THAT EVIL WILL INFECT AN UNBORN FETUS ON EARTH, GIVING RISE TO A HITLER OR A BIN LADEN.
MOST OFTEN, EVIL INFECTS ADULTS.
THIS IS ONE EXPLANATION WHY PEOPLE THAT ONCE SEEMED SO NICE...OUT OF NOWHERE... ACTUALLY TURN OUT TO BE SERIAL KILLERS.
THE GRAY AREA EXISTS PARTLY TO KEEP EVIL IN CHECK.
IF ALL THE SOULS ON THE CUSP OF EVIL WERE SENT TO THE CLOUD, IT WOULD BLOW APART...AND ALL EXISTENCE WOULD BE ENVELOPED IN DARKNESS.
THE GRAY AREA IS HERE TO OFFER IN-BETWEEN SOULS...
...A SECOND CHANCE AT REDEMPTION.
BECAUSE EVERY SOUL WE LOSE INCREASES THE MASS OF THE DARK CLOUD.
GRAY WATCH WAS FORMED AS AN ADDITIONAL DETERRENT TO KEEP SOULS FROM GOING BAD.
WHEN LEFT WITH NO CHOICE, GRAY WATCH MUST CONDEMN DARK SOULS TO THE CLOUD FOR ALL ETERNITY.
ARE YOU GRAY WATCH, JORDAN?
NO. I'M JUST YOUR GUIDE. IT'S MY JOB TO LOOK AFTER YOU.
THIS DOESN'T CHANGE ANYTHING.
IF YOU EXPECT ME TO BE AN AFTERLIFE BADGE, YOU CAN FORGET IT.
I MEAN, LIKE... WHAT ARE YOU GONNA DO--KILL ME? I'M ALREADY DEAD.
I'M VERY SORRY YOU STILL FEEL THIS WAY.
ALLOW ME TO SHOW YOU WHERE THIS ROAD TO APATHY YOU'RE ON WILL LEAD.

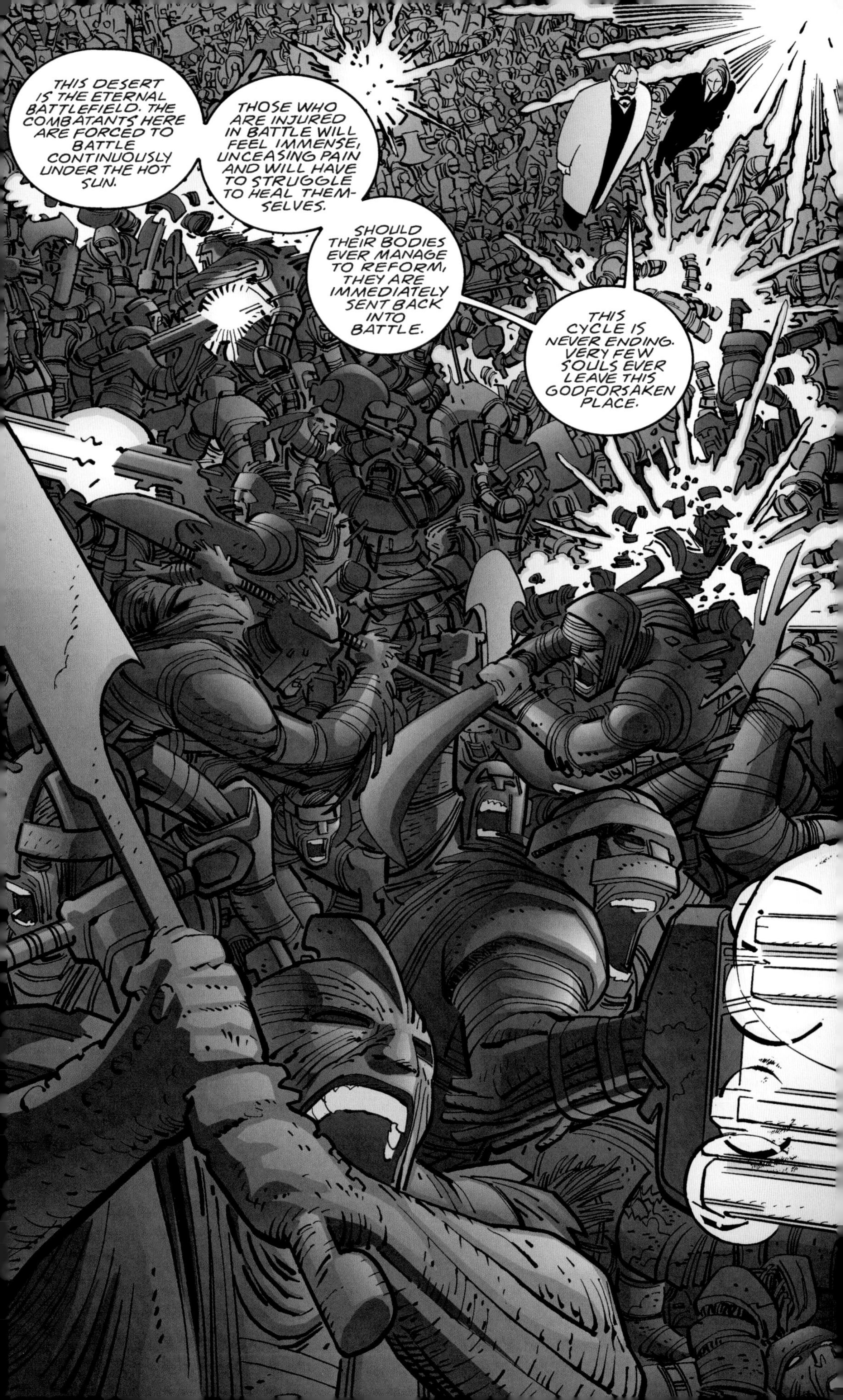
THIS DESERT IS THE ETERNAL BATTLEFIELD. THE COMBATANTS HERE ARE FORCED TO BATTLE CONTINUOUSLY UNDER THE HOT SUN.
THOSE WHO ARE INJURED IN BATTLE WILL FEEL IMMENSE, UNCEASING PAIN AND WILL HAVE TO STRUGGLE TO HEAL THEM-SELVES.
SHOULD THEIR BODIES EVER MANAGE TO REFORM, THEY ARE IMMEDIATELY SENT BACK INTO BATTLE.
THIS CYCLE IS NEVER ENDING. VERY FEW SOULS EVER LEAVE THIS GODFORSAKEN PLACE.

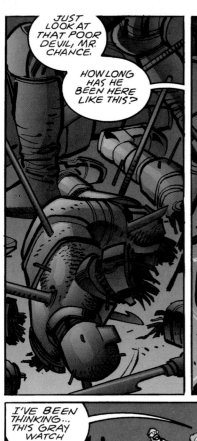

JUST LOOK AT THAT POOR DEVIL, MR. CHANCE.

HOW LONG HAS HE BEEN HERE LIKE THIS?

I CAN HEAL HIS WOUNDS...

...BUT I CAN'T ALTER HIS FATE.

IF YOU REFUSE SERVICE IN GRAY WATCH, I HAVE NO CHOICE BUT TO SEND YOU HERE.

IS THIS YOUR DESIRE?

I'VE BEEN THINKING... THIS GRAY WATCH THING?

THAT MIGHT NOT BE A BAD VOCATION AFTER ALL.

YOU'RE KIND OF A PAIN IN THE ASS. YOU KNOW THAT, JORDAN?

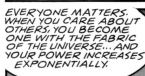

EXCELLENT. NOW, IF I COULD JUST GET YOU TO SHAVE. GRAY WATCH SHAVE.

WHY DO I MATTER SO MUCH TO YOU, ANYWAY?

EVERYONE MATTERS. WHEN YOU CARE ABOUT OTHERS, YOU BECOME ONE WITH THE FABRIC OF THE UNIVERSE... AND YOUR POWER INCREASES EXPONENTIALLY.

YOU REALLY EXPECT ME TO SWALLOW THAT CRAP?

YOU BETTER!

YOUR FOCUS ON EARTH WAS ALWAYS YOURSELF. TO SIMPLY SURVIVE HERE, YOU WILL HAVE TO IMPLEMENT A SEVERE INTERNAL CHANGE.

I'LL GIVE YOU THE FIFTY-CENT TOUR, MR. CHANCE. WE'RE FLYING OVER GRAY AREA CITY NOW.

IT LOOKS A LOT LIKE NEW YORK. THE PIZZA STINKS, BUT THE HOT DOGS ARE AWESOME. THEY KICK THE CRAP OUT OF PAPAYA KING.

I REALIZE YOU DON'T HAVE A BODY TO SUSTAIN, BUT, SEEING AS YOU STILL ENJOY THE PLEASURES OF THE FLESH, YOU'LL PROBABLY STILL ENJOY EATING, AS WELL.

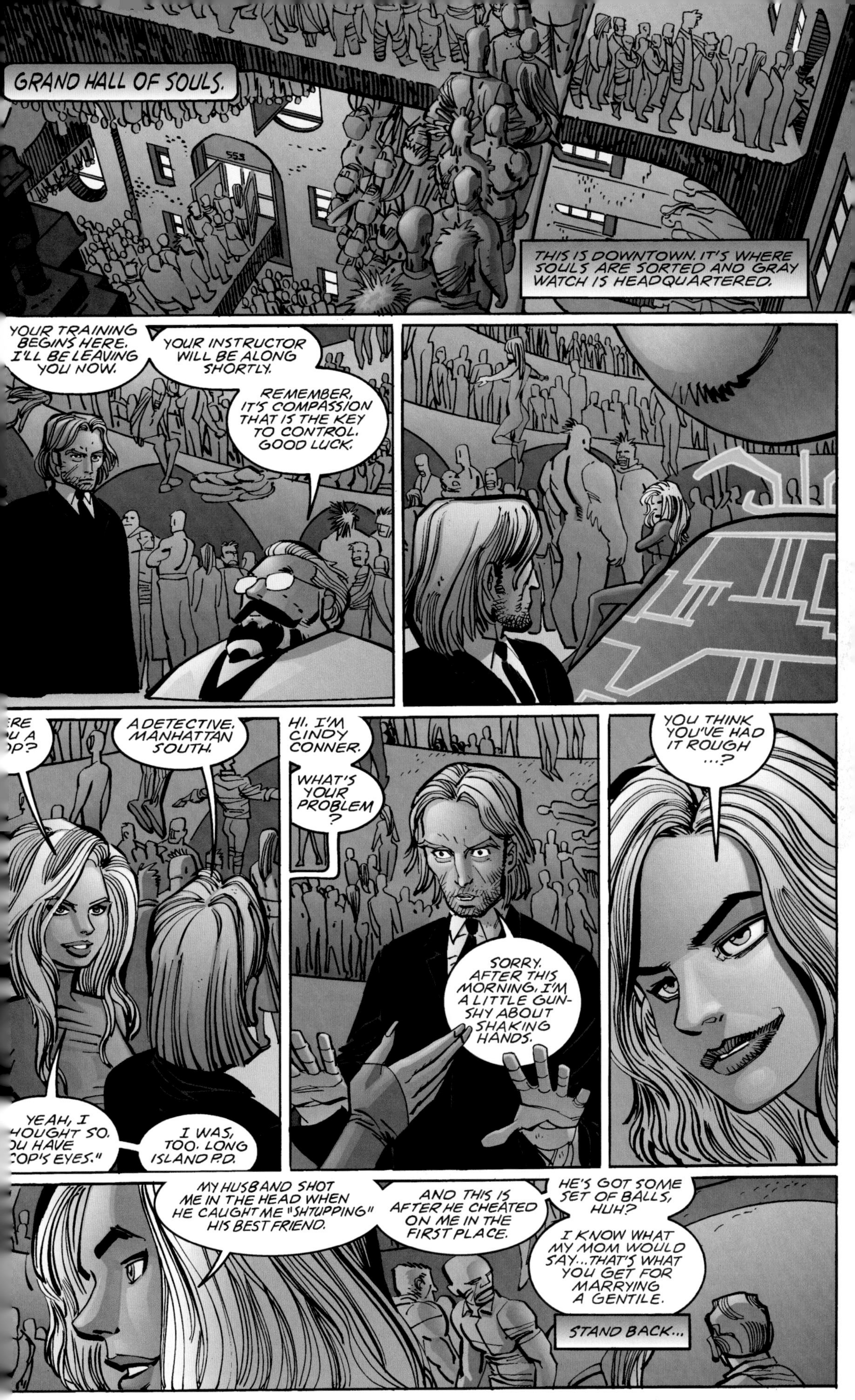
GRAND HALL OF SOULS.
THIS IS DOWNTOWN. IT'S WHERE SOULS ARE SORTED AND GRAY WATCH IS HEADQUARTERED.
YOUR TRAINING BEGINS HERE. I'LL BE LEAVING YOU NOW.
YOUR INSTRUCTOR WILL BE ALONG SHORTLY.
REMEMBER, IT'S COMPASSION THAT IS THE KEY TO CONTROL. GOOD LUCK.
ERE U A OP?
A DETECTIVE. MANHATTAN SOUTH.
YEAH, I HOUGHT SO. OU HAVE COP'S EYES."
I WAS, TOO. LONG ISLAND P.D.
HI. I'M CINDY CONNER.
WHAT'S YOUR PROBLEM?
SORRY. AFTER THIS MORNING, I'M A LITTLE GUN-SHY ABOUT SHAKING HANDS.
YOU THINK YOU'VE HAD IT ROUGH ...?
MY HUSBAND SHOT ME IN THE HEAD WHEN HE CAUGHT ME "SHTUPPING" HIS BEST FRIEND.
AND THIS IS AFTER HE CHEATED ON ME IN THE FIRST PLACE.
HE'S GOT SOME SET OF BALLS, HUH?
I KNOW WHAT MY MOM WOULD SAY...THAT'S WHAT YOU GET FOR MARRYING A GENTILE.
STAND BACK...

LIEUTENANT BEEBONOCK IS IN COMMAND.

ALL YOU MISFITS GATHER AROUND.

I CAN'T REMEMBER THE LAST TIME I SAW A WORSE-LOOKING BUNCH OF RECRUITS.

I'M YOUR DRILL INSTRUCTOR.

IT'S MY JOB TO TURN YOUR SORRY BUTTS INTO GRAY WATCH.

EVERY-BODY WISH ME LUCK.

LATER--A TRAINING FIELD.

YOU ALL WILL BE FITTED WITH A SHOULDER HARNESS THAT PIERCES THE SOUL AND CANNOT BE REMOVED WITH-OUT THE PROPER DEVICE.

THE HARNESS WILL ENHANCE YOUR ABILITIES.

WHEN YOUR POWER FULLY DEVELOPS, IT WILL BE REMOVED.

THIS PIECE W... ALLOW YOU T... USE YOUR MI... TO MOVE MATT... TRANSPORT YO... SELF ANYWHE... AND HEAL... INJURIES.

UHHH!

THWAK!

AWW, NO! MORE PAIN? CAN'T I GET A BREAK HERE?

IN TIME, MOST OF YOU WILL DEVELOP THE POWER TO SHOOT AN ENERGY BLAST STRONG ENOUGH TO DESTROY OBJECTS AND VANQUISH OPPONENTS.

DAMN! DOES EVERYTHING HAVE TO HURT LIKE A BITCH?

BUT DON'T GET DISCOURAGED. SOME RECRUITS OBVIOUSLY WILL TAKE MUCH LONGER TO DEVELOP THAN OTHERS.

TRAINING BEGINS...

THIS WILL BE YOUR FIRST EXERCISE, CHANCE. WAIT HERE AND BE READY FOR ANYTHING.

ACTUALLY, I LEARNED A LOT ON THE JOB. LIKE HOW TO KEEP YOUR FOCUS ON ALL THE EXIT AND ENTRY POINTS.

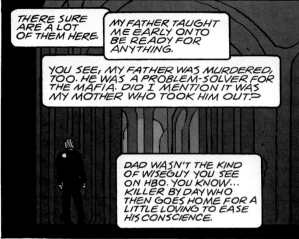

THERE SURE ARE A LOT OF THEM HERE.

MY FATHER TAUGHT ME EARLY ON TO BE READY FOR ANYTHING.

YOU SEE, MY FATHER WAS MURDERED, TOO. HE WAS A PROBLEM-SOLVER FOR THE MAFIA. DID I MENTION IT WAS MY MOTHER WHO TOOK HIM OUT?

DAD WASN'T THE KIND OF WISEGUY YOU SEE ON HBO. YOU KNOW... KILLER BY DAY WHO THEN GOES HOME FOR A LITTLE LOVING TO EASE HIS CONSCIENCE.

BEATING ON MOM AND MY YOUNGER BROTHER PETER WAS DAD'S FAVORITE RECREATION.

HE'D PUMMEL ME, TOO, IF I GOT IN THE WAY.

LET'S SEE IF I CAN CREATE A LITTLE DISTRACTION HERE.

NOTHIN'. NOT EVEN A NIBBLE.

MOM DRANK A LOT AND, AS IT TURNED OUT, PETER HAD A DIFFERENT FATHER.

ONE DAY DAD DECIDED TO REMIND HER OF HER INDISCRETION.

SHE JUST COULDN'T TAKE IT ANYMORE. SHE SHOT HIM POINT BLANK. PROBLEM WAS SHE FORGOT TO STOP SQUEEZING THE TRIGGER.

IN HER DRUNKEN HAZE, ONE OF HER SHOTS STRUCK PETER AND KILLED HIM.

MOM'S DOING CONSECUTIVE LIFE SENTENCES.

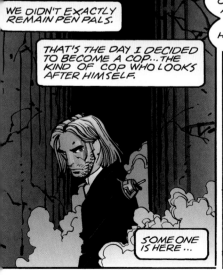

WE DIDN'T EXACTLY REMAIN PEN PALS.

THAT'S THE DAY I DECIDED TO BECOME A COP...THE KIND OF COP WHO LOOKS AFTER HIMSELF.

SOMEONE IS HERE...

RIGHT CROSS? THAT'S ALL YOU GOT?

YOU'RE GONNA HAVE TO DO BETTER THAN THAT.

JUST SLIDE BEHIND HIS PUNCH...

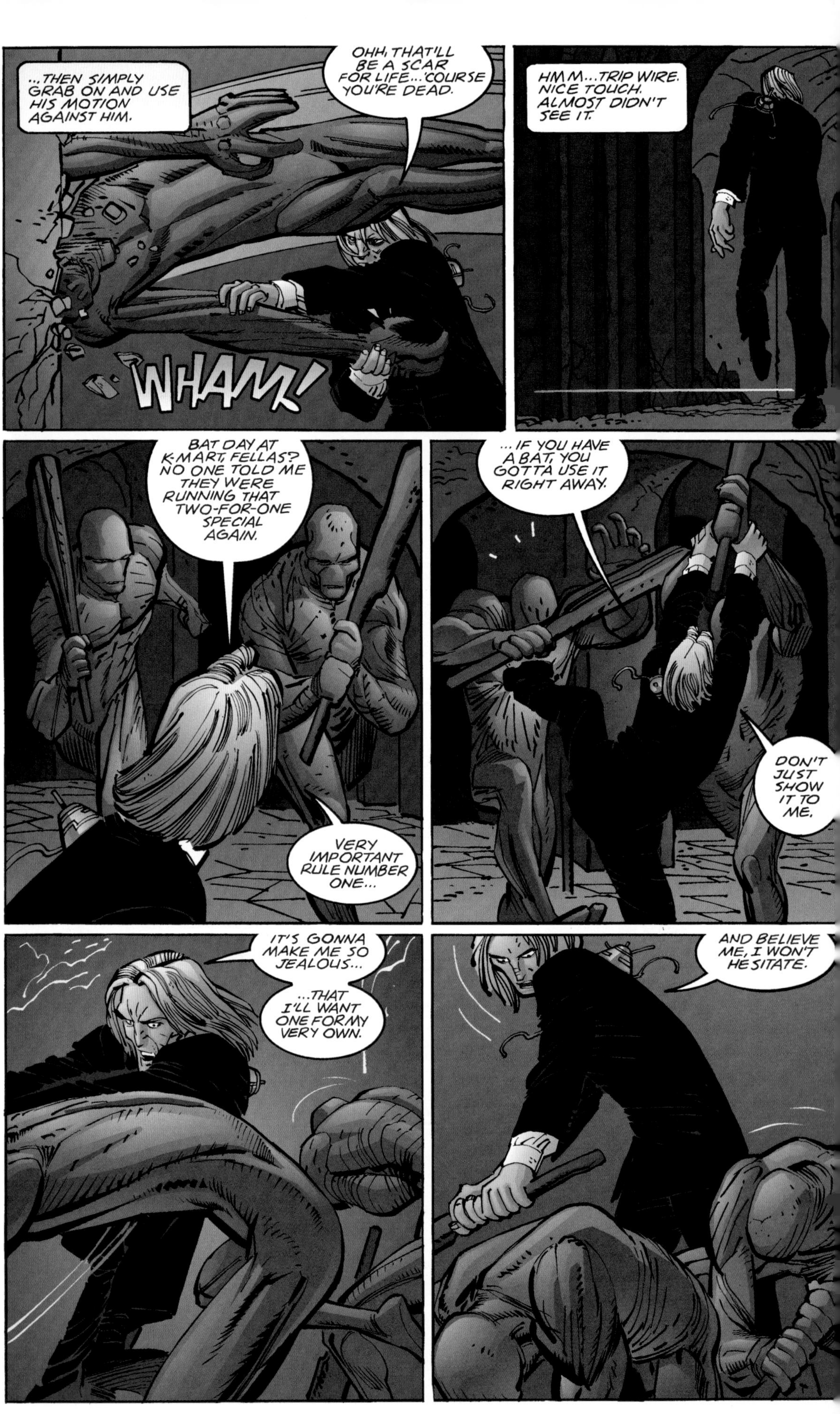
...THEN SIMPLY GRAB ON AND USE HIS MOTION AGAINST HIM.
OHH, THAT'LL BE A SCAR FOR LIFE...'COURSE YOU'RE DEAD.
WHAM!
HMM...TRIP WIRE. NICE TOUCH. ALMOST DIDN'T SEE IT.
BAT DAY AT K-MART, FELLAS? NO ONE TOLD ME THEY WERE RUNNING THAT TWO-FOR-ONE SPECIAL AGAIN.
VERY IMPORTANT RULE NUMBER ONE...
...IF YOU HAVE A BAT, YOU GOTTA USE IT RIGHT AWAY.
DON'T JUST SHOW IT TO ME.
IT'S GONNA MAKE ME SO JEALOUS...
...THAT I'LL WANT ONE FOR MY VERY OWN.
AND BELIEVE ME, I WON'T HESITATE.

I KNOW JUST HOW TO USE IT.

WHACK!

WHACK!

HAD ENOUGH, DIRT-BAGS?

YOU FRICKIN' PUNKS ARE FOLDING BEFORE THE STAKES EVEN GET INTERESTING.

OKAY, I'VE BEEN ON DEFENSE LONG ENOUGH. TIME TO TAKE THE BALL TO THE HOOP.

FEELS SO GREAT TO REALLY CUT LOOSE AND TAKE NO PRISONERS. I COULD GET USED TO THIS.

WHOA! DON'T NEED TO GET CAUGHT IN THE MIDDLE OF THAT MESS.

FIRST UNWRITTEN RULE YOU LEARN AT THE ACADEMY... IF YOU WANT TO SURVIVE... AVOID RIOT PATROL.

T THEN... THERE'S WAYS A COUPLE OF YS IN A CROWD WHO INK THEY'RE TOUGHER THAN THE REST.

ALLOW ME TO EDUCATE YOU.

I HOPE I DON'T COME OFF LIKE A BRAGGART HERE...

...BUT I'M THE MVP...

...EVERY SUNDAY ON THE EAST HAMPTON SOFTBALL LEAGUE.

THUMP!

SMACK!

I REALIZE IT'S NOT MAJOR LEAGUE STUFF, BUT BRAD PITT PLAYED WITH US LAST SUMMER.

DON'T HATE ME FOR BEING SUCH A NAME-DROPPER WHILE I'M KICKIN' YOUR TAIL.

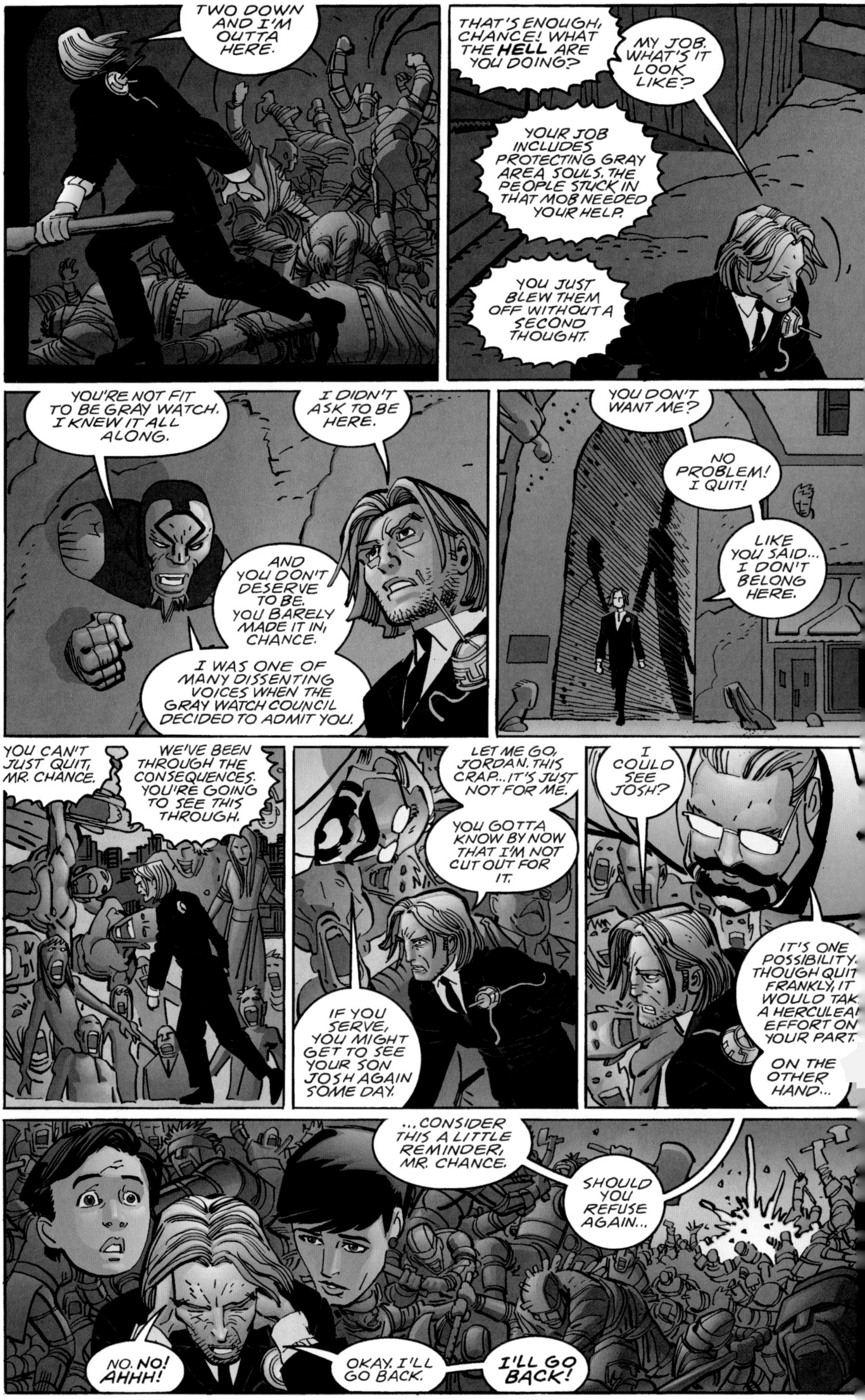
TWO DOWN AND I'M OUTTA HERE.
THAT'S ENOUGH, CHANCE! WHAT THE HELL ARE YOU DOING?
MY JOB. WHAT'S IT LOOK LIKE?
YOUR JOB INCLUDES PROTECTING GRAY AREA SOULS. THE PEOPLE STUCK IN THAT MOB NEEDED YOUR HELP.
YOU JUST BLEW THEM OFF WITHOUT A SECOND THOUGHT.
YOU'RE NOT FIT TO BE GRAY WATCH. I KNEW IT ALL ALONG.
I DIDN'T ASK TO BE HERE.
AND YOU DON'T DESERVE TO BE. YOU BARELY MADE IT IN, CHANCE.
I WAS ONE OF MANY DISSENTING VOICES WHEN THE GRAY WATCH COUNCIL DECIDED TO ADMIT YOU.
YOU DON'T WANT ME?
NO PROBLEM! I QUIT!
LIKE YOU SAID... I DON'T BELONG HERE.
YOU CAN'T JUST QUIT, MR. CHANCE.
WE'VE BEEN THROUGH THE CONSEQUENCES. YOU'RE GOING TO SEE THIS THROUGH.
LET ME GO, JORDAN. THIS CRAP... IT'S JUST NOT FOR ME.
YOU GOTTA KNOW BY NOW THAT I'M NOT CUT OUT FOR IT.
IF YOU SERVE, YOU MIGHT GET TO SEE YOUR SON JOSH AGAIN SOME DAY.
I COULD SEE JOSH?
IT'S ONE POSSIBILITY. THOUGH QUIT FRANKLY, IT WOULD TAK A HERCULEA EFFORT ON YOUR PART.
ON THE OTHER HAND...
...CONSIDER THIS A LITTLE REMINDER, MR. CHANCE.
SHOULD YOU REFUSE AGAIN...
NO. NO! AHHH!
OKAY. I'LL GO BACK.
I'LL GO BACK!

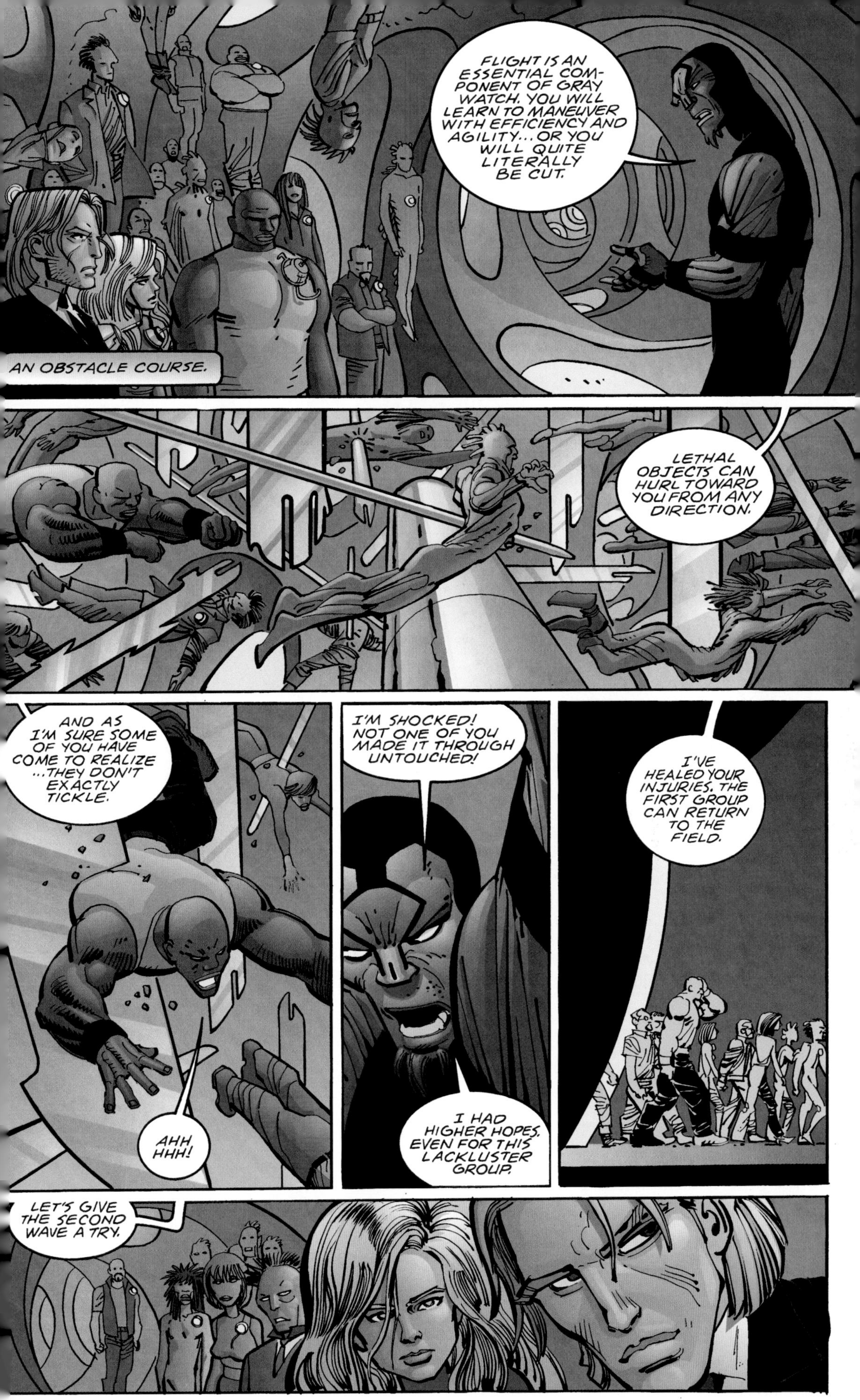
FLIGHT IS AN ESSENTIAL COMPONENT OF GRAY WATCH. YOU WILL LEARN TO MANEUVER WITH EFFICIENCY AND AGILITY... OR YOU WILL QUITE LITERALLY BE CUT.
AN OBSTACLE COURSE.
LETHAL OBJECTS CAN HURL TOWARD YOU FROM ANY DIRECTION.
AND AS I'M SURE SOME OF YOU HAVE COME TO REALIZE ...THEY DON'T EXACTLY TICKLE.
AHH HHH!
I'M SHOCKED! NOT ONE OF YOU MADE IT THROUGH UNTOUCHED!
I HAD HIGHER HOPES. EVEN FOR THIS LACKLUSTER GROUP.
I'VE HEALED YOUR INJURIES. THE FIRST GROUP CAN RETURN TO THE FIELD.
LET'S GIVE THE SECOND WAVE A TRY.

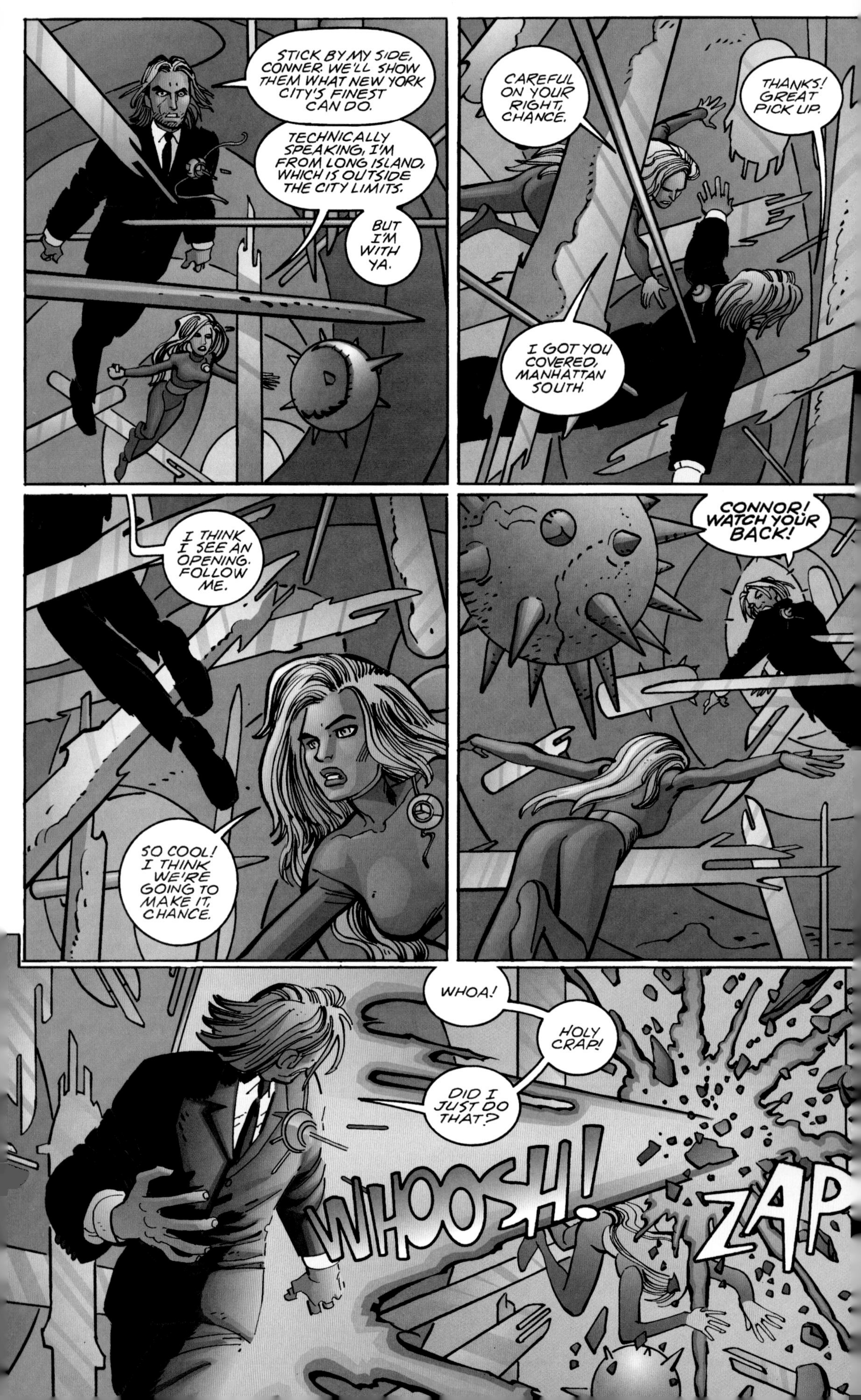
STICK BY MY SIDE, CONNER. WE'LL SHOW THEM WHAT NEW YORK CITY'S FINEST CAN DO.
TECHNICALLY SPEAKING, I'M FROM LONG ISLAND, WHICH IS OUTSIDE THE CITY LIMITS.
BUT I'M WITH YA.
CAREFUL ON YOUR RIGHT, CHANCE.
THANKS! GREAT PICK UP.
I GOT YOU COVERED, MANHATTAN SOUTH.
I THINK I SEE AN OPENING. FOLLOW ME.
SO COOL! I THINK WE'RE GOING TO MAKE IT, CHANCE.
CONNOR! WATCH YOUR BACK!
WHOA!
HOLY CRAP!
DID I JUST DO THAT?
WHOOSH!
ZAP

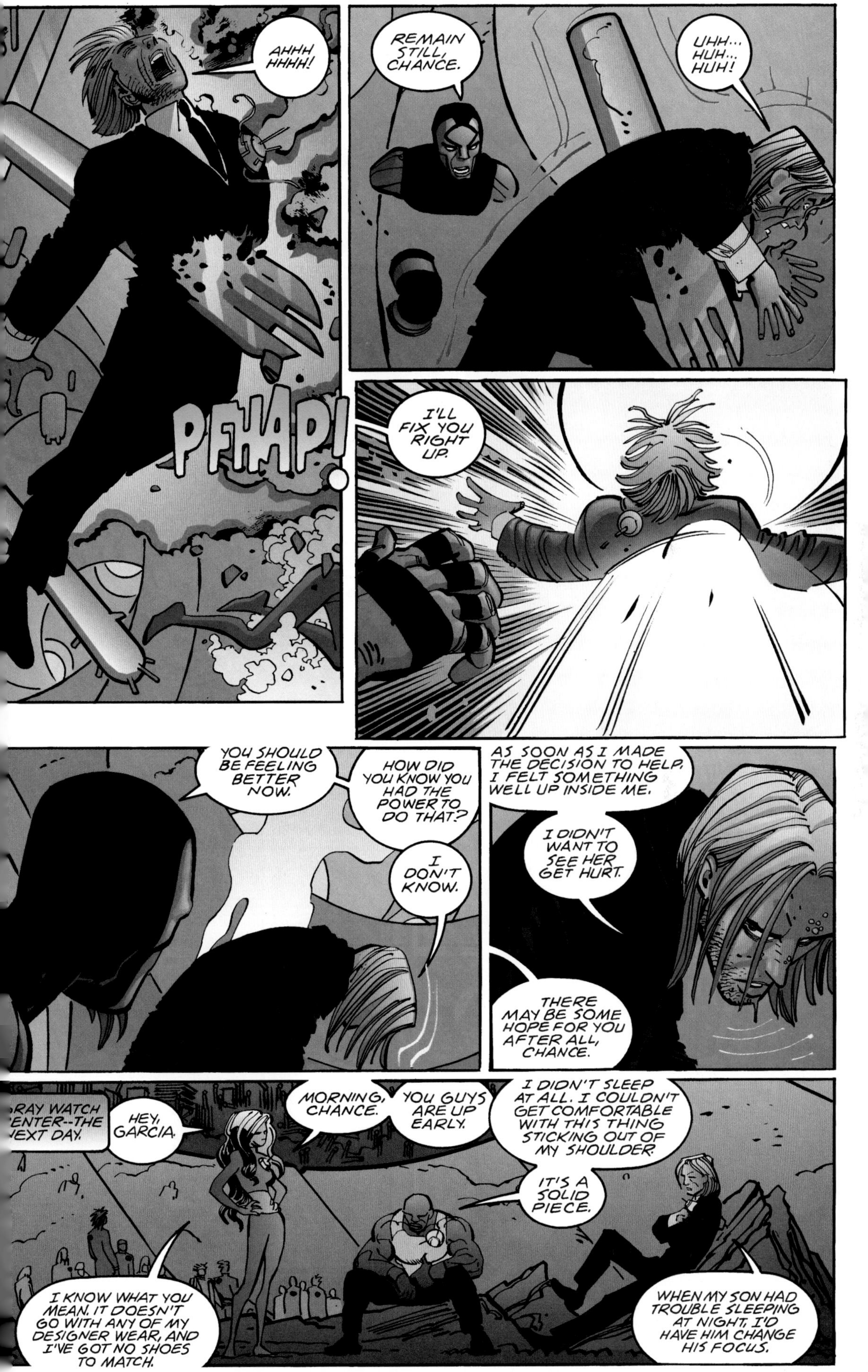
AHHH HHHH!
PFHAP!
REMAIN STILL, CHANCE.
UHH... HUH... HUH!
I'LL FIX YOU RIGHT UP.
YOU SHOULD BE FEELING BETTER NOW.
HOW DID YOU KNOW YOU HAD THE POWER TO DO THAT?
I DON'T KNOW.
AS SOON AS I MADE THE DECISION TO HELP, I FELT SOMETHING WELL UP INSIDE ME.
I DIDN'T WANT TO SEE HER GET HURT.
THERE MAY BE SOME HOPE FOR YOU AFTER ALL, CHANCE.
RAY WATCH ENTER--THE NEXT DAY.
HEY, GARCIA.
MORNING, CHANCE.
YOU GUYS ARE UP EARLY.
I DIDN'T SLEEP AT ALL. I COULDN'T GET COMFORTABLE WITH THIS THING STICKING OUT OF MY SHOULDER.
IT'S A SOLID PIECE.
I KNOW WHAT YOU MEAN. IT DOESN'T GO WITH ANY OF MY DESIGNER WEAR, AND I'VE GOT NO SHOES TO MATCH.
WHEN MY SON HAD TROUBLE SLEEPING AT NIGHT, I'D HAVE HIM CHANGE HIS FOCUS.

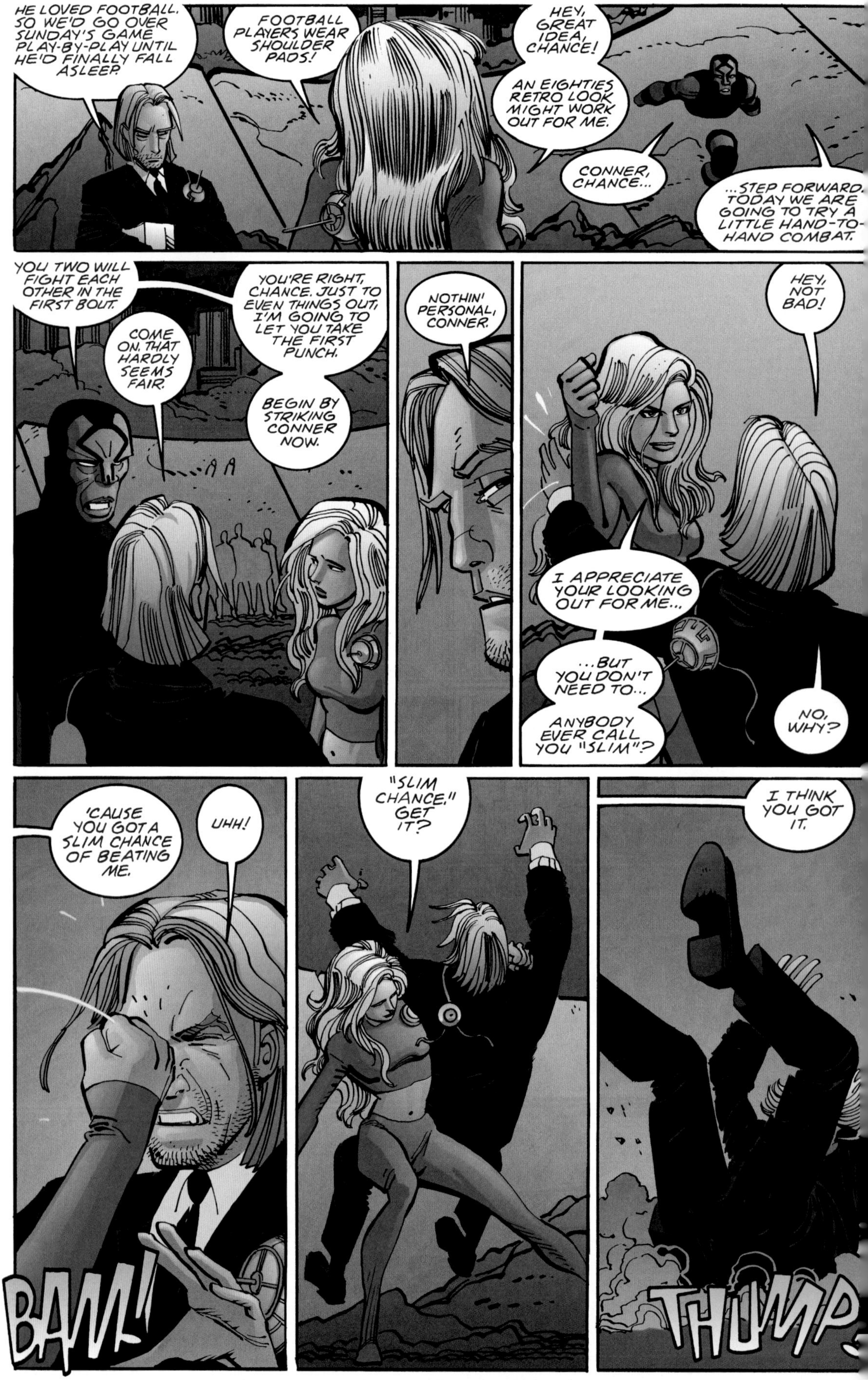
HE LOVED FOOTBALL. SO WE'D GO OVER SUNDAY'S GAME PLAY-BY-PLAY UNTIL HE'D FINALLY FALL ASLEEP.
FOOTBALL PLAYERS WEAR SHOULDER PADS!
HEY, GREAT IDEA, CHANCE!
AN EIGHTIES RETRO LOOK MIGHT WORK OUT FOR ME.
CONNER, CHANCE...
...STEP FORWARD. TODAY WE ARE GOING TO TRY A LITTLE HAND-TO-HAND COMBAT.
YOU TWO WILL FIGHT EACH OTHER IN THE FIRST BOUT.
COME ON. THAT HARDLY SEEMS FAIR.
YOU'RE RIGHT, CHANCE. JUST TO EVEN THINGS OUT, I'M GOING TO LET YOU TAKE THE FIRST PUNCH.
BEGIN BY STRIKING CONNER NOW.
NOTHIN' PERSONAL, CONNER.
HEY, NOT BAD!
I APPRECIATE YOUR LOOKING OUT FOR ME...
...BUT YOU DON'T NEED TO...
ANYBODY EVER CALL YOU "SLIM"?
NO, WHY?
'CAUSE YOU GOT A SLIM CHANCE OF BEATING ME.
UHH!
BAM!
"SLIM CHANCE." GET IT?
I THINK YOU GOT IT.
THUMP

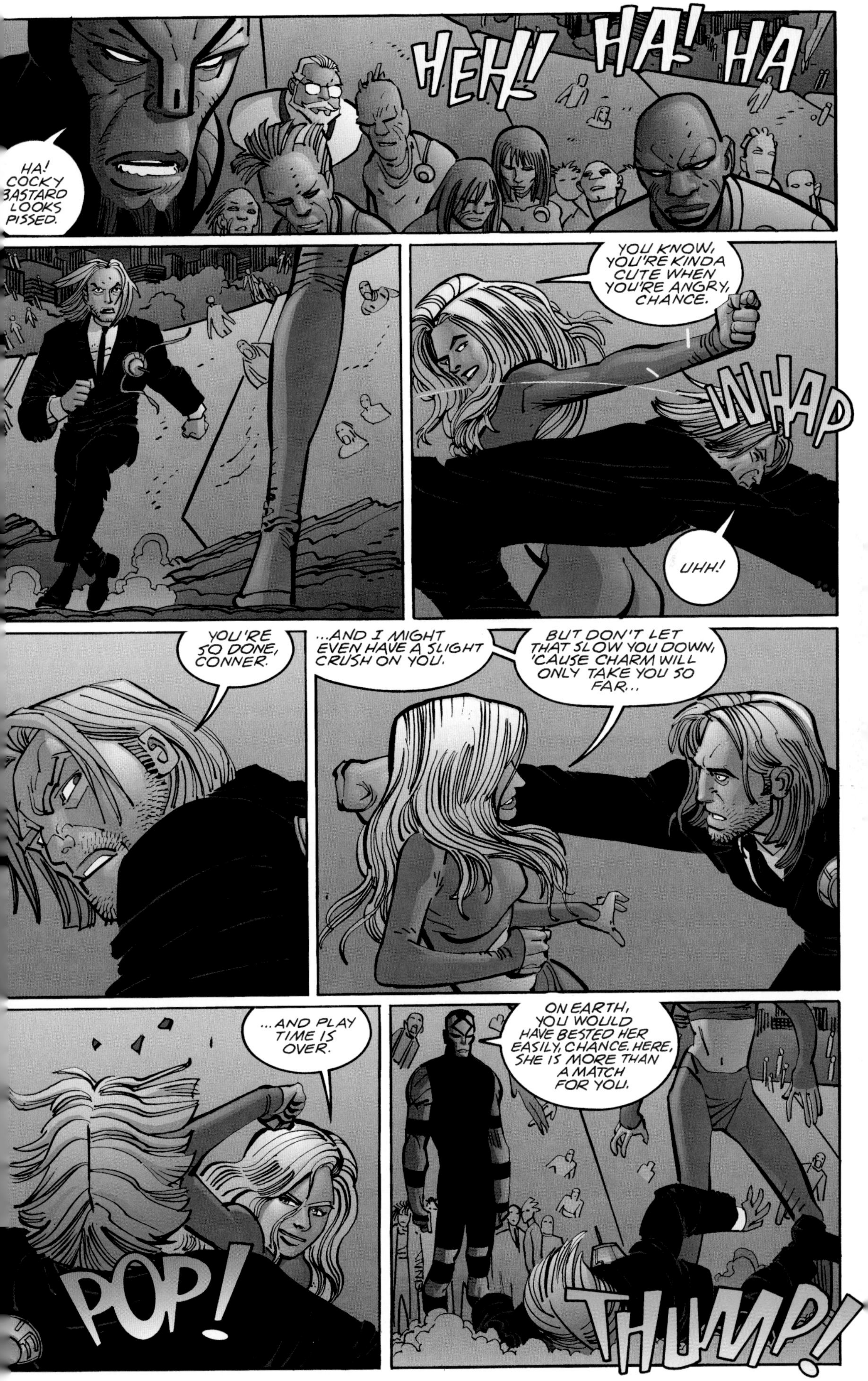
HEH! HA! HA
HA! COCKY BASTARD LOOKS PISSED.
YOU KNOW, YOU'RE KINDA CUTE WHEN YOU'RE ANGRY, CHANCE.
WHAP
UHH!
YOU'RE SO DONE, CONNER.
...AND I MIGHT EVEN HAVE A SLIGHT CRUSH ON YOU.
BUT DON'T LET THAT SLOW YOU DOWN, 'CAUSE CHARM WILL ONLY TAKE YOU SO FAR...
...AND PLAY TIME IS OVER.
POP!
ON EARTH, YOU WOULD HAVE BESTED HER EASILY, CHANCE. HERE, SHE IS MORE THAN A MATCH FOR YOU.
THUMP!

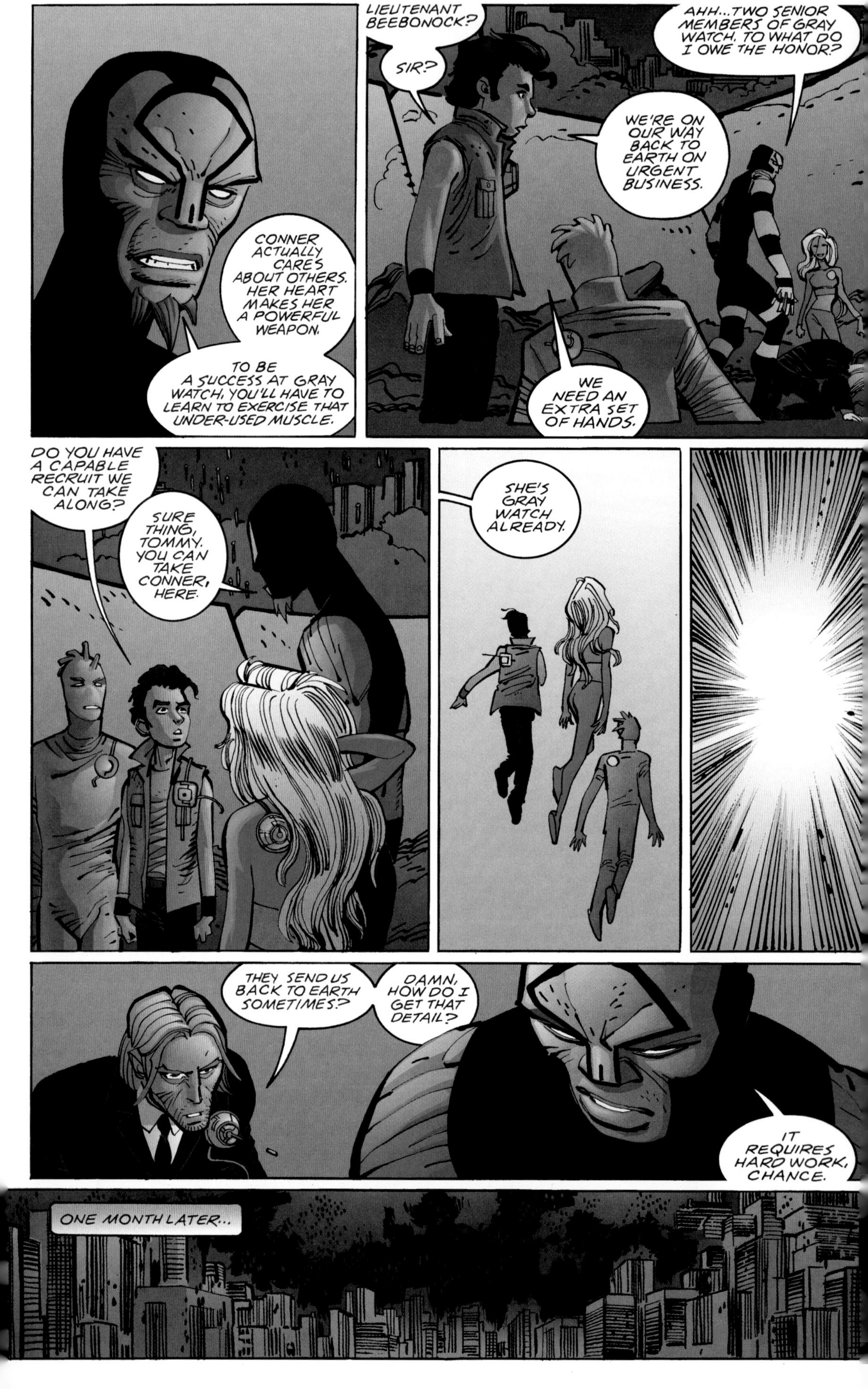
CONNER ACTUALLY CARES ABOUT OTHERS. HER HEART MAKES HER A POWERFUL WEAPON.
TO BE A SUCCESS AT GRAY WATCH, YOU'LL HAVE TO LEARN TO EXERCISE THAT UNDER-USED MUSCLE.
LIEUTENANT BEEBONOCK?
SIR?
AHH...TWO SENIOR MEMBERS OF GRAY WATCH. TO WHAT DO I OWE THE HONOR?
WE'RE ON OUR WAY BACK TO EARTH ON URGENT BUSINESS.
WE NEED AN EXTRA SET OF HANDS.
DO YOU HAVE A CAPABLE RECRUIT WE CAN TAKE ALONG?
SURE THING, TOMMY. YOU CAN TAKE CONNER, HERE.
SHE'S GRAY WATCH ALREADY.
THEY SEND US BACK TO EARTH SOMETIMES?
DAMN, HOW DO I GET THAT DETAIL?
IT REQUIRES HARD WORK, CHANCE.
ONE MONTH LATER...

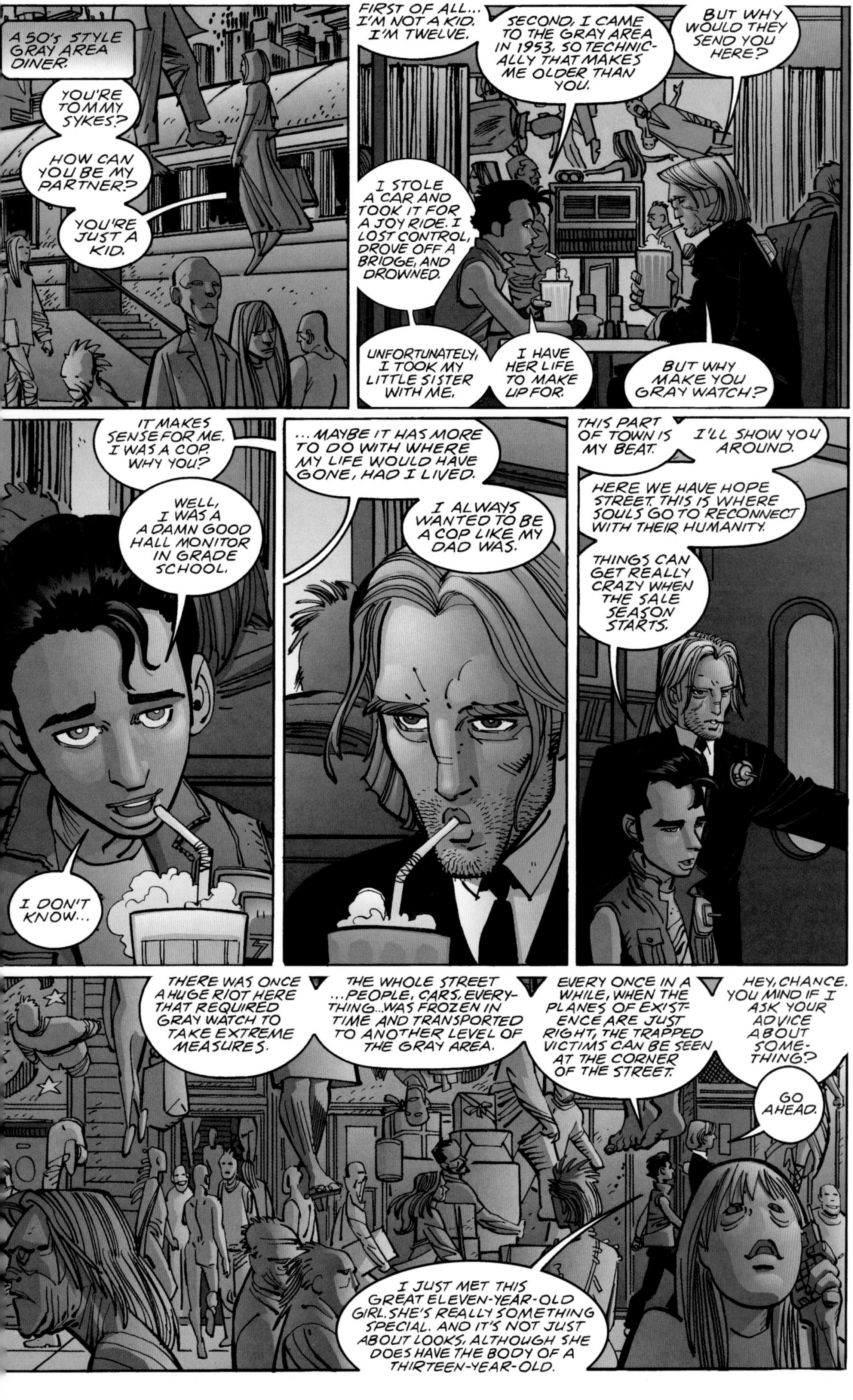

A 50's STYLE GRAY AREA DINER.
YOU'RE TOMMY SYKES?
HOW CAN YOU BE MY PARTNER?
YOU'RE JUST A KID.
FIRST OF ALL... I'M NOT A KID. I'M TWELVE.
SECOND, I CAME TO THE GRAY AREA IN 1953, SO TECHNICALLY THAT MAKES ME OLDER THAN YOU.
BUT WHY WOULD THEY SEND YOU HERE?
I STOLE A CAR AND TOOK IT FOR A JOY RIDE. I LOST CONTROL, DROVE OFF A BRIDGE, AND DROWNED.
UNFORTUNATELY, I TOOK MY LITTLE SISTER WITH ME.
I HAVE HER LIFE TO MAKE UP FOR.
BUT WHY MAKE YOU GRAY WATCH?
IT MAKES SENSE FOR ME. I WAS A COP. WHY YOU?
WELL, I WAS A DAMN GOOD HALL MONITOR IN GRADE SCHOOL.
I DON'T KNOW...
...MAYBE IT HAS MORE TO DO WITH WHERE MY LIFE WOULD HAVE GONE, HAD I LIVED.
I ALWAYS WANTED TO BE A COP LIKE MY DAD WAS.
THIS PART OF TOWN IS MY BEAT.
I'LL SHOW YOU AROUND.
HERE WE HAVE HOPE STREET. THIS IS WHERE SOULS GO TO RECONNECT WITH THEIR HUMANITY.
THINGS CAN GET REALLY CRAZY WHEN THE SALE SEASON STARTS.
THERE WAS ONCE A HUGE RIOT HERE THAT REQUIRED GRAY WATCH TO TAKE EXTREME MEASURES.
THE WHOLE STREET ...PEOPLE, CARS, EVERYTHING...WAS FROZEN IN TIME AND TRANSPORTED TO ANOTHER LEVEL OF THE GRAY AREA.
EVERY ONCE IN A WHILE, WHEN THE PLANES OF EXISTENCE ARE JUST RIGHT, THE TRAPPED VICTIMS CAN BE SEEN AT THE CORNER OF THE STREET.
HEY, CHANCE. YOU MIND IF I ASK YOUR ADVICE ABOUT SOMETHING?
GO AHEAD.
I JUST MET THIS GREAT ELEVEN-YEAR-OLD GIRL. SHE'S REALLY SOMETHING SPECIAL. AND IT'S NOT JUST ABOUT LOOKS, ALTHOUGH SHE DOES HAVE THE BODY OF A THIRTEEN-YEAR-OLD.

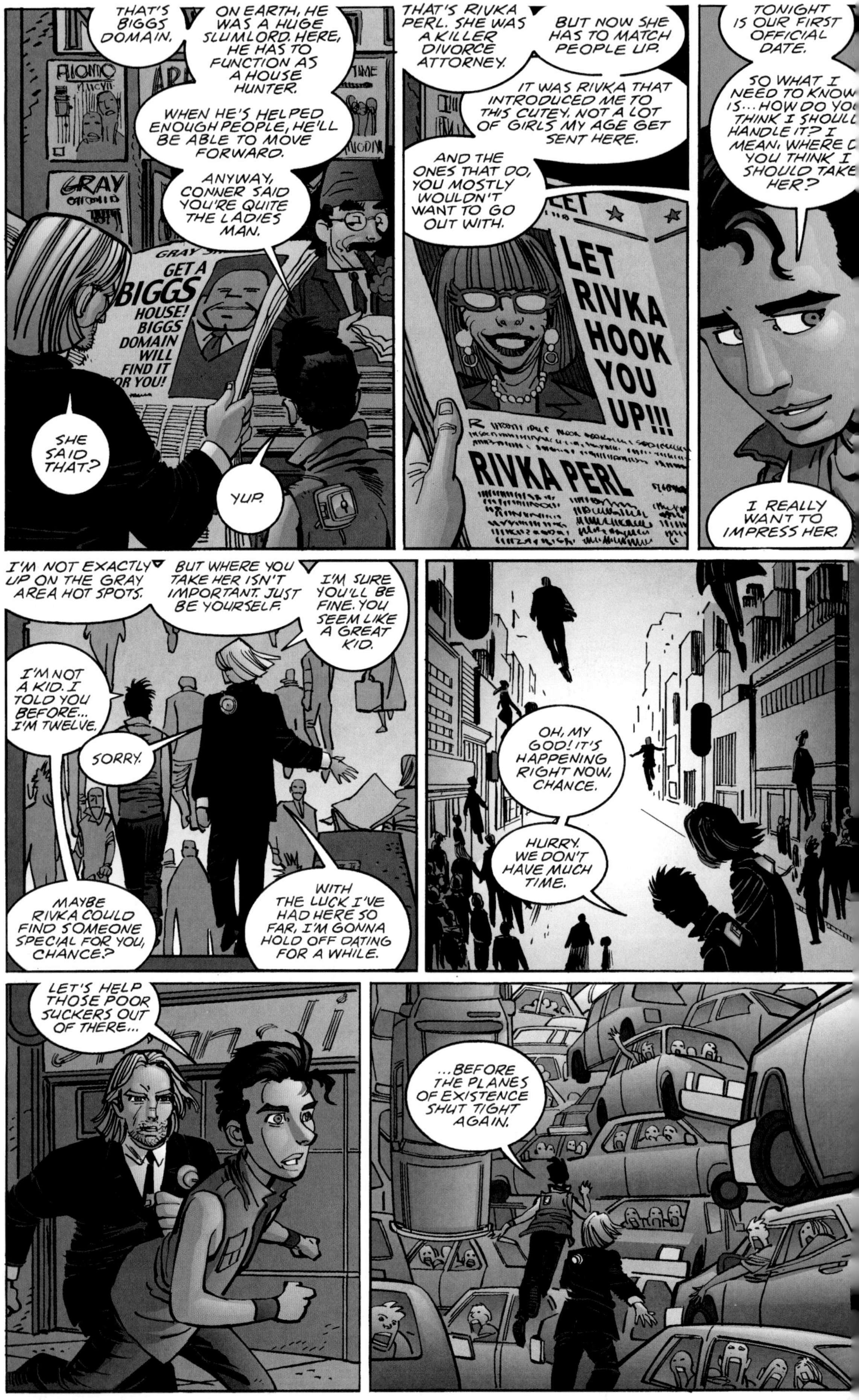
THAT'S BIGGS DOMAIN.
ON EARTH, HE WAS A HUGE SLUMLORD. HERE, HE HAS TO FUNCTION AS A HOUSE HUNTER.
WHEN HE'S HELPED ENOUGH PEOPLE, HE'LL BE ABLE TO MOVE FORWARD.
ANYWAY, CONNER SAID YOU'RE QUITE THE LADIES MAN.
GRAY
GET A BIGGS HOUSE! BIGGS DOMAIN WILL
OR YOU!
SHE SAID THAT?
YUP.
THAT'S RIVKA PERL. SHE WAS A KILLER DIVORCE ATTORNEY.
BUT NOW SHE HAS TO MATCH PEOPLE UP.
IT WAS RIVKA THAT INTRODUCED ME TO THIS CUTEY. NOT A LOT OF GIRLS MY AGE GET SENT HERE.
AND THE ONES THAT DO, YOU MOSTLY WOULDN'T WANT TO GO OUT WITH.
LET RIVKA HOOK YOU UP!!!
RIVKA PERL
TONIGHT IS OUR FIRST OFFICIAL DATE.
SO WHAT I NEED TO KNOW IS... HOW DO YOU THINK I SHOULD HANDLE IT? I MEAN, WHERE DO YOU THINK I SHOULD TAKE HER?
I REALLY WANT TO IMPRESS HER.
I'M NOT EXACTLY UP ON THE GRAY AREA HOT SPOTS.
BUT WHERE YOU TAKE HER ISN'T IMPORTANT. JUST BE YOURSELF.
I'M SURE YOU'LL BE FINE. YOU SEEM LIKE A GREAT KID.
I'M NOT A KID. I TOLD YOU BEFORE... I'M TWELVE.
SORRY.
MAYBE RIVKA COULD FIND SOMEONE SPECIAL FOR YOU, CHANCE?
WITH THE LUCK I'VE HAD HERE SO FAR, I'M GONNA HOLD OFF DATING FOR A WHILE.
OH, MY GOD! IT'S HAPPENING RIGHT NOW, CHANCE.
HURRY. WE DON'T HAVE MUCH TIME.
LET'S HELP THOSE POOR SUCKERS OUT OF THERE...
...BEFORE THE PLANES OF EXISTENCE SHUT TIGHT AGAIN.

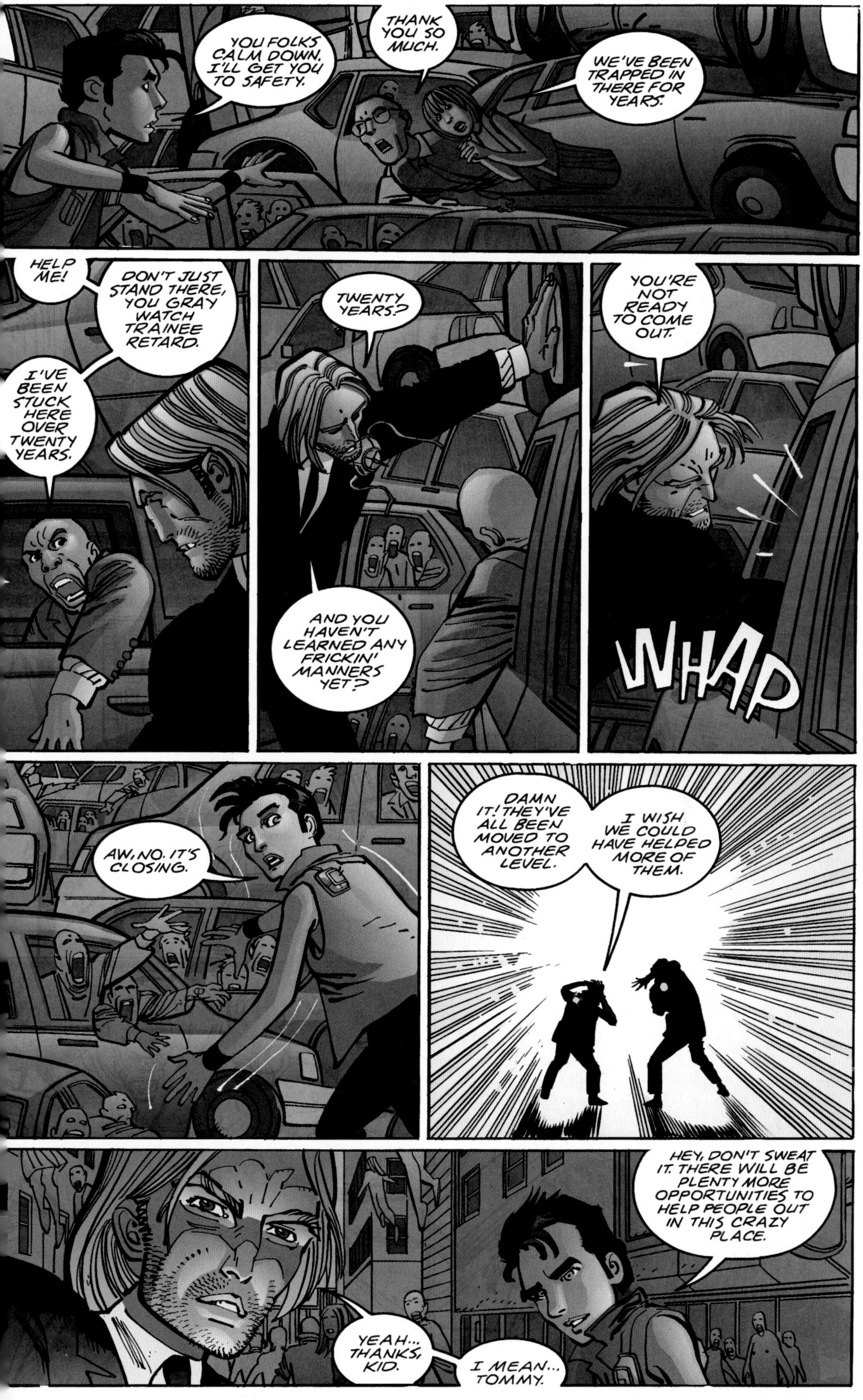
YOU FOLKS CALM DOWN. I'LL GET YOU TO SAFETY.
THANK YOU SO MUCH.
WE'VE BEEN TRAPPED IN THERE FOR YEARS.
HELP ME!
DON'T JUST STAND THERE, YOU GRAY WATCH TRAINEE RETARD.
I'VE BEEN STUCK HERE OVER TWENTY YEARS.
TWENTY YEARS?
AND YOU HAVEN'T LEARNED ANY FRICKIN' MANNERS YET?
YOU'RE NOT READY TO COME OUT.
WHAP
AW, NO. IT'S CLOSING.
DAMN IT! THEY'VE ALL BEEN MOVED TO ANOTHER LEVEL.
I WISH WE COULD HAVE HELPED MORE OF THEM.
HEY, DON'T SWEAT IT. THERE WILL BE PLENTY MORE OPPORTUNITIES TO HELP PEOPLE OUT IN THIS CRAZY PLACE.
YEAH... THANKS, KID.
I MEAN... TOMMY.

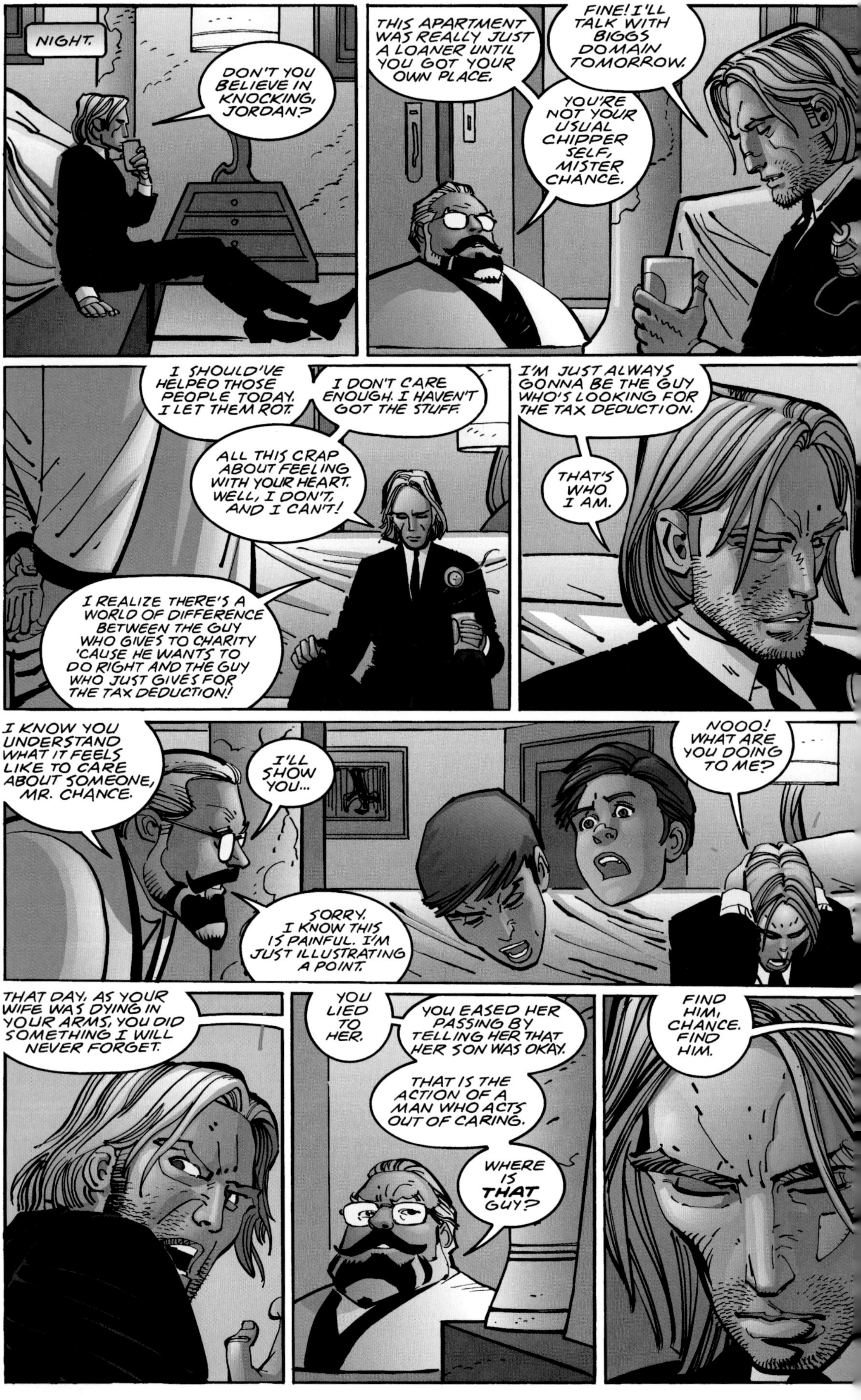
NIGHT.
DON'T YOU BELIEVE IN KNOCKING, JORDAN?
THIS APARTMENT WAS REALLY JUST A LOANER UNTIL YOU GOT YOUR OWN PLACE.
FINE! I'LL TALK WITH BIGGS DOMAIN TOMORROW.
YOU'RE NOT YOUR USUAL CHIPPER SELF, MISTER CHANCE.
I SHOULD'VE HELPED THOSE PEOPLE TODAY. I LET THEM ROT.
I DON'T CARE ENOUGH. I HAVEN'T GOT THE STUFF.
ALL THIS CRAP ABOUT FEELING WITH YOUR HEART. WELL, I DON'T, AND I CAN'T!
I REALIZE THERE'S A WORLD OF DIFFERENCE BETWEEN THE GUY WHO GIVES TO CHARITY 'CAUSE HE WANTS TO DO RIGHT AND THE GUY WHO JUST GIVES FOR THE TAX DEDUCTION!
I'M JUST ALWAYS GONNA BE THE GUY WHO'S LOOKING FOR THE TAX DEDUCTION.
THAT'S WHO I AM.
I KNOW YOU UNDERSTAND WHAT IT FEELS LIKE TO CARE ABOUT SOMEONE, MR. CHANCE.
I'LL SHOW YOU...
SORRY. I KNOW THIS IS PAINFUL. I'M JUST ILLUSTRATING A POINT.
NOOO! WHAT ARE YOU DOING TO ME?
THAT DAY, AS YOUR WIFE WAS DYING IN YOUR ARMS, YOU DID SOMETHING I WILL NEVER FORGET.
YOU LIED TO HER.
YOU EASED HER PASSING BY TELLING HER THAT HER SON WAS OKAY.
THAT IS THE ACTION OF A MAN WHO ACTS OUT OF CARING.
WHERE IS **THAT** GUY?
FIND HIM, CHANCE. FIND HIM.

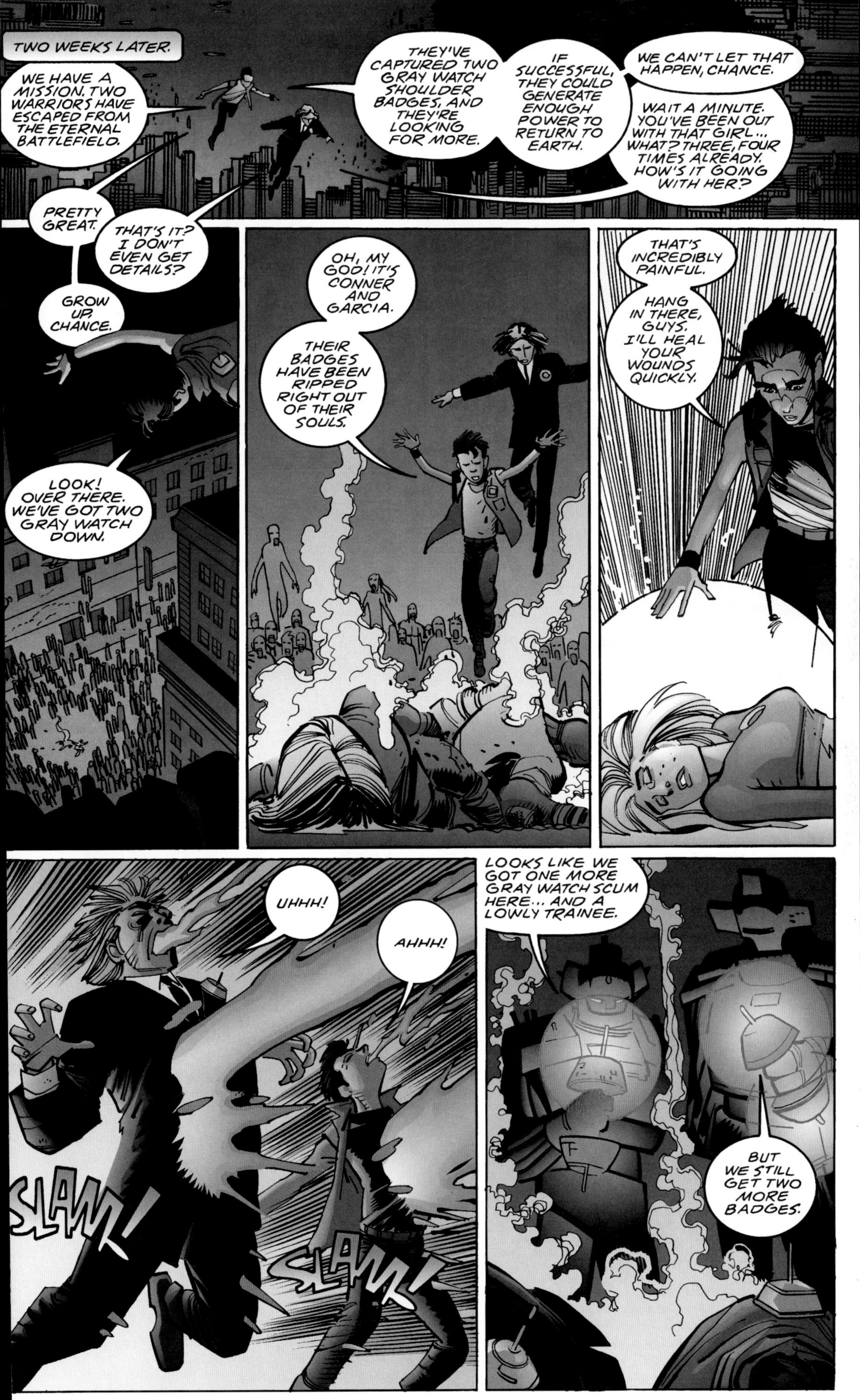
TWO WEEKS LATER.
WE HAVE A MISSION. TWO WARRIORS HAVE ESCAPED FROM THE ETERNAL BATTLEFIELD.
THEY'VE CAPTURED TWO GRAY WATCH SHOULDER BADGES, AND THEY'RE LOOKING FOR MORE.
IF SUCCESSFUL, THEY COULD GENERATE ENOUGH POWER TO RETURN TO EARTH.
WE CAN'T LET THAT HAPPEN, CHANCE.
WAIT A MINUTE. YOU'VE BEEN OUT WITH THAT GIRL... WHAT? THREE, FOUR TIMES ALREADY. HOW'S IT GOING WITH HER?
PRETTY GREAT.
THAT'S IT? I DON'T EVEN GET DETAILS?
GROW UP, CHANCE.
LOOK! OVER THERE. WE'VE GOT TWO GRAY WATCH DOWN.
OH, MY GOD! IT'S CONNER AND GARCIA.
THEIR BADGES HAVE BEEN RIPPED RIGHT OUT OF THEIR SOULS.
THAT'S INCREDIBLY PAINFUL.
HANG IN THERE, GUYS. I'LL HEAL YOUR WOUNDS QUICKLY.
UHHH!
AHHH!
SLAM!
SLAM!
LOOKS LIKE WE GOT ONE MORE GRAY WATCH SCUM HERE... AND A LOWLY TRAINEE.
BUT WE STILL GET TWO MORE BADGES.

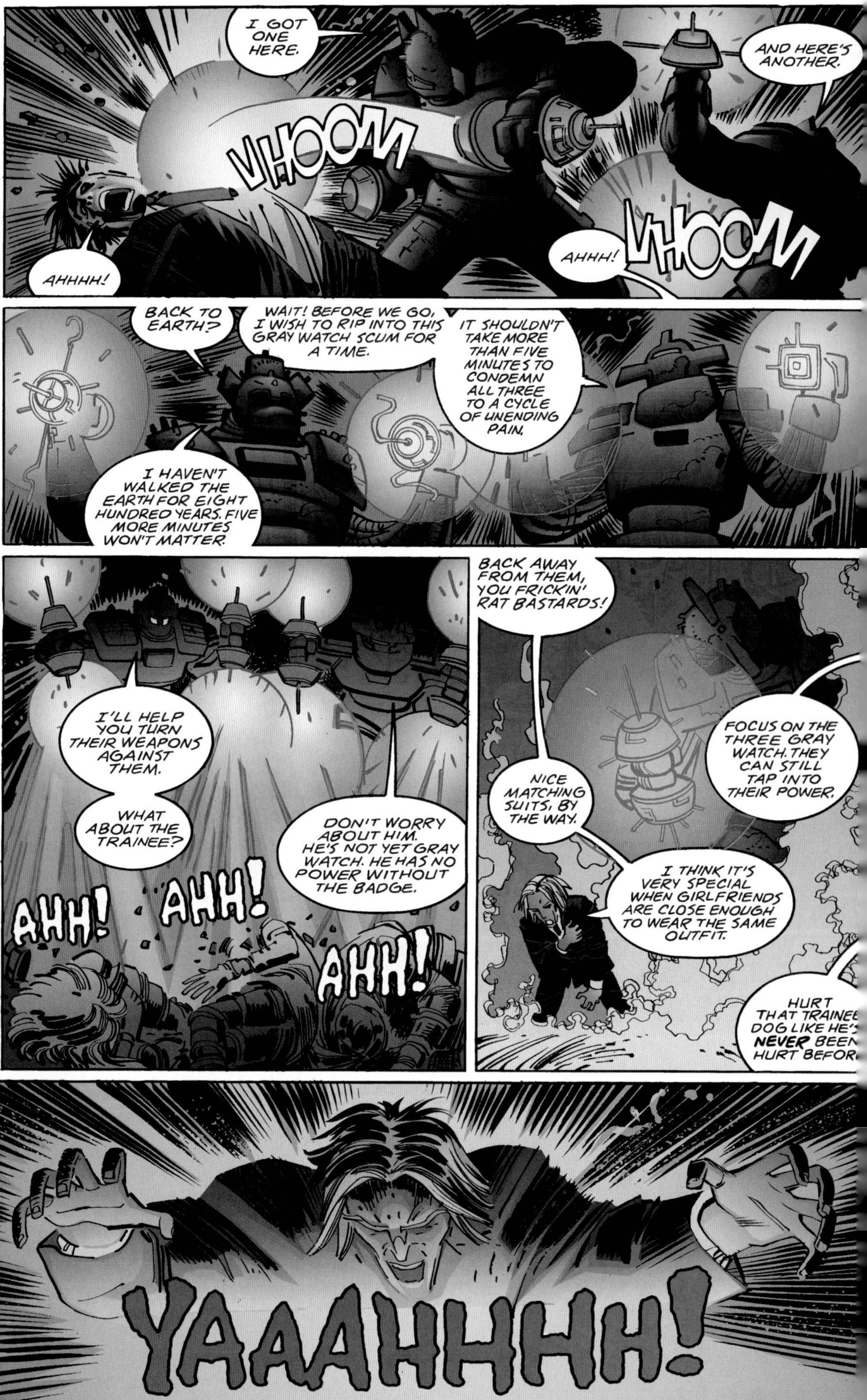

I GOT ONE HERE.
AND HERE'S ANOTHER.
VHOOM
AHHHH!
VHOOM
AHHH!
BACK TO EARTH?
WAIT! BEFORE WE GO, I WISH TO RIP INTO THIS GRAY WATCH SCUM FOR A TIME.
IT SHOULDN'T TAKE MORE THAN FIVE MINUTES TO CONDEMN ALL THREE TO A CYCLE OF UNENDING PAIN.
I HAVEN'T WALKED THE EARTH FOR EIGHT HUNDRED YEARS. FIVE MORE MINUTES WON'T MATTER.
I'LL HELP YOU TURN THEIR WEAPONS AGAINST THEM.
WHAT ABOUT THE TRAINEE?
DON'T WORRY ABOUT HIM. HE'S NOT YET GRAY WATCH. HE HAS NO POWER WITHOUT THE BADGE.
AHH!
AHH!
AHH!
BACK AWAY FROM THEM, YOU FRICKIN' RAT BASTARDS!
FOCUS ON THE THREE GRAY WATCH. THEY CAN STILL TAP INTO THEIR POWER.
NICE MATCHING SUITS, BY THE WAY.
I THINK IT'S VERY SPECIAL WHEN GIRLFRIENDS ARE CLOSE ENOUGH TO WEAR THE SAME OUTFIT.
HURT THAT TRAINEE DOG LIKE HE'S NEVER BEEN HURT BEFOR
YAAAHHHH!

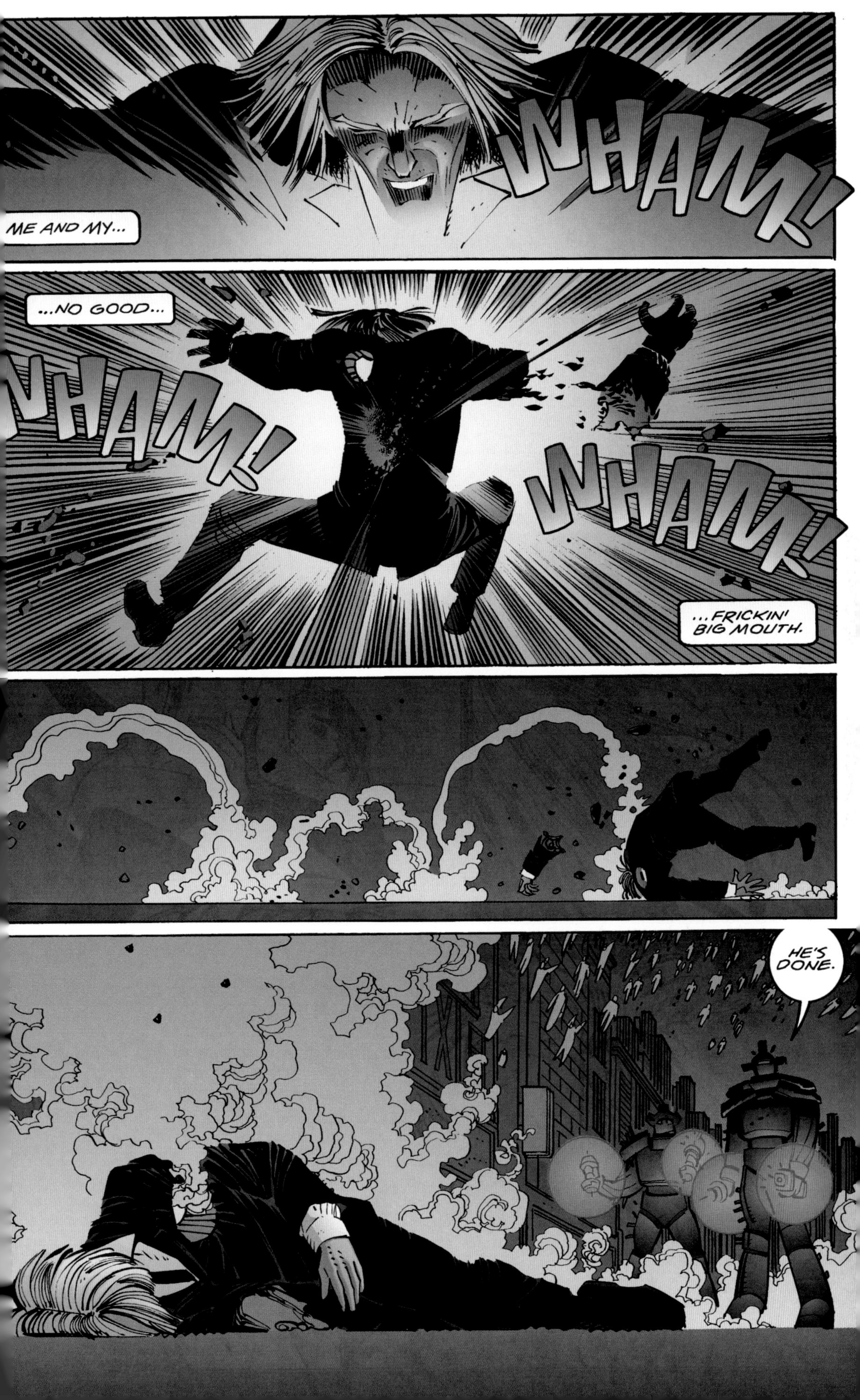
WHAM!
ME AND MY...
...NO GOOD...
WHAM!
WHAM!
...FRICKIN' BIG MOUTH.
HE'S DONE.

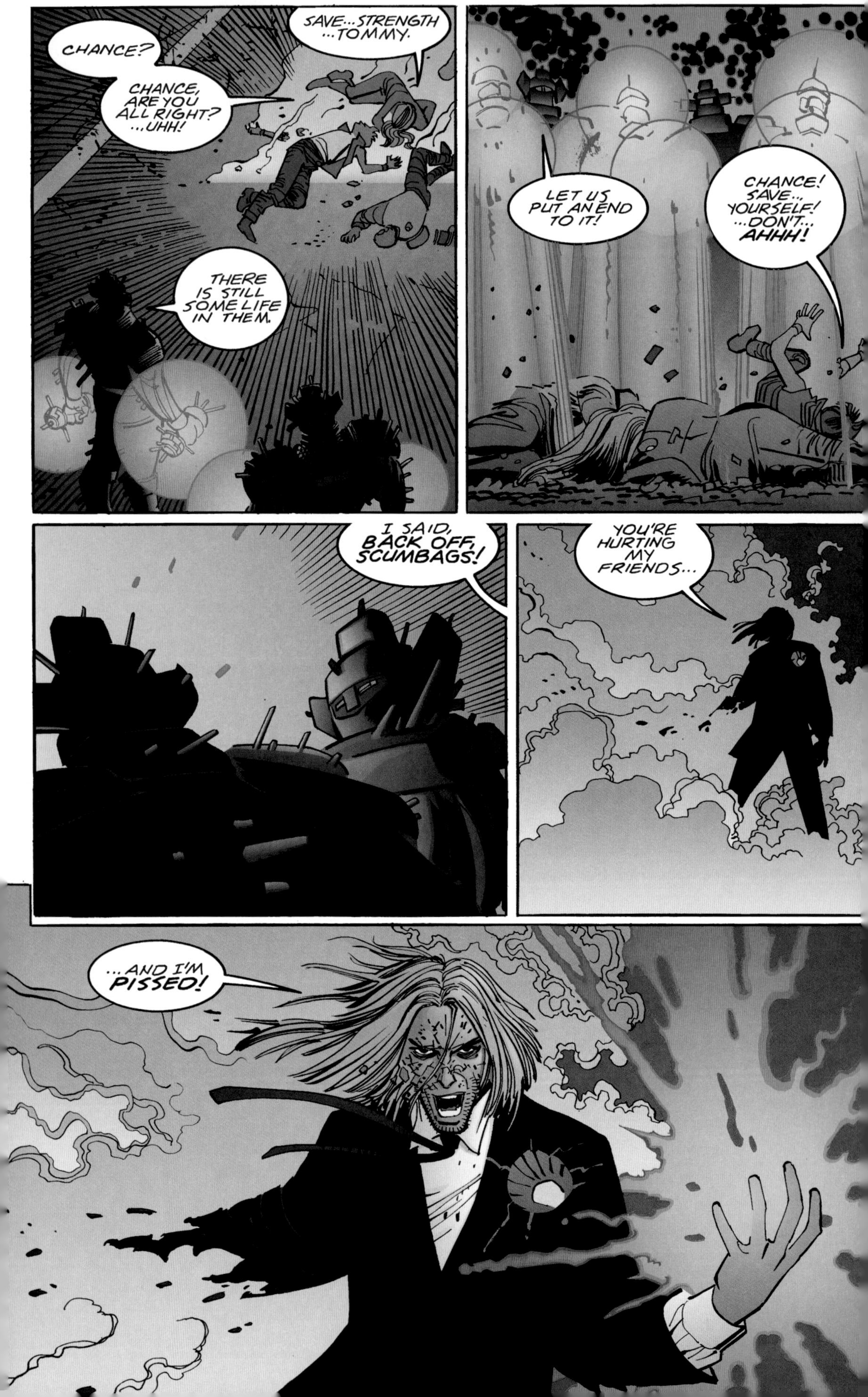
CHANCE?
SAVE...STRENGTH ...TOMMY.
CHANCE, ARE YOU ALL RIGHT? ...UHH!
THERE IS STILL SOME LIFE IN THEM.
LET US PUT AN END TO IT!
CHANCE! SAVE... YOURSELF! ...DON'T... AHHH!
I SAID, BACK OFF, SCUMBAGS!
YOU'RE HURTING MY FRIENDS...
...AND I'M PISSED!

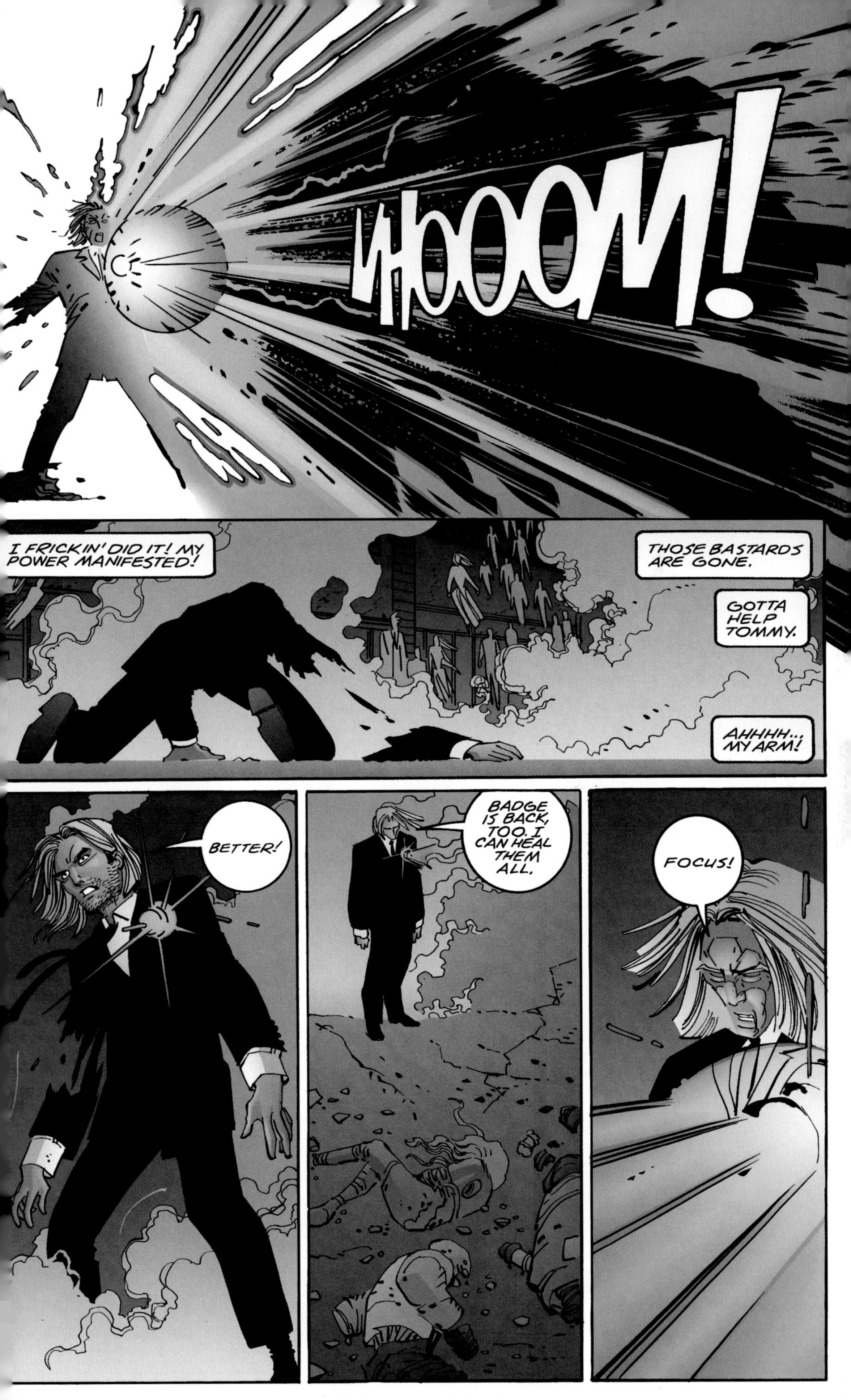
WHOOM!
I FRICKIN' DID IT! MY POWER MANIFESTED!
THOSE BASTARDS ARE GONE.
GOTTA HELP TOMMY.
AHHHH... MY ARM!
BETTER!
BADGE IS BACK, TOO. I CAN HEAL THEM ALL.
FOCUS!

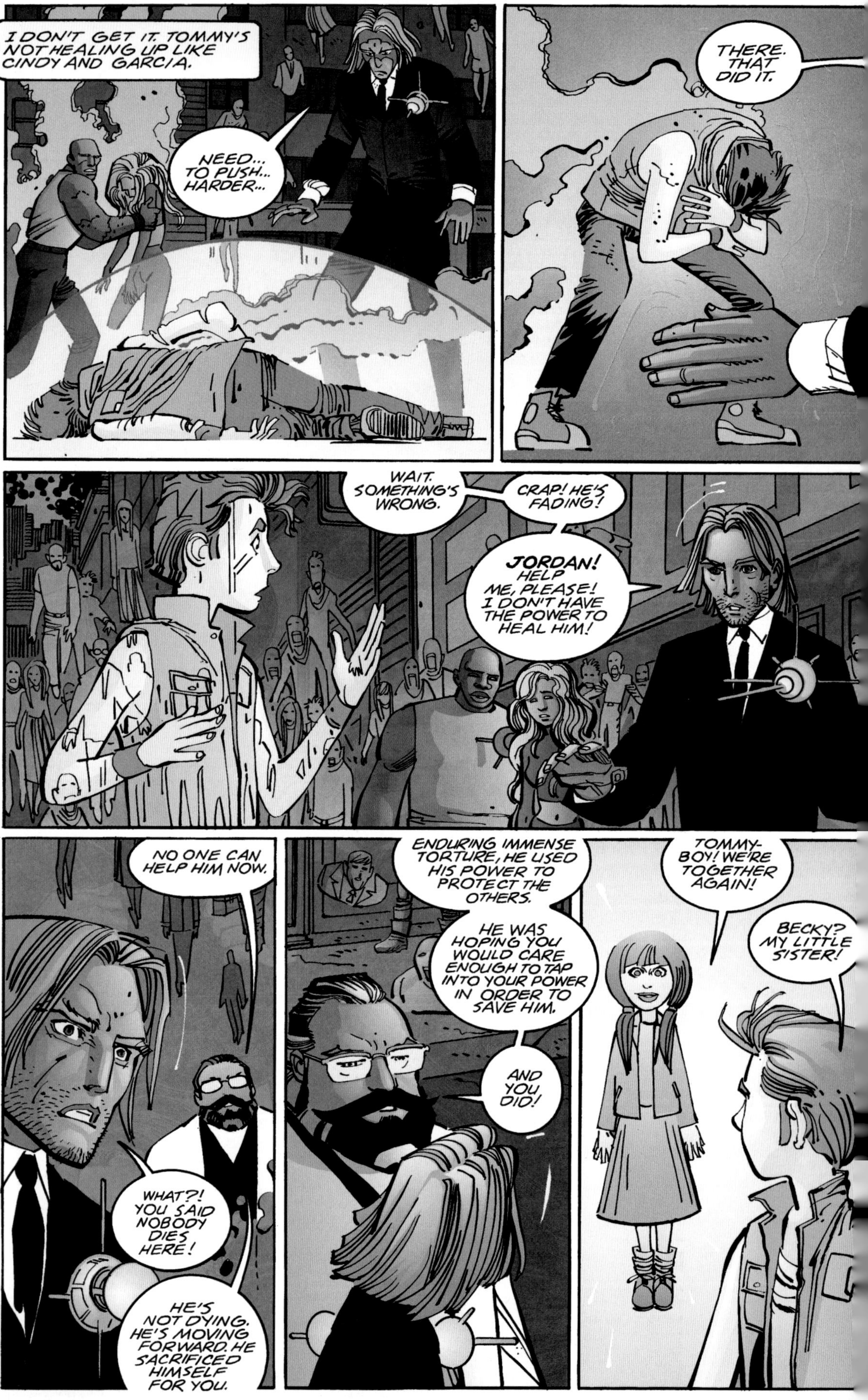
I DON'T GET IT. TOMMY'S NOT HEALING UP LIKE CINDY AND GARCIA.
NEED... TO PUSH... HARDER...
THERE. THAT DID IT.
WAIT. SOMETHING'S WRONG.
CRAP! HE'S FADING!
JORDAN! HELP ME, PLEASE! I DON'T HAVE THE POWER TO HEAL HIM!
NO ONE CAN HELP HIM NOW.
WHAT?! YOU SAID NOBODY DIES HERE!
HE'S NOT DYING. HE'S MOVING FORWARD. HE SACRIFICED HIMSELF FOR YOU.
ENDURING IMMENSE TORTURE, HE USED HIS POWER TO PROTECT THE OTHERS.
HE WAS HOPING YOU WOULD CARE ENOUGH TO TAP INTO YOUR POWER IN ORDER TO SAVE HIM.
AND YOU DID!
TOMMY-BOY! WE'RE TOGETHER AGAIN!
BECKY? MY LITTLE SISTER!

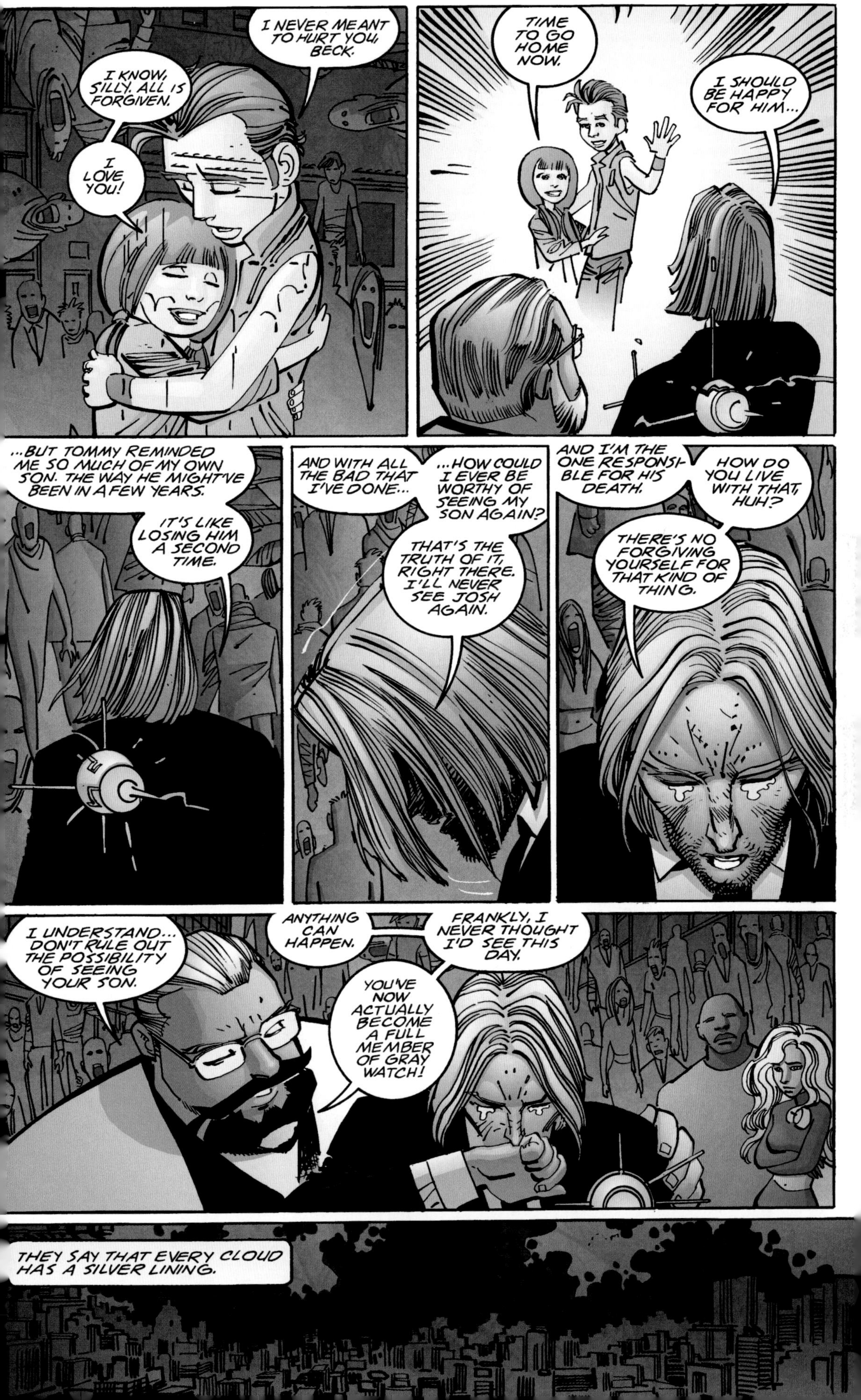
I NEVER MEANT TO HURT YOU, BECK.
I KNOW, SILLY. ALL IS FORGIVEN.
I LOVE YOU!
TIME TO GO HOME NOW.
I SHOULD BE HAPPY FOR HIM...
...BUT TOMMY REMINDED ME SO MUCH OF MY OWN SON. THE WAY HE MIGHT'VE BEEN IN A FEW YEARS.
IT'S LIKE LOSING HIM A SECOND TIME.
AND WITH ALL THE BAD THAT I'VE DONE...
...HOW COULD I EVER BE WORTHY OF SEEING MY SON AGAIN?
THAT'S THE TRUTH OF IT, RIGHT THERE. I'LL NEVER SEE JOSH AGAIN.
AND I'M THE ONE RESPONSIBLE FOR HIS DEATH.
HOW DO YOU LIVE WITH THAT, HUH?
THERE'S NO FORGIVING YOURSELF FOR THAT KIND OF THING.
I UNDERSTAND... DON'T RULE OUT THE POSSIBILITY OF SEEING YOUR SON.
ANYTHING CAN HAPPEN.
FRANKLY, I NEVER THOUGHT I'D SEE THIS DAY.
YOU'VE NOW ACTUALLY BECOME A FULL MEMBER OF GRAY WATCH!
THEY SAY THAT EVERY CLOUD HAS A SILVER LINING.

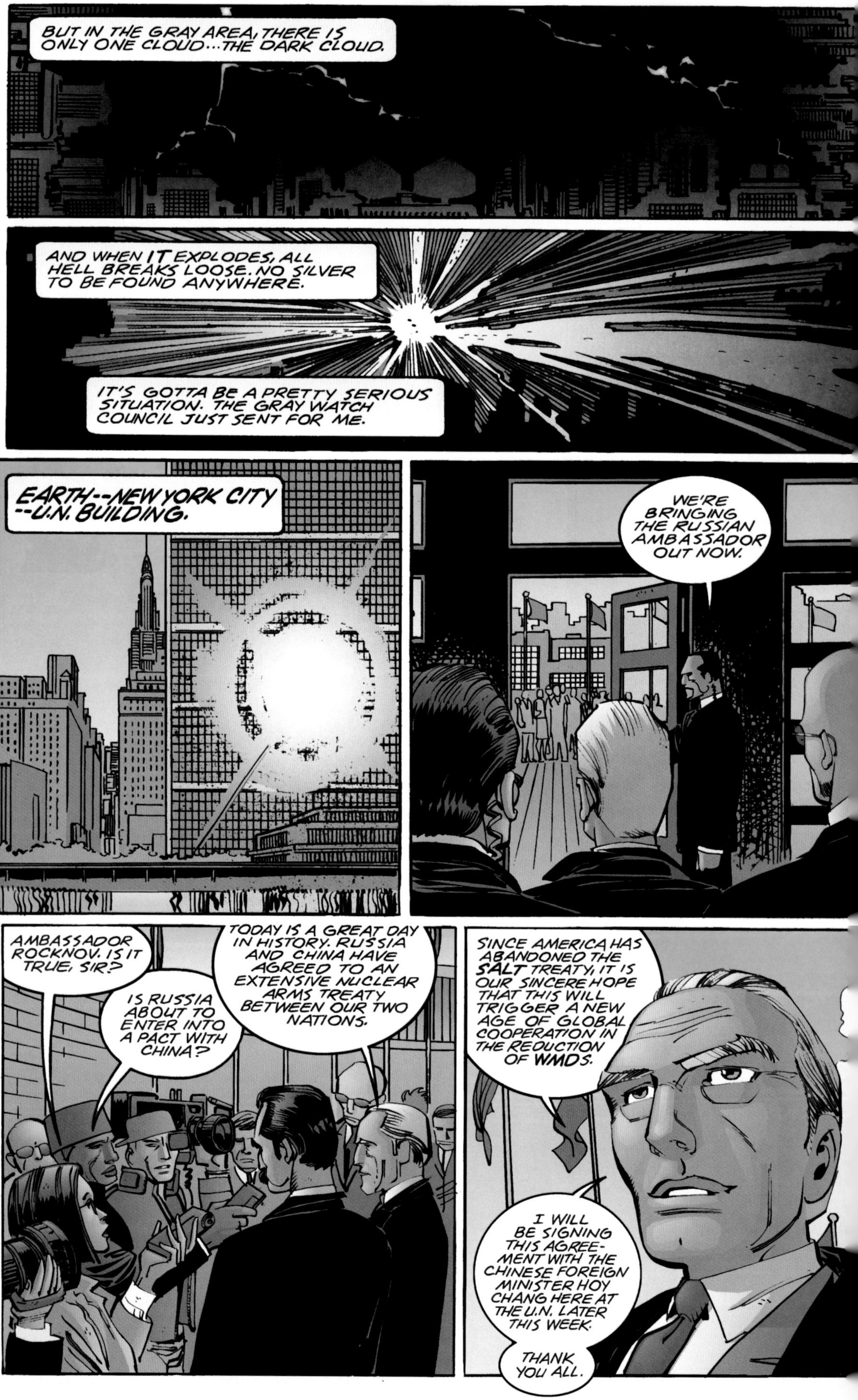

BUT IN THE GRAY AREA, THERE IS ONLY ONE CLOUD... THE DARK CLOUD.
AND WHEN IT EXPLODES, ALL HELL BREAKS LOOSE. NO SILVER TO BE FOUND ANYWHERE.
IT'S GOTTA BE A PRETTY SERIOUS SITUATION. THE GRAY WATCH COUNCIL JUST SENT FOR ME.
EARTH--NEW YORK CITY --U.N. BUILDING.
WE'RE BRINGING THE RUSSIAN AMBASSADOR OUT NOW.
AMBASSADOR ROCKNOV. IS IT TRUE, SIR?
IS RUSSIA ABOUT TO ENTER INTO A PACT WITH CHINA?
TODAY IS A GREAT DAY IN HISTORY. RUSSIA AND CHINA HAVE AGREED TO AN EXTENSIVE NUCLEAR ARMS TREATY BETWEEN OUR TWO NATIONS.
SINCE AMERICA HAS ABANDONED THE SALT TREATY, IT IS OUR SINCERE HOPE THAT THIS WILL TRIGGER A NEW AGE OF GLOBAL COOPERATION IN THE REDUCTION OF WMDS.
I WILL BE SIGNING THIS AGREE-MENT WITH THE CHINESE FOREIGN MINISTER HOY CHANG HERE AT THE U.N. LATER THIS WEEK.
THANK YOU ALL.

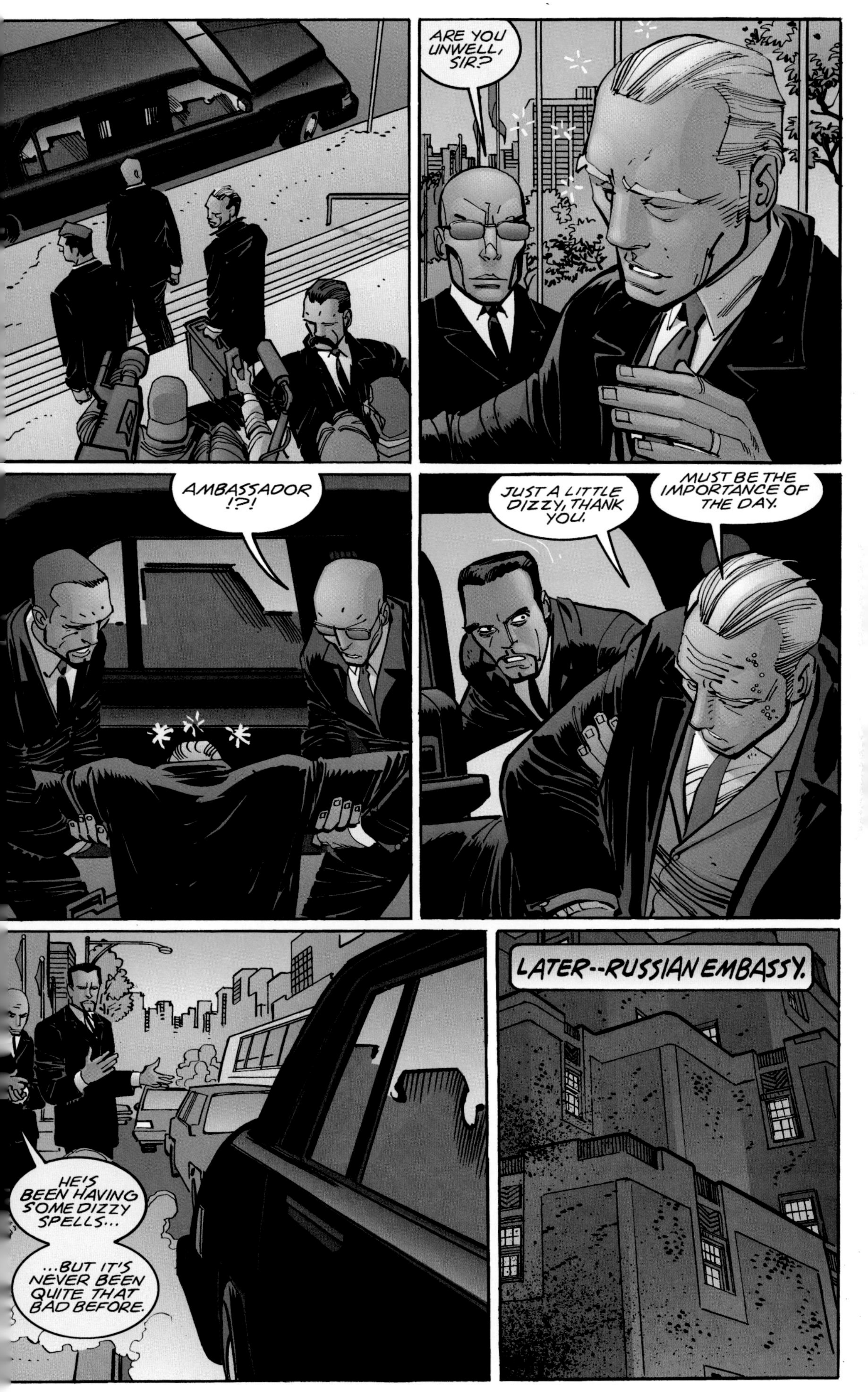
ARE YOU UNWELL, SIR?
AMBASSADOR !?!
JUST A LITTLE DIZZY, THANK YOU.
MUST BE THE IMPORTANCE OF THE DAY.
HE'S BEEN HAVING SOME DIZZY SPELLS...
...BUT IT'S NEVER BEEN QUITE THAT BAD BEFORE.
LATER--RUSSIAN EMBASSY.

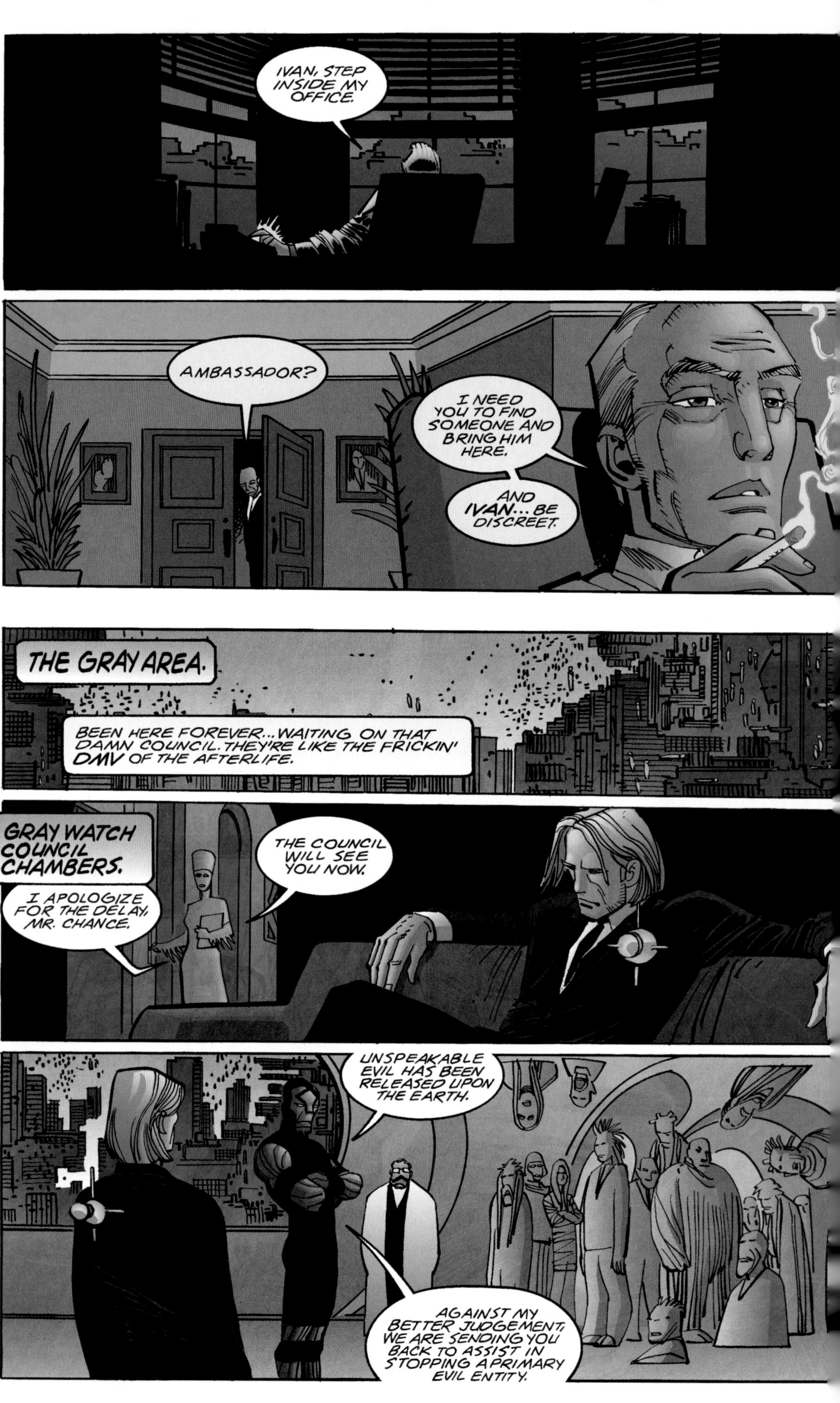
IVAN, STEP INSIDE MY OFFICE.
AMBASSADOR?
I NEED YOU TO FIND SOMEONE AND BRING HIM HERE.
AND IVAN... BE DISCREET.
THE GRAY AREA.
BEEN HERE FOREVER...WAITING ON THAT DAMN COUNCIL. THEY'RE LIKE THE FRICKIN' DMV OF THE AFTERLIFE.
GRAY WATCH COUNCIL CHAMBERS.
I APOLOGIZE FOR THE DELAY, MR. CHANCE.
THE COUNCIL WILL SEE YOU NOW.
UNSPEAKABLE EVIL HAS BEEN RELEASED UPON THE EARTH.
AGAINST MY BETTER JUDGEMENT, WE ARE SENDING YOU BACK TO ASSIST IN STOPPING A PRIMARY EVIL ENTITY.

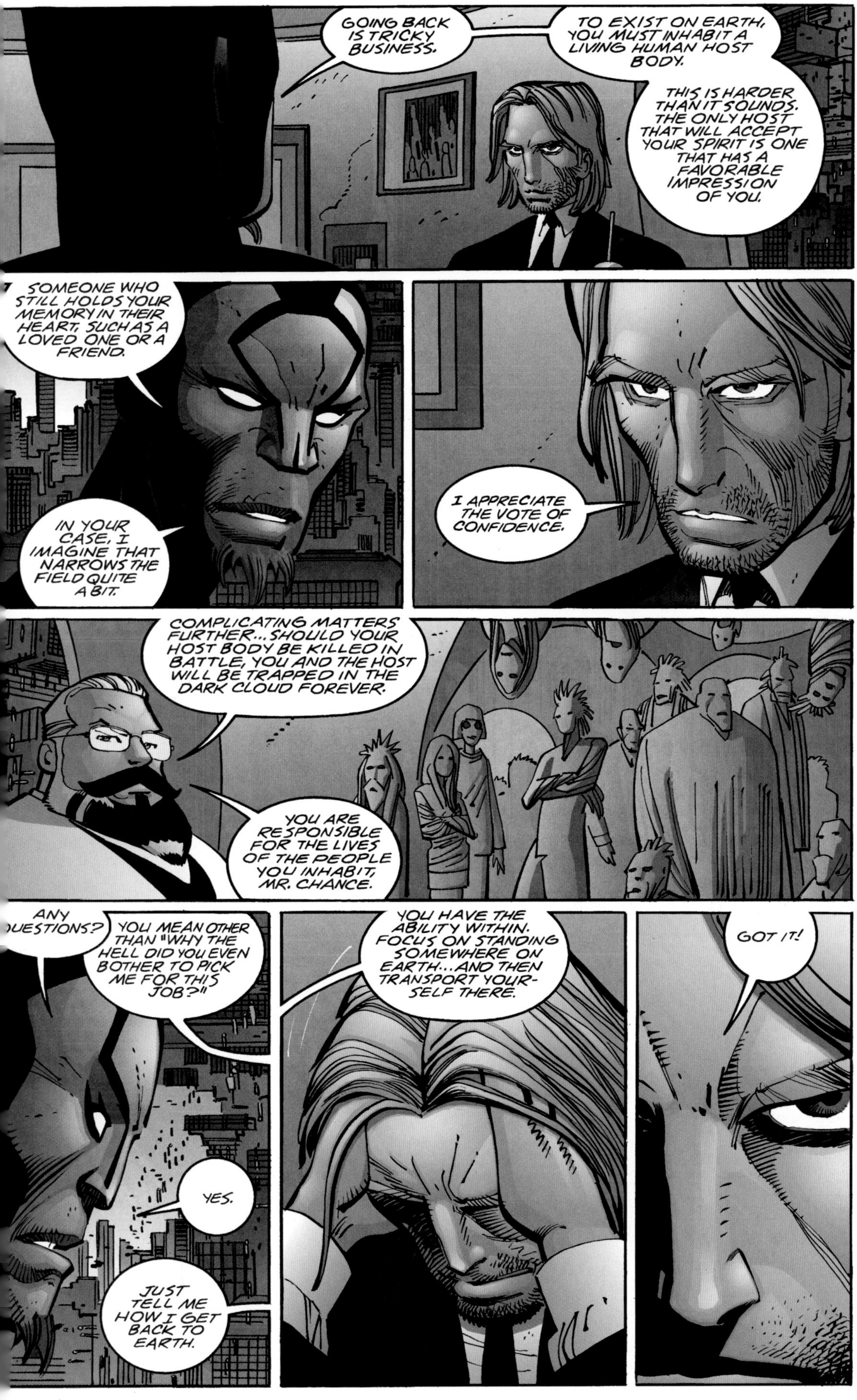
GOING BACK IS TRICKY BUSINESS.
TO EXIST ON EARTH, YOU MUST INHABIT A LIVING HUMAN HOST BODY.
THIS IS HARDER THAN IT SOUNDS. THE ONLY HOST THAT WILL ACCEPT YOUR SPIRIT IS ONE THAT HAS A FAVORABLE IMPRESSION OF YOU.
SOMEONE WHO STILL HOLDS YOUR MEMORY IN THEIR HEART, SUCH AS A LOVED ONE OR A FRIEND.
IN YOUR CASE, I IMAGINE THAT NARROWS THE FIELD QUITE A BIT.
I APPRECIATE THE VOTE OF CONFIDENCE.
COMPLICATING MATTERS FURTHER... SHOULD YOUR HOST BODY BE KILLED IN BATTLE, YOU AND THE HOST WILL BE TRAPPED IN THE DARK CLOUD FOREVER.
YOU ARE RESPONSIBLE FOR THE LIVES OF THE PEOPLE YOU INHABIT, MR. CHANCE.
ANY QUESTIONS?
YOU MEAN OTHER THAN "WHY THE HELL DID YOU EVEN BOTHER TO PICK ME FOR THIS JOB?"
YES.
JUST TELL ME HOW I GET BACK TO EARTH.
YOU HAVE THE ABILITY WITHIN. FOCUS ON STANDING SOMEWHERE ON EARTH... AND THEN TRANSPORT YOURSELF THERE.
GOT IT!

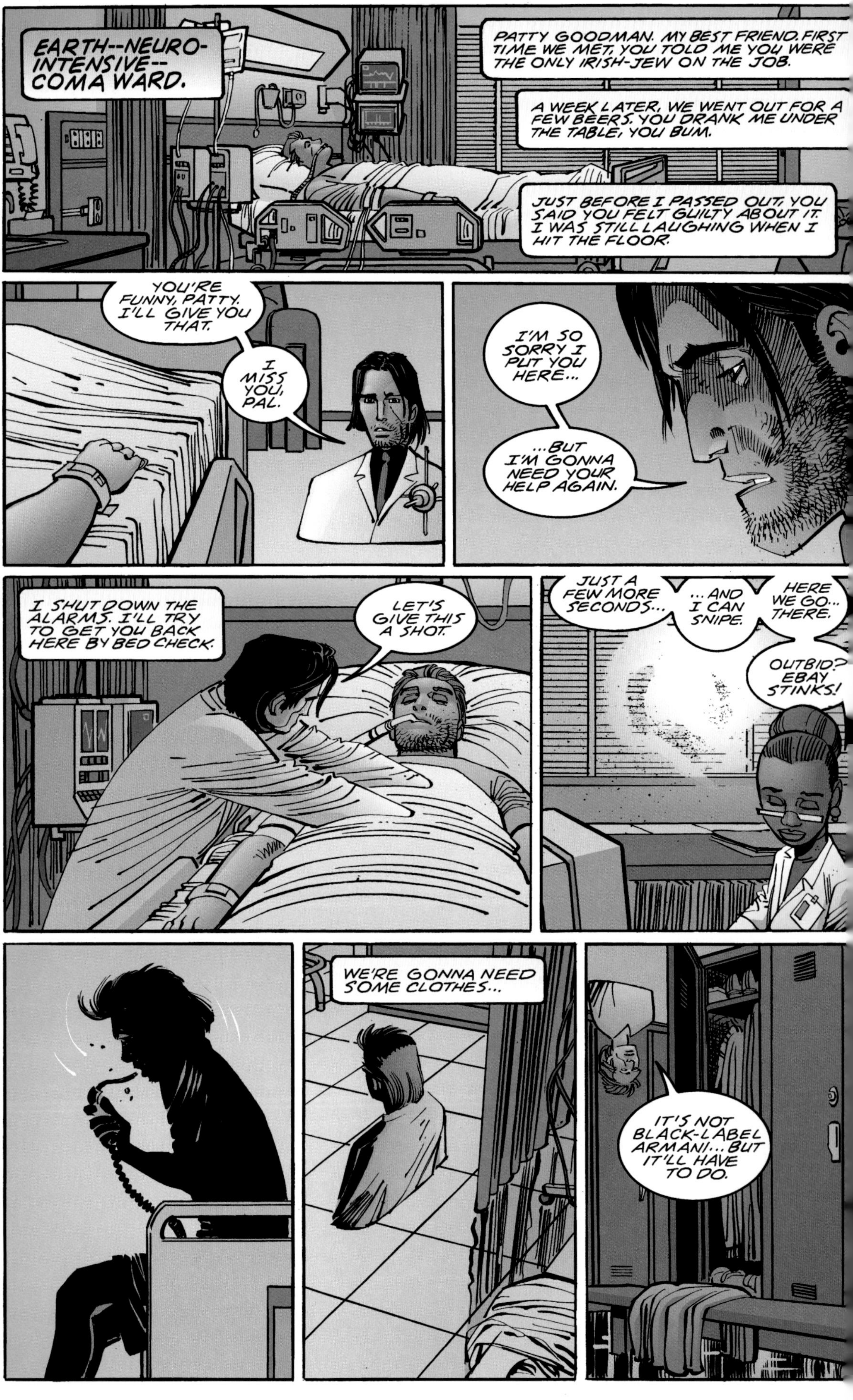
EARTH--NEURO-INTENSIVE--COMA WARD.
PATTY GOODMAN. MY BEST FRIEND. FIRST TIME WE MET, YOU TOLD ME YOU WERE THE ONLY IRISH-JEW ON THE JOB.
A WEEK LATER, WE WENT OUT FOR A FEW BEERS. YOU DRANK ME UNDER THE TABLE, YOU BUM.
JUST BEFORE I PASSED OUT, YOU SAID YOU FELT GUILTY ABOUT IT. I WAS STILL LAUGHING WHEN I HIT THE FLOOR.
YOU'RE FUNNY, PATTY. I'LL GIVE YOU THAT.
I MISS YOU, PAL.
I'M SO SORRY I PUT YOU HERE...
...BUT I'M GONNA NEED YOUR HELP AGAIN.
I SHUT DOWN THE ALARMS. I'LL TRY TO GET YOU BACK HERE BY BED CHECK.
LET'S GIVE THIS A SHOT.
JUST A FEW MORE SECONDS...
...AND I CAN SNIPE.
HERE WE GO... THERE.
OUTBID? EBAY STINKS!
WE'RE GONNA NEED SOME CLOTHES...
IT'S NOT BLACK-LABEL ARMANI... BUT IT'LL HAVE TO DO.

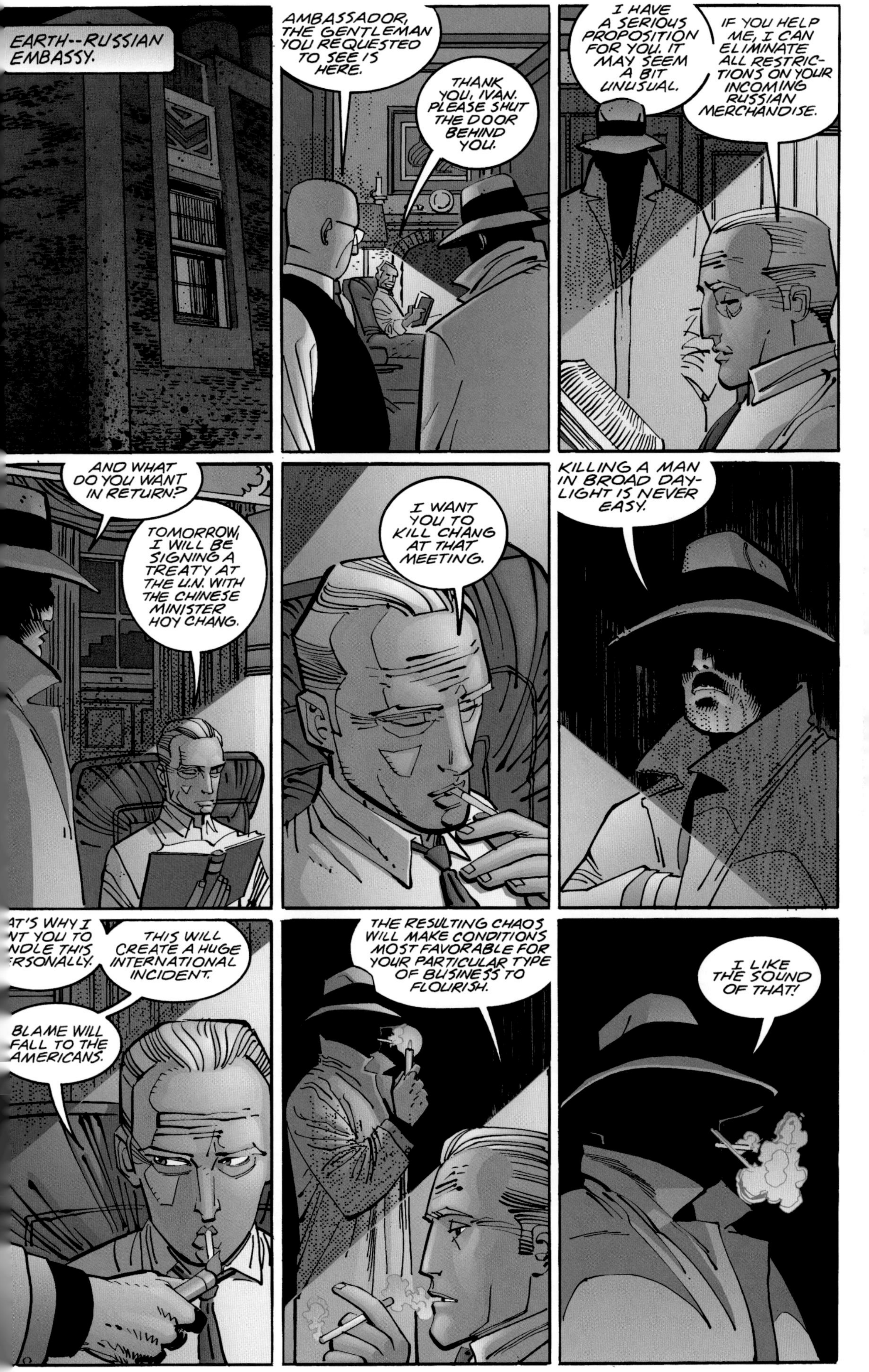
EARTH--RUSSIAN EMBASSY.
AMBASSADOR, THE GENTLEMAN YOU REQUESTED TO SEE IS HERE.
THANK YOU, IVAN. PLEASE SHUT THE DOOR BEHIND YOU.
I HAVE A SERIOUS PROPOSITION FOR YOU. IT MAY SEEM A BIT UNUSUAL.
IF YOU HELP ME, I CAN ELIMINATE ALL RESTRICTIONS ON YOUR INCOMING RUSSIAN MERCHANDISE.
AND WHAT DO YOU WANT IN RETURN?
TOMORROW, I WILL BE SIGNING A TREATY AT THE U.N. WITH THE CHINESE MINISTER HOY CHANG.
I WANT YOU TO KILL CHANG AT THAT MEETING.
KILLING A MAN IN BROAD DAYLIGHT IS NEVER EASY.
AT'S WHY I
NT YOU TO
NDLE THIS
ERSONALLY.
THIS WILL CREATE A HUGE INTERNATIONAL INCIDENT.
BLAME WILL FALL TO THE AMERICANS.
THE RESULTING CHAOS WILL MAKE CONDITIONS MOST FAVORABLE FOR YOUR PARTICULAR TYPE OF BUSINESS TO FLOURISH.
I LIKE THE SOUND OF THAT!

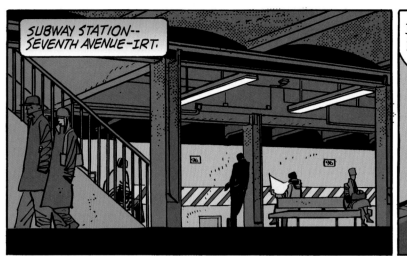

SUBWAY STATION--
SEVENTH AVENUE--IRT.

I THINK I CAN SPEAK FREELY NOW.

LET'S DO ROLL CALL FOR THE SAKE OF CLARITY. I'M LT. BEEBONOCK IN THIS BODY.

I'M NICK GARCIA.

CINDY CONNER HERE.

I'M JERRY RUBENSTEIN. I'M A GRAY WATCH TRAINEE.

THIS IS MY FIRST REAL MISSION.

PRETTY EXCITING STUFF, HUH?

THIS ISN'T GOING TO BE A JOYRIDE, ROOKIE.

OKAY, WHERE THE HELL IS CHANCE?

I'M CHANCE.

OVER HERE, LIEUTENANT.

MY FRIEND'S BODY NEEDED A LITTLE LUNCH.

I FORGOT HOW GOOD THESE THINGS ARE.

ANYBODY WANT A BITE?

WE BELIEVE THE ENTITY IS HERE IN MANHATTAN.

WE'LL EACH CANVAS DIFFERENT NEIGHBORHOODS.

WE'RE SEARCHING FOR ANYTHING THAT DOESN'T SEEM EARTHBOUND IN NATURE.

EXCUSE MY IGNORANCE, HERE, BUT SHOULDN'T WE BE USING OUR POWERS TO LOCATE THIS SOB.

YOU ARE ALL DETECTIVES. BE RESOURCEFUL.

USE YOUR POWER ONLY IF ABSOLUTELY NECESSARY.

THE HUMAN BODY IS FAR TOO FRAGILE TO HANDLE THE FORCE OF YOUR POWER LONG TERM.

A SMALL BURST OF POWER WILL AGE YOUR BODY ONE ENTIRE EARTH YEAR.

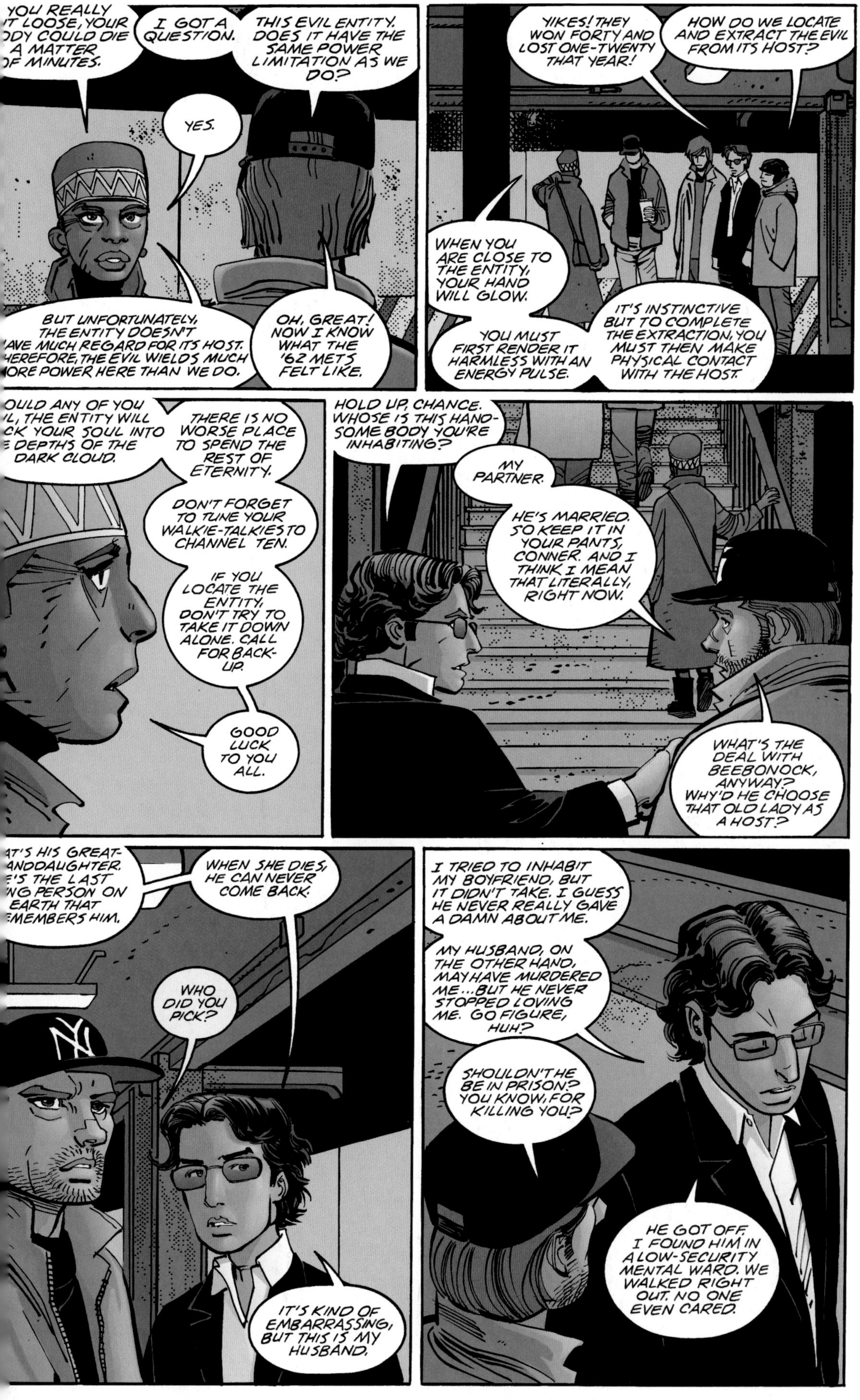

YOU REALLY
IT LOOSE, YOUR
ODY COULD DIE
A MATTER
OF MINUTES.
I GOT A QUESTION.
THIS EVIL ENTITY. DOES IT HAVE THE SAME POWER LIMITATION AS WE DO?
YES.
BUT UNFORTUNATELY, THE ENTITY DOESN'T
AVE MUCH REGARD FOR ITS HOST.
HEREFORE, THE EVIL WIELDS MUCH
ORE POWER HERE THAN WE DO.
OH, GREAT! NOW I KNOW WHAT THE '62 METS FELT LIKE.
YIKES! THEY WON FORTY AND LOST ONE-TWENTY THAT YEAR!
HOW DO WE LOCATE AND EXTRACT THE EVIL FROM ITS HOST?
WHEN YOU ARE CLOSE TO THE ENTITY, YOUR HAND WILL GLOW.
YOU MUST FIRST RENDER IT HARMLESS WITH AN ENERGY PULSE.
IT'S INSTINCTIVE BUT TO COMPLETE THE EXTRACTION, YOU MUST THEN MAKE PHYSICAL CONTACT WITH THE HOST.
OULD ANY OF YOU
IL, THE ENTITY WILL
CK YOUR SOUL INTO
E DEPTHS OF THE
DARK CLOUD.
THERE IS NO WORSE PLACE TO SPEND THE REST OF ETERNITY.
DON'T FORGET TO TUNE YOUR WALKIE-TALKIES TO CHANNEL TEN.
IF YOU LOCATE THE ENTITY, DON'T TRY TO TAKE IT DOWN ALONE. CALL FOR BACK-UP.
GOOD LUCK TO YOU ALL.
HOLD UP, CHANCE. WHOSE IS THIS HANDSOME BODY YOU'RE INHABITING?
MY PARTNER.
HE'S MARRIED. SO KEEP IT IN YOUR PANTS, CONNER. AND I THINK I MEAN THAT LITERALLY, RIGHT NOW.
WHAT'S THE DEAL WITH BEEBONOCK, ANYWAY? WHY'D HE CHOOSE THAT OLD LADY AS A HOST?
AT'S HIS GREAT-
ANDDAUGHTER.
E'S THE LAST
NG PERSON ON
EARTH THAT
EMEMBERS HIM.
WHEN SHE DIES, HE CAN NEVER COME BACK.
WHO DID YOU PICK?
IT'S KIND OF EMBARRASSING, BUT THIS IS MY HUSBAND.
I TRIED TO INHABIT MY BOYFRIEND, BUT IT DIDN'T TAKE. I GUESS HE NEVER REALLY GAVE A DAMN ABOUT ME.
MY HUSBAND, ON THE OTHER HAND, MAY HAVE MURDERED ME... BUT HE NEVER STOPPED LOVING ME. GO FIGURE, HUH?
SHOULDN'T HE BE IN PRISON? YOU KNOW, FOR KILLING YOU?
HE GOT OFF. I FOUND HIM IN A LOW-SECURITY MENTAL WARD. WE WALKED RIGHT OUT. NO ONE EVEN CARED.

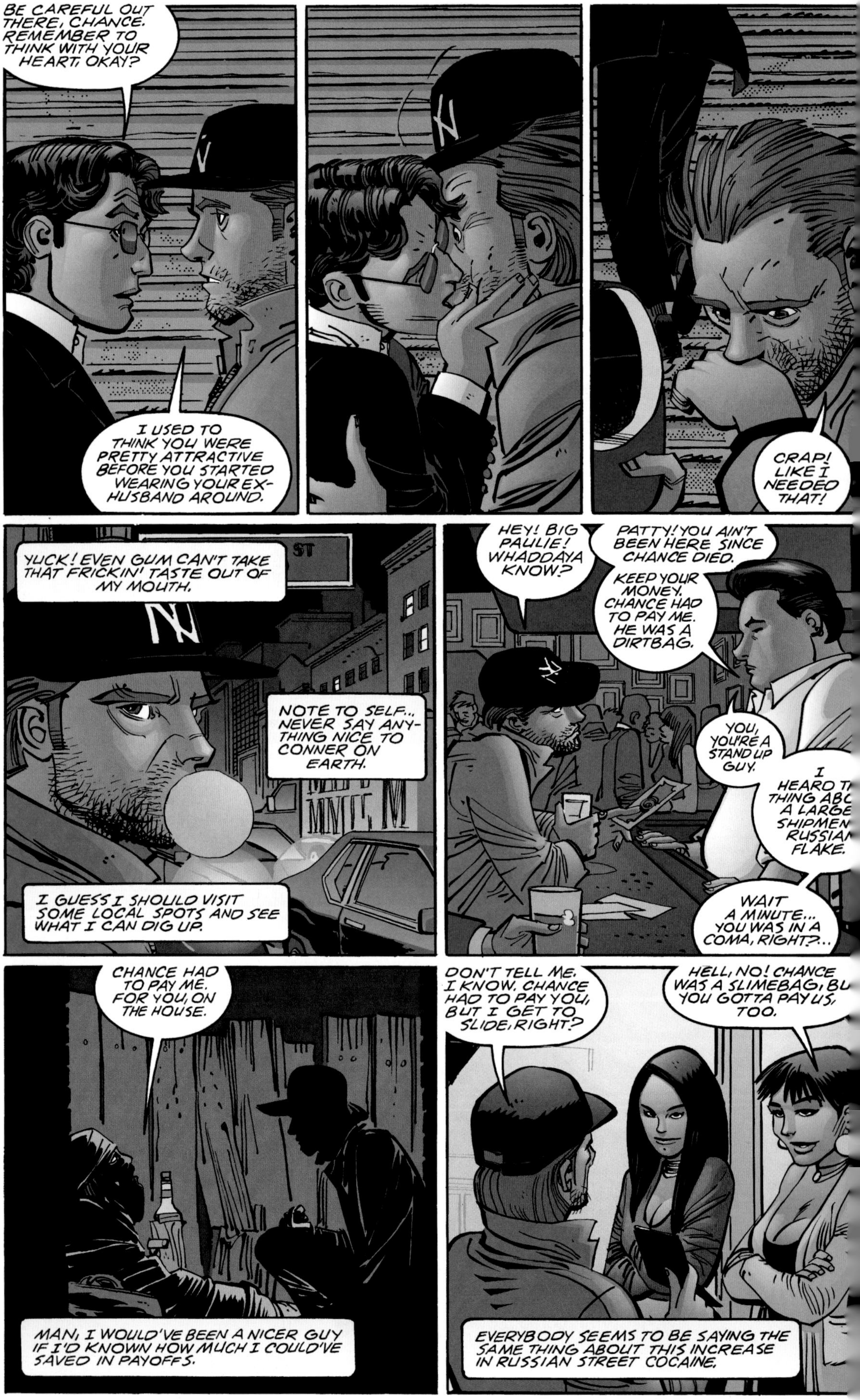
BE CAREFUL OUT THERE, CHANCE. REMEMBER TO THINK WITH YOUR HEART, OKAY?
I USED TO THINK YOU WERE PRETTY ATTRACTIVE BEFORE YOU STARTED WEARING YOUR EX-HUSBAND AROUND.
CRAP! LIKE I NEEDED THAT!
YUCK! EVEN GUM CAN'T TAKE THAT FRICKIN' TASTE OUT OF MY MOUTH.
ST
NOTE TO SELF... NEVER SAY ANYTHING NICE TO CONNER ON EARTH.
I GUESS I SHOULD VISIT SOME LOCAL SPOTS AND SEE WHAT I CAN DIG UP.
HEY! BIG PAULIE! WHADDAYA KNOW?
PATTY! YOU AIN'T BEEN HERE SINCE CHANCE DIED.
KEEP YOUR MONEY. CHANCE HAD TO PAY ME. HE WAS A DIRTBAG.
YOU, YOU'RE A STAND UP GUY.
I HEARD T THING ABO A LARGE SHIPMEN RUSSIAN FLAKE.
WAIT A MINUTE... YOU WAS IN A COMA, RIGHT?...
CHANCE HAD TO PAY ME. FOR YOU, ON THE HOUSE.
MAN, I WOULD'VE BEEN A NICER GUY IF I'D KNOWN HOW MUCH I COULD'VE SAVED IN PAYOFFS.
DON'T TELL ME. I KNOW. CHANCE HAD TO PAY YOU, BUT I GET TO SLIDE, RIGHT?
HELL, NO! CHANCE WAS A SLIMEBAG, BU YOU GOTTA PAY US, TOO.
EVERYBODY SEEMS TO BE SAYING THE SAME THING ABOUT THIS INCREASE IN RUSSIAN STREET COCAINE.

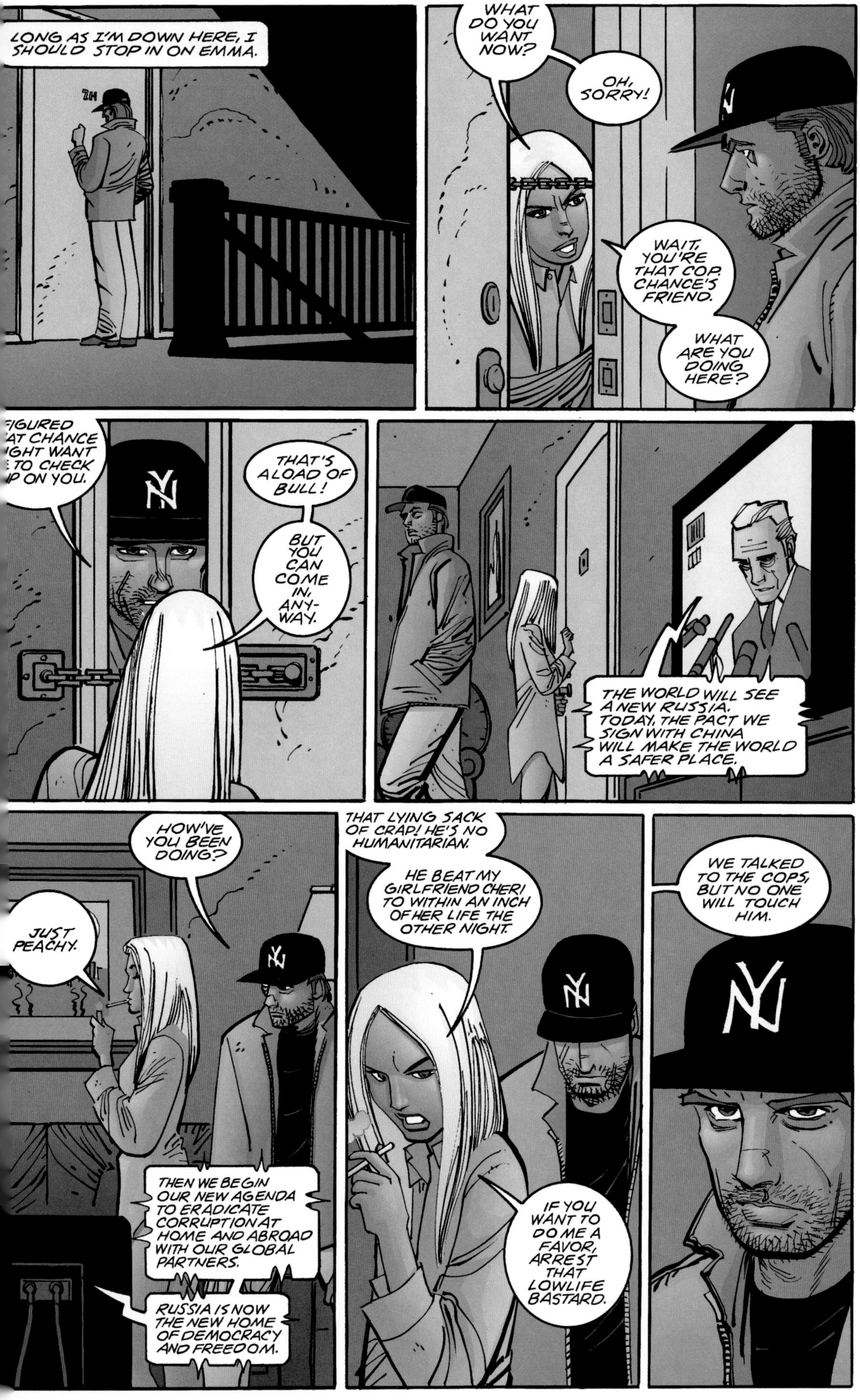
LONG AS I'M DOWN HERE, I SHOULD STOP IN ON EMMA.
WHAT DO YOU WANT NOW?
OH, SORRY!
WAIT, YOU'RE THAT COP. CHANCE'S FRIEND.
WHAT ARE YOU DOING HERE?
FIGURED AT CHANCE IGHT WANT E TO CHECK P ON YOU.
THAT'S A LOAD OF BULL!
BUT YOU CAN COME IN, ANYWAY.
THE WORLD WILL SEE A NEW RUSSIA. TODAY, THE PACT WE SIGN WITH CHINA WILL MAKE THE WORLD A SAFER PLACE.
HOW'VE YOU BEEN DOING?
JUST PEACHY.
THEN WE BEGIN OUR NEW AGENDA TO ERADICATE CORRUPTION AT HOME AND ABROAD WITH OUR GLOBAL PARTNERS.
RUSSIA IS NOW THE NEW HOME OF DEMOCRACY AND FREEDOM.
THAT LYING SACK OF CRAP! HE'S NO HUMANITARIAN.
HE BEAT MY GIRLFRIEND CHERI TO WITHIN AN INCH OF HER LIFE THE OTHER NIGHT.
IF YOU WANT TO DO ME A FAVOR, ARREST THAT LOWLIFE BASTARD.
WE TALKED TO THE COPS, BUT NO ONE WILL TOUCH HIM.

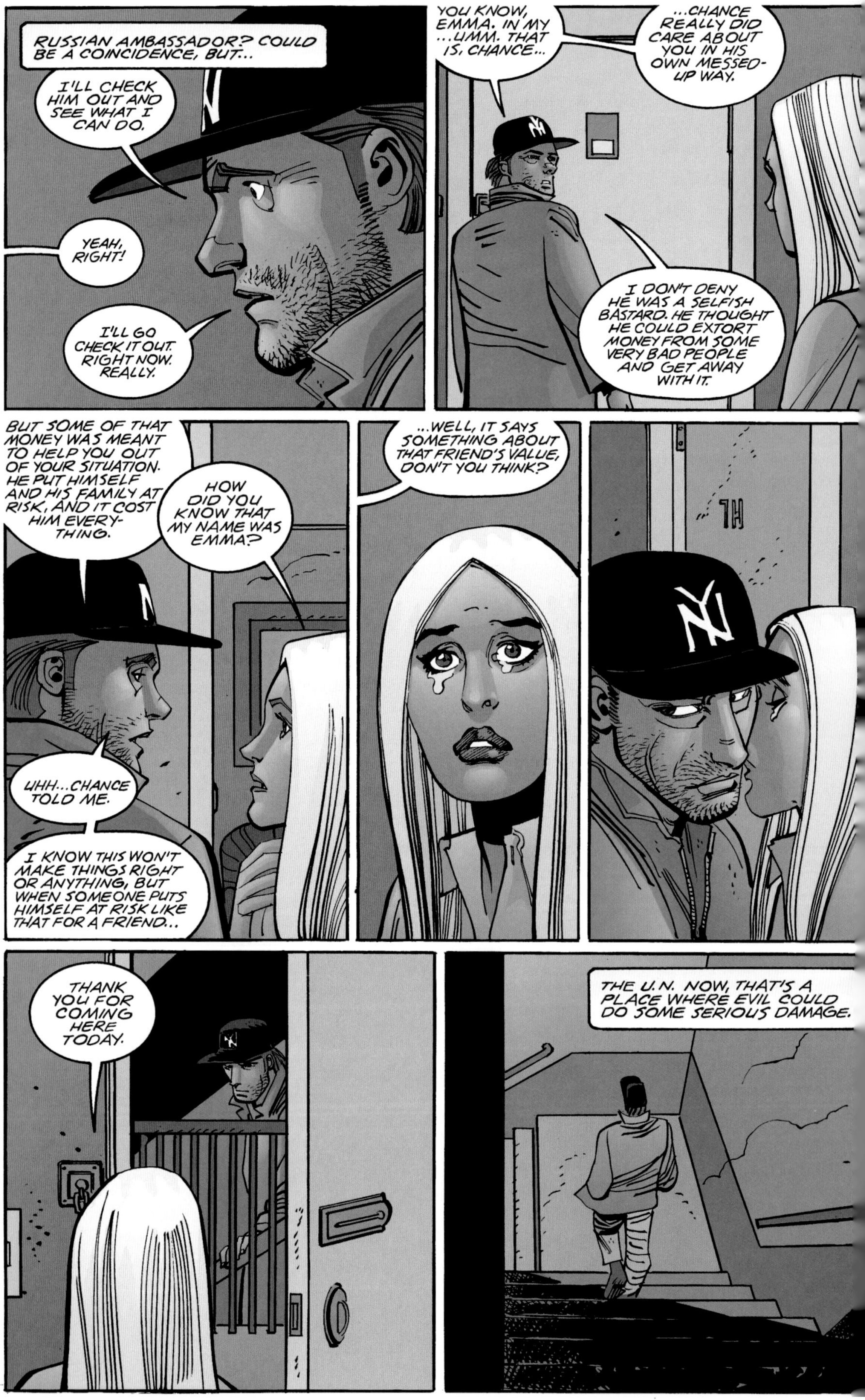
RUSSIAN AMBASSADOR? COULD BE A COINCIDENCE, BUT...
I'LL CHECK HIM OUT AND SEE WHAT I CAN DO.
YEAH, RIGHT!
I'LL GO CHECK IT OUT. RIGHT NOW. REALLY.
YOU KNOW, EMMA. IN MY ...UMM. THAT IS, CHANCE...
...CHANCE REALLY DID CARE ABOUT YOU IN HIS OWN MESSED-UP WAY.
I DON'T DENY HE WAS A SELFISH BASTARD. HE THOUGHT HE COULD EXTORT MONEY FROM SOME VERY BAD PEOPLE AND GET AWAY WITH IT.
BUT SOME OF THAT MONEY WAS MEANT TO HELP YOU OUT OF YOUR SITUATION. HE PUT HIMSELF AND HIS FAMILY AT RISK, AND IT COST HIM EVERY-THING.
HOW DID YOU KNOW THAT MY NAME WAS EMMA?
UHH...CHANCE TOLD ME.
I KNOW THIS WON'T MAKE THINGS RIGHT OR ANYTHING, BUT WHEN SOMEONE PUTS HIMSELF AT RISK LIKE THAT FOR A FRIEND...
...WELL, IT SAYS SOMETHING ABOUT THAT FRIEND'S VALUE, DON'T YOU THINK?
7H
THANK YOU FOR COMING HERE TODAY.
THE U.N. NOW, THAT'S A PLACE WHERE EVIL COULD DO SOME SERIOUS DAMAGE.

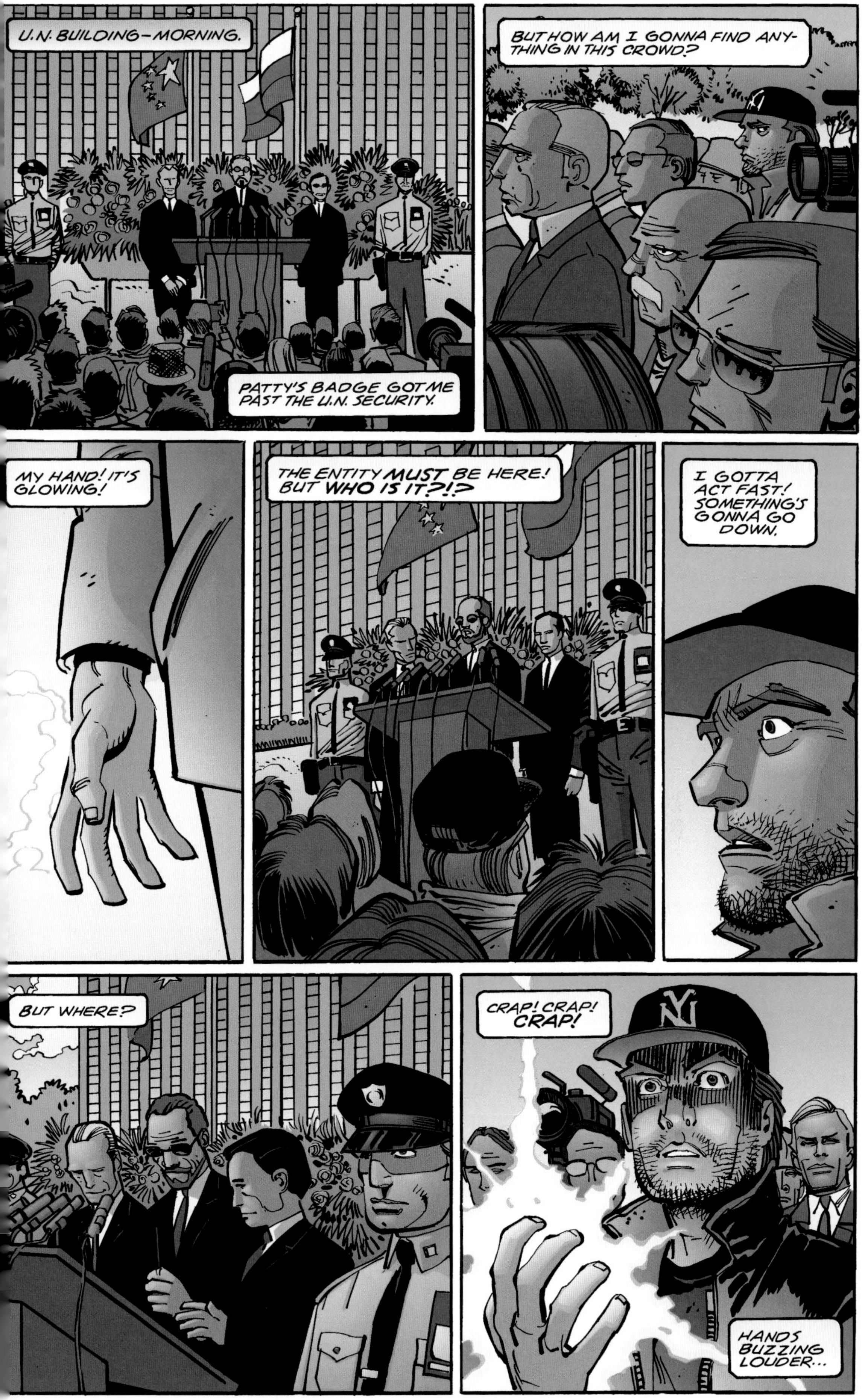
U.N. BUILDING—MORNING.
PATTY'S BADGE GOT ME PAST THE U.N. SECURITY.
BUT HOW AM I GONNA FIND ANY-THING IN THIS CROWD?
MY HAND! IT'S GLOWING!
THE ENTITY MUST BE HERE! BUT WHO IS IT?!?
I GOTTA ACT FAST! SOMETHING'S GONNA GO DOWN.
BUT WHERE?
CRAP! CRAP! CRAP!
HANDS BUZZING LOUDER...

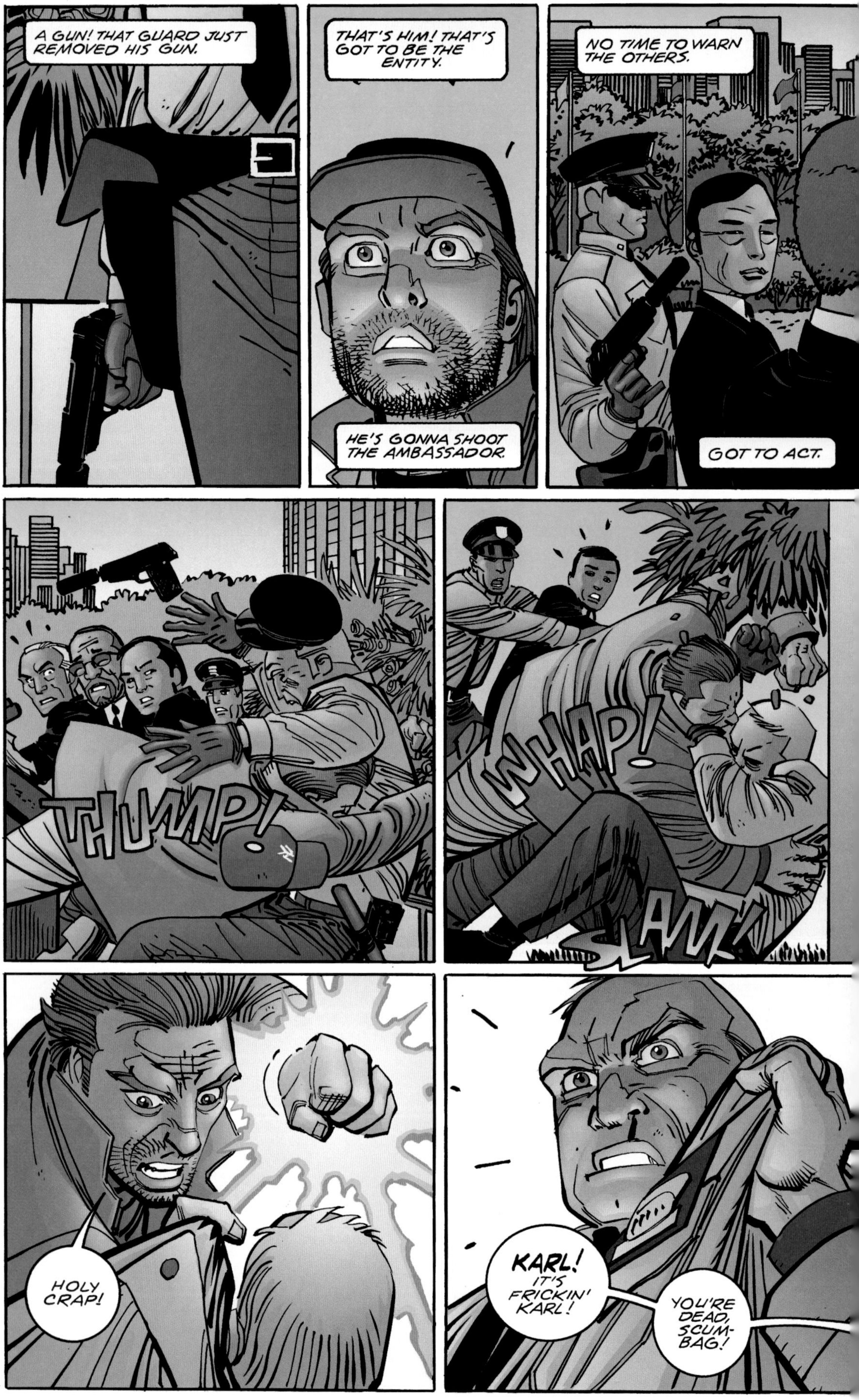
A GUN! THAT GUARD JUST REMOVED HIS GUN.
THAT'S HIM! THAT'S GOT TO BE THE ENTITY.
HE'S GONNA SHOOT THE AMBASSADOR.
NO TIME TO WARN THE OTHERS.
GOT TO ACT.
THUMP!
WHAP!
SLAM!
HOLY CRAP!
KARL! IT'S FRICKIN' KARL!
YOU'RE DEAD, SCUMBAG!

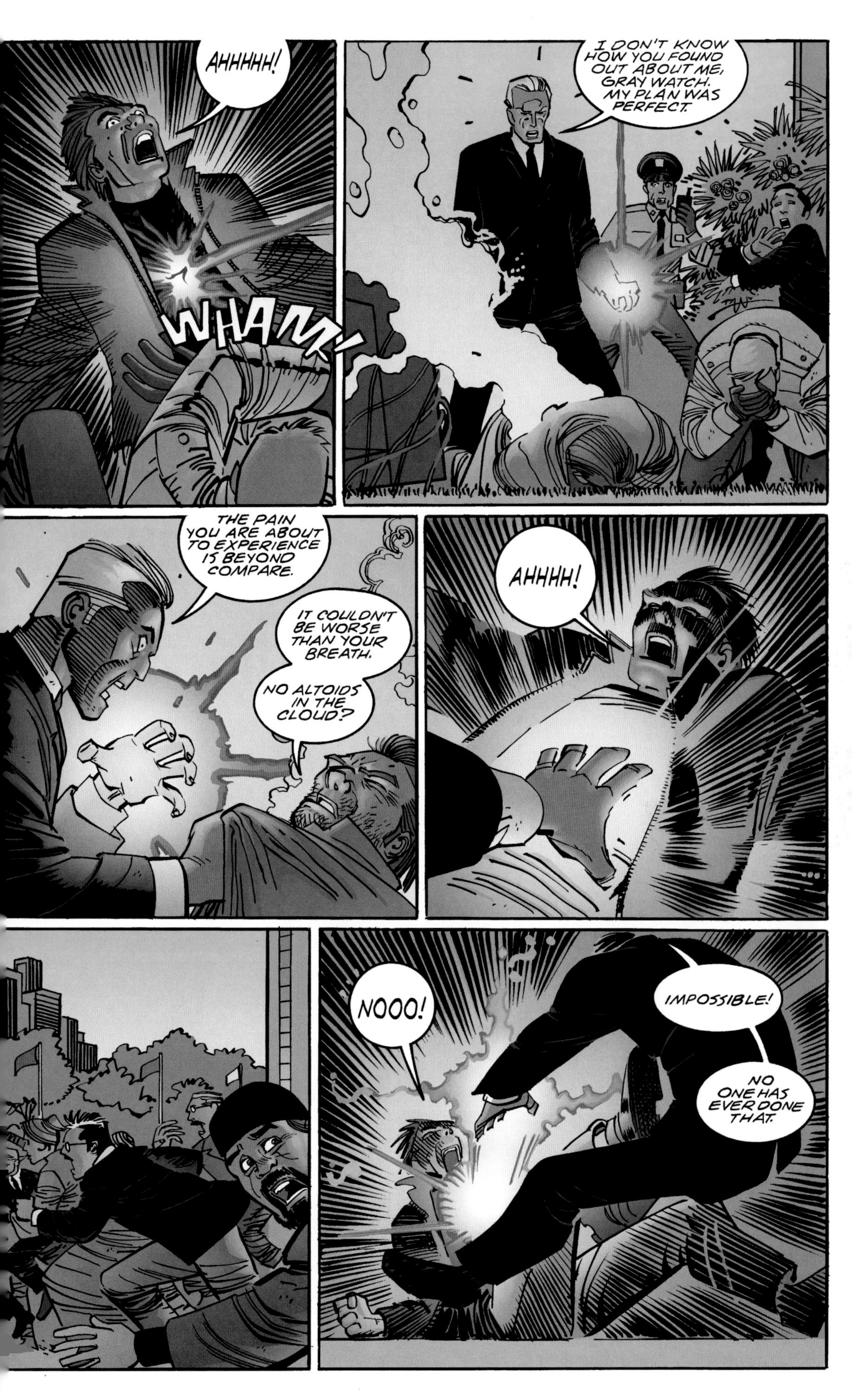
AHHHHH!
WHAM!
I DON'T KNOW HOW YOU FOUND OUT ABOUT ME, GRAY WATCH. MY PLAN WAS PERFECT.
THE PAIN YOU ARE ABOUT TO EXPERIENCE IS BEYOND COMPARE.
IT COULDN'T BE WORSE THAN YOUR BREATH.
NO ALTOIDS IN THE CLOUD?
AHHHH!
NOOO!
IMPOSSIBLE!
NO ONE HAS EVER DONE THAT.

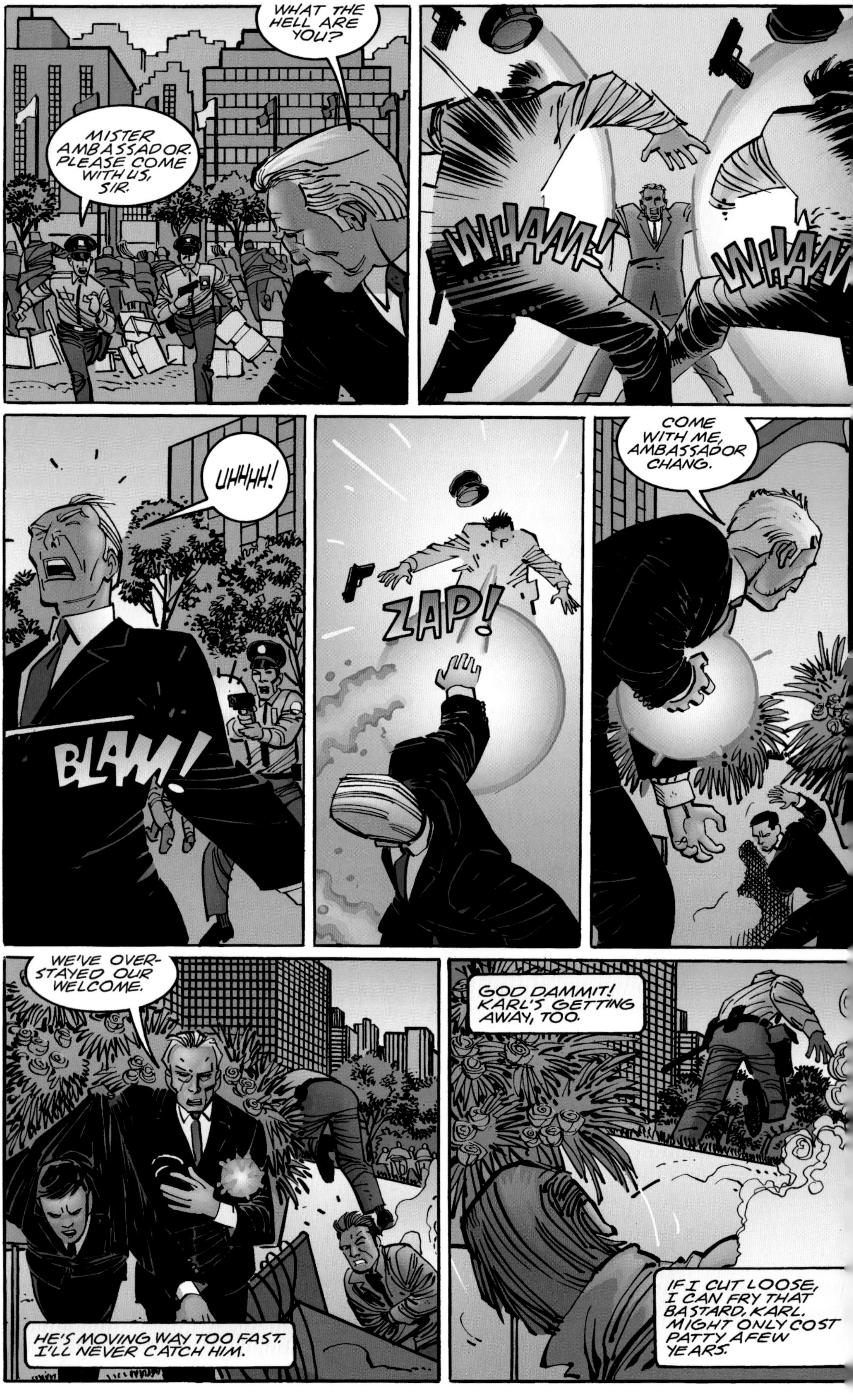
WHAT THE HELL ARE YOU?
MISTER AMBASSADOR. PLEASE COME WITH US, SIR.
WHAM!
WHAM
UHHHH!
BLAM!
ZAP!
COME WITH ME, AMBASSADOR CHANG.
WE'VE OVER-STAYED OUR WELCOME.
HE'S MOVING WAY TOO FAST. I'LL NEVER CATCH HIM.
GOD DAMMIT! KARL'S GETTING AWAY, TOO.
IF I CUT LOOSE, I CAN FRY THAT BASTARD, KARL. MIGHT ONLY COST PATTY A FEW YEARS.

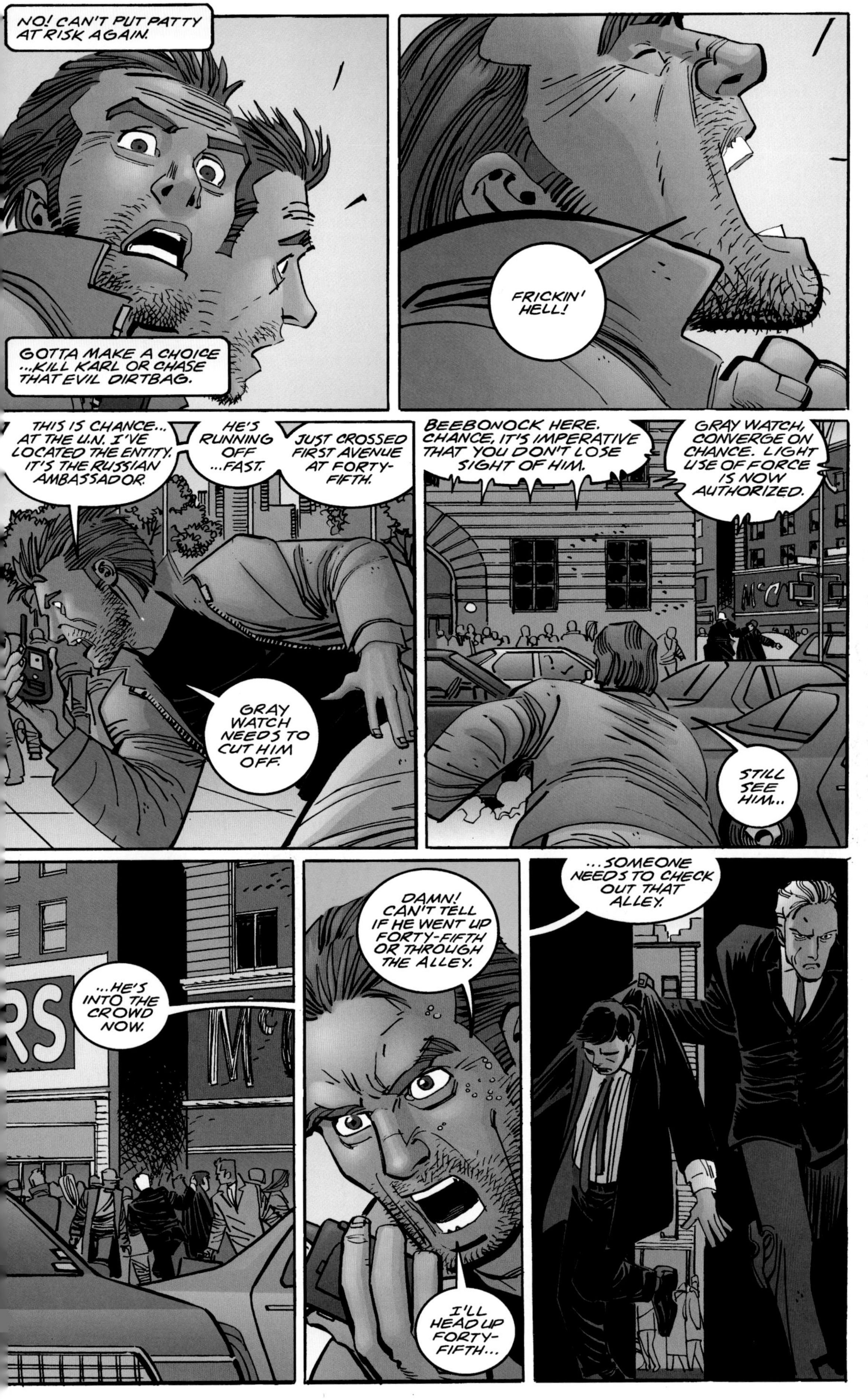
NO! CAN'T PUT PATTY AT RISK AGAIN.
GOTTA MAKE A CHOICE ...KILL KARL OR CHASE THAT EVIL DIRTBAG.
FRICKIN' HELL!
THIS IS CHANCE... AT THE U.N. I'VE LOCATED THE ENTITY. IT'S THE RUSSIAN AMBASSADOR.
HE'S RUNNING OFF ...FAST.
JUST CROSSED FIRST AVENUE AT FORTY-FIFTH.
GRAY WATCH NEEDS TO CUT HIM OFF.
BEEBONOCK HERE. CHANCE, IT'S IMPERATIVE THAT YOU DON'T LOSE SIGHT OF HIM.
GRAY WATCH, CONVERGE ON CHANCE. LIGHT USE OF FORCE IS NOW AUTHORIZED.
STILL SEE HIM...
...HE'S INTO THE CROWD NOW.
DAMN! CAN'T TELL IF HE WENT UP FORTY-FIFTH OR THROUGH THE ALLEY.
I'LL HEAD UP FORTY-FIFTH...
...SOMEONE NEEDS TO CHECK OUT THAT ALLEY.

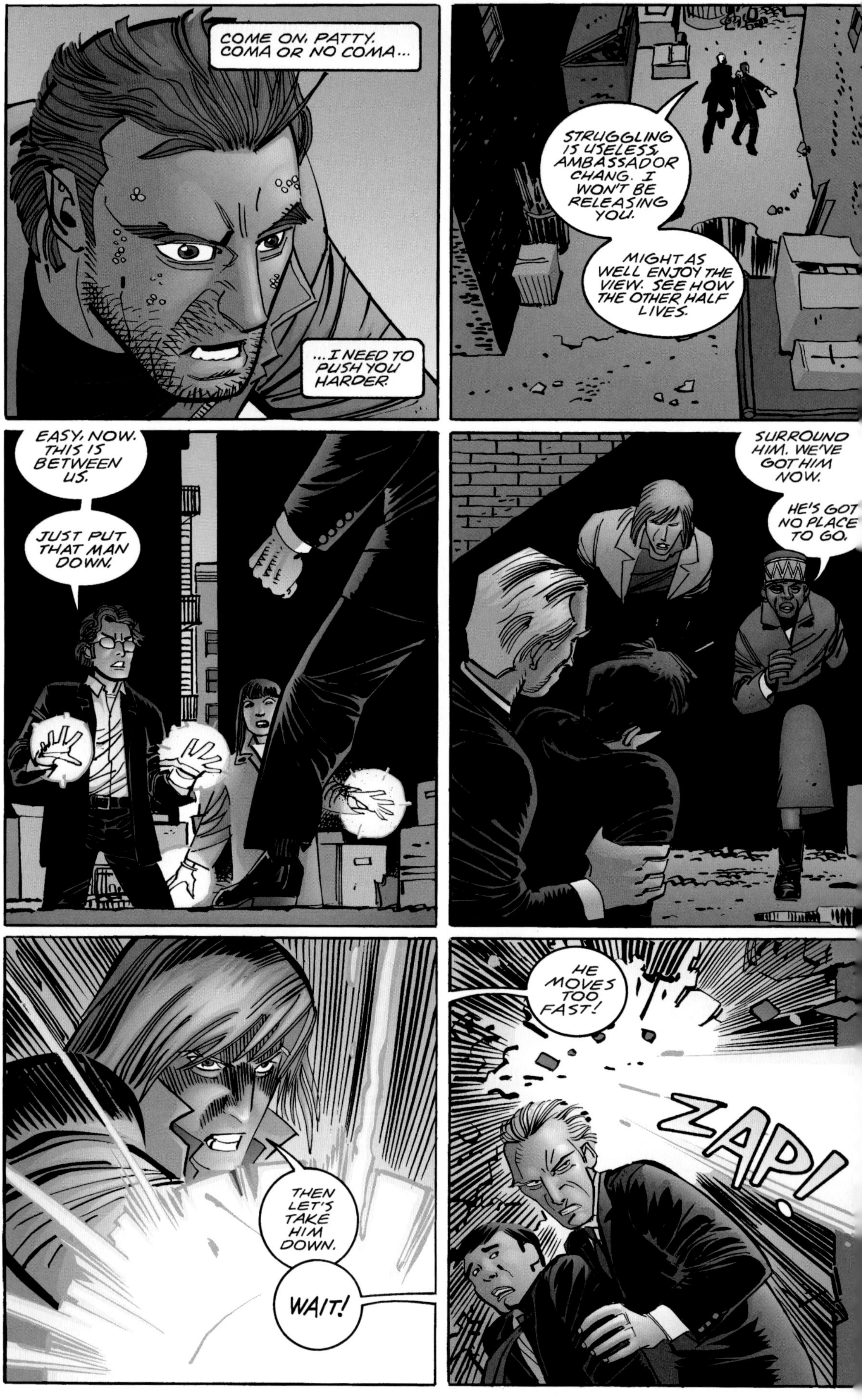

COME ON, PATTY. COMA OR NO COMA...
...I NEED TO PUSH YOU HARDER.
STRUGGLING IS USELESS, AMBASSADOR CHANG. I WON'T BE RELEASING YOU.
MIGHT AS WELL ENJOY THE VIEW. SEE HOW THE OTHER HALF LIVES.
EASY, NOW. THIS IS BETWEEN US.
JUST PUT THAT MAN DOWN.
SURROUND HIM. WE'VE GOT HIM NOW.
HE'S GOT NO PLACE TO GO.
THEN LET'S TAKE HIM DOWN.
WAIT!
HE MOVES TOO FAST!
ZAP!

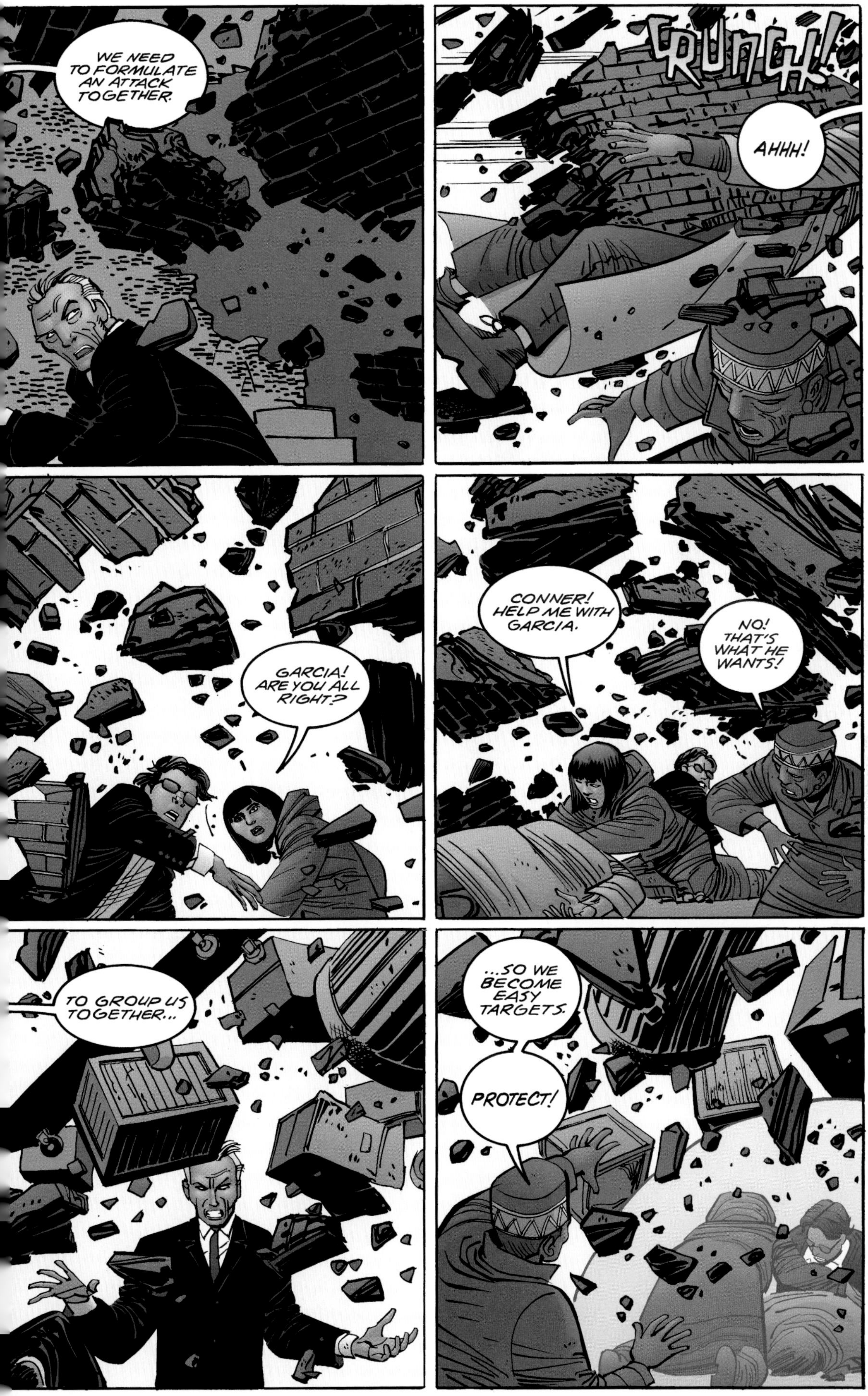
WE NEED TO FORMULATE AN ATTACK TOGETHER.
CRUNCH!!
AHHH!
GARCIA! ARE YOU ALL RIGHT?
CONNER! HELP ME WITH GARCIA.
NO! THAT'S WHAT HE WANTS!
TO GROUP US TOGETHER...
...SO WE BECOME EASY TARGETS.
PROTECT!

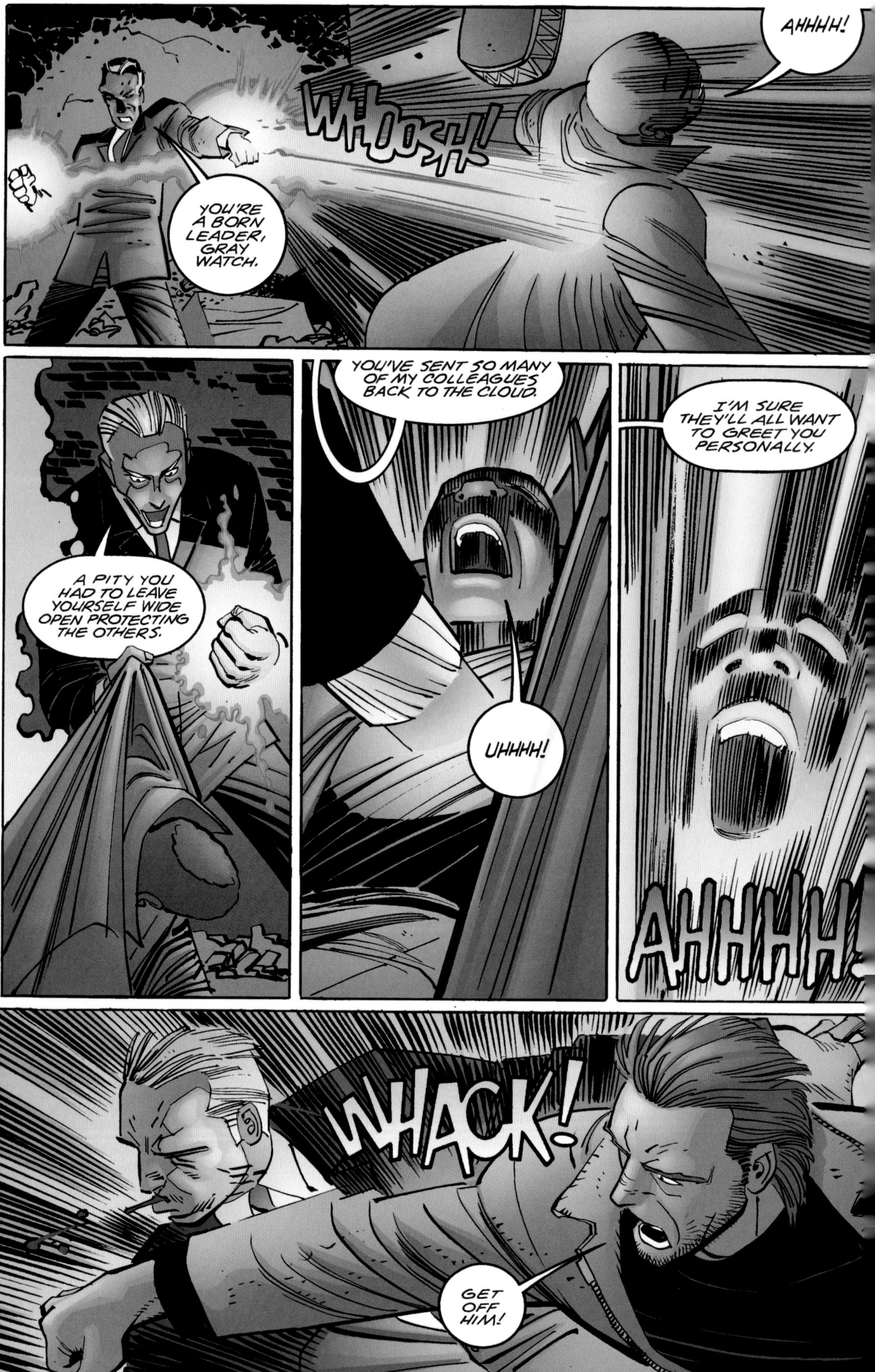
WHOOSH!
AHHHH!
YOU'RE A BORN LEADER, GRAY WATCH.
A PITY YOU HAD TO LEAVE YOURSELF WIDE OPEN PROTECTING THE OTHERS.
YOU'VE SENT SO MANY OF MY COLLEAGUES BACK TO THE CLOUD.
UHHHH!
I'M SURE THEY'LL ALL WANT TO GREET YOU PERSONALLY.
AHHHH!
WHACK!
GET OFF HIM!

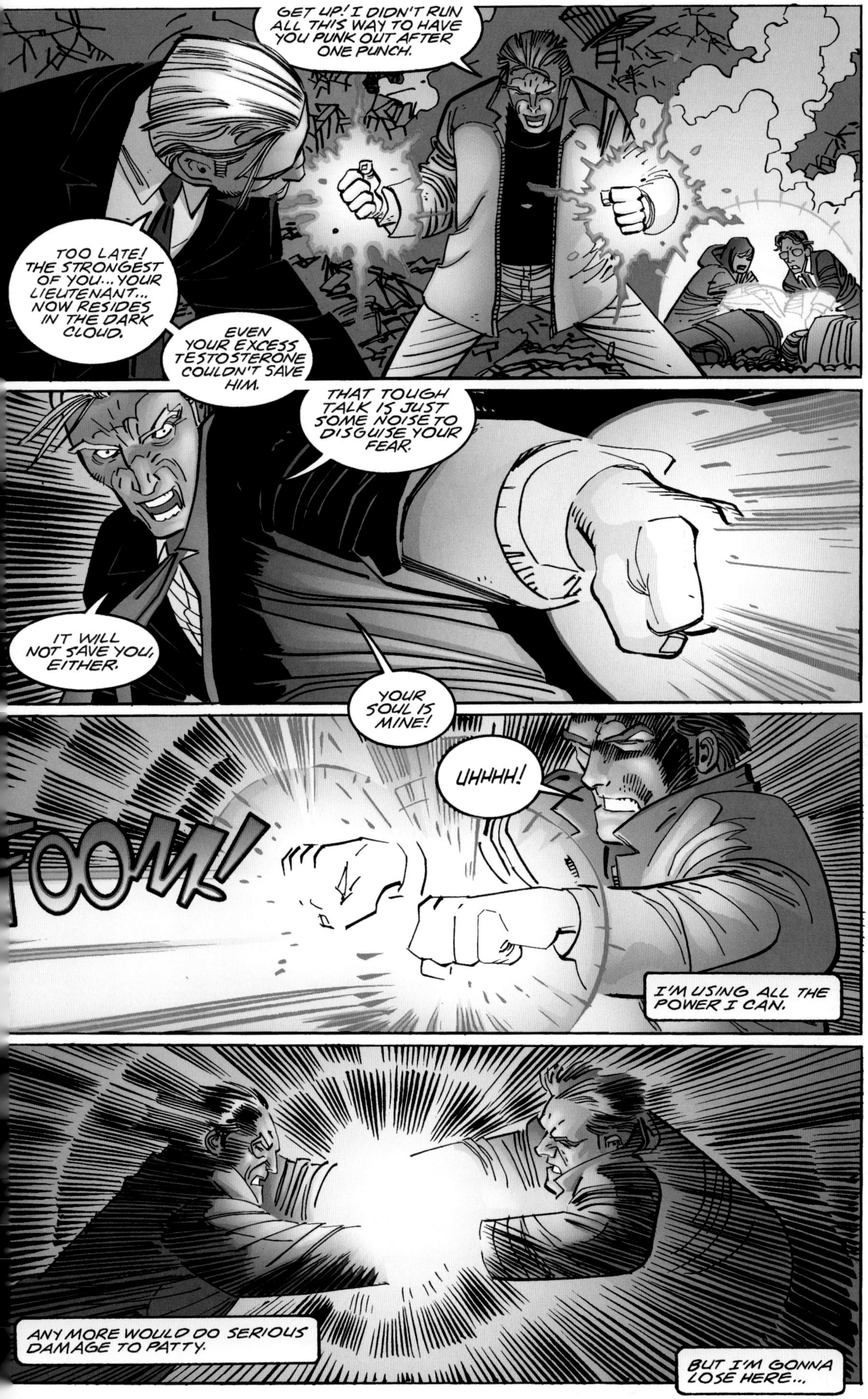
GET UP! I DIDN'T RUN ALL THIS WAY TO HAVE YOU PUNK OUT AFTER ONE PUNCH.
TOO LATE! THE STRONGEST OF YOU... YOUR LIEUTENANT... NOW RESIDES IN THE DARK CLOUD.
EVEN YOUR EXCESS TESTOSTERONE COULDN'T SAVE HIM.
THAT TOUGH TALK IS JUST SOME NOISE TO DISGUISE YOUR FEAR.
IT WILL NOT SAVE YOU, EITHER.
YOUR SOUL IS MINE!
UHHHH!
OOM!
I'M USING ALL THE POWER I CAN.
ANY MORE WOULD DO SERIOUS DAMAGE TO PATTY.
BUT I'M GONNA LOSE HERE...

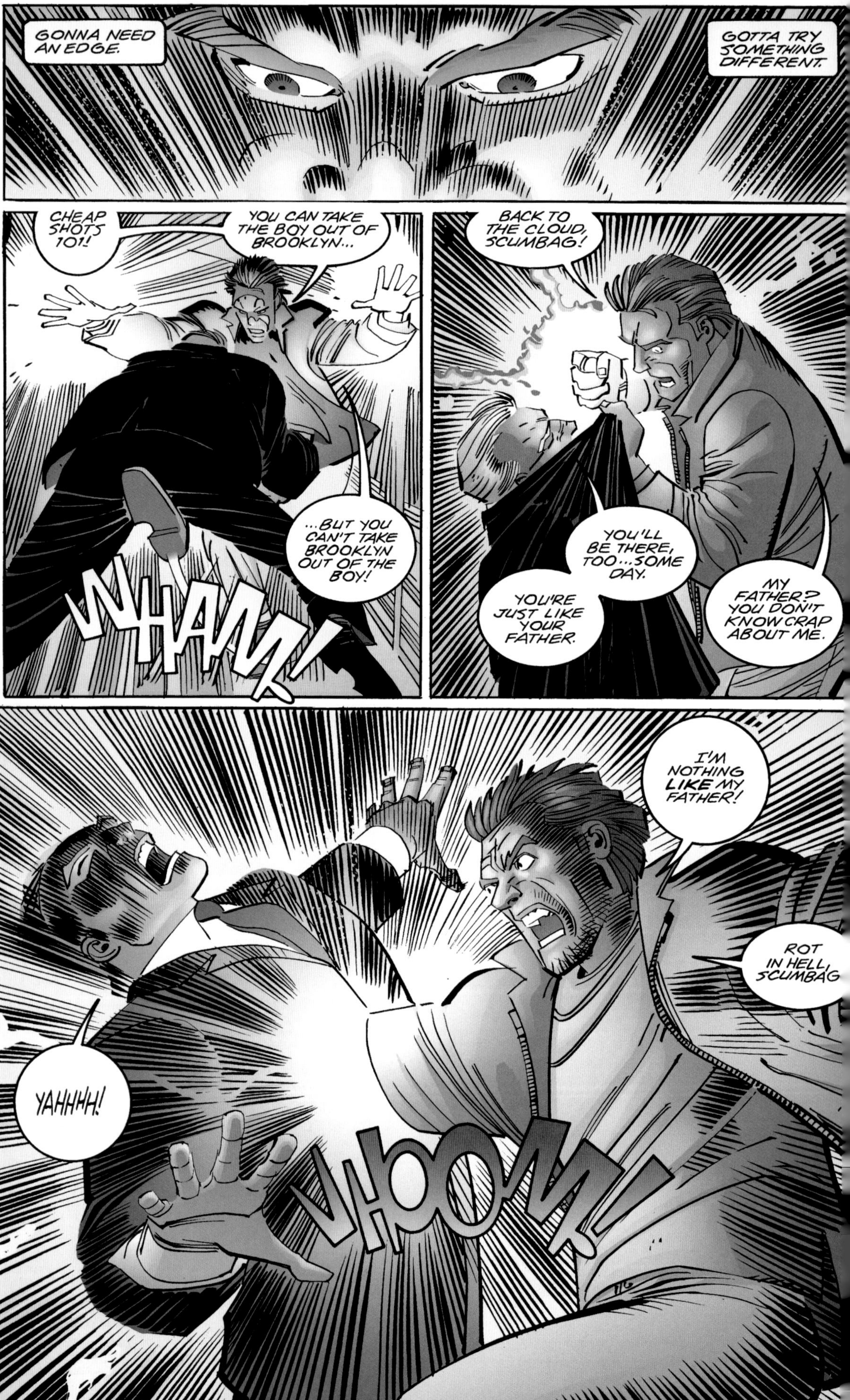
GONNA NEED AN EDGE.
GOTTA TRY SOMETHING DIFFERENT.
CHEAP SHOTS 101!
YOU CAN TAKE THE BOY OUT OF BROOKLYN...
...BUT YOU CAN'T TAKE BROOKLYN OUT OF THE BOY!
WHAM!
BACK TO THE CLOUD, SCUMBAG!
YOU'RE JUST LIKE YOUR FATHER.
YOU'LL BE THERE, TOO...SOME DAY.
MY FATHER? YOU DON'T KNOW CRAP ABOUT ME.
I'M NOTHING LIKE MY FATHER!
ROT IN HELL, SCUMBAG
YAHHHH!
VHOOM!

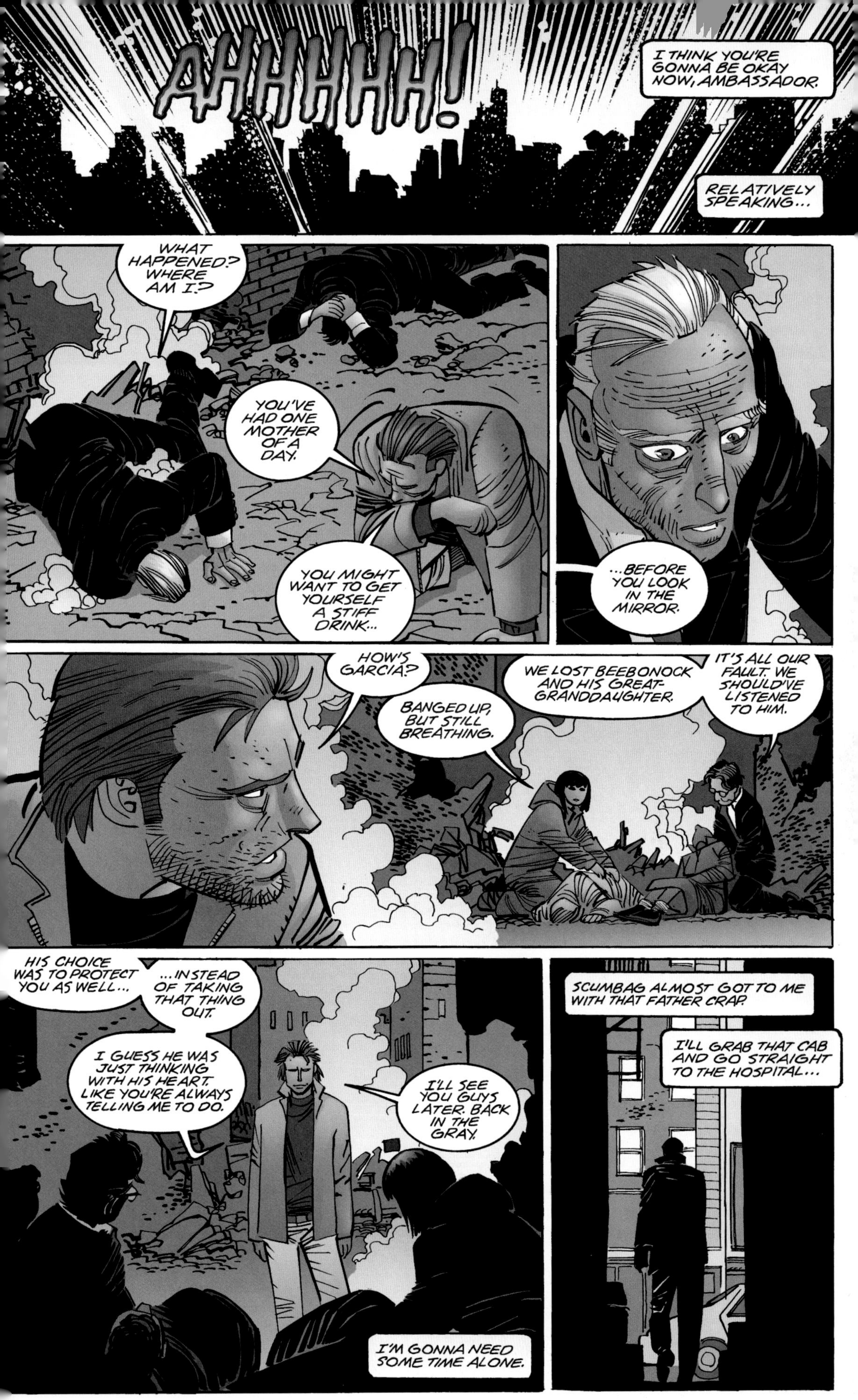
AHHHHH!
I THINK YOU'RE GONNA BE OKAY NOW, AMBASSADOR.
RELATIVELY SPEAKING...
WHAT HAPPENED? WHERE AM I?
YOU'VE HAD ONE MOTHER OF A DAY.
YOU MIGHT WANT TO GET YOURSELF A STIFF DRINK...
...BEFORE YOU LOOK IN THE MIRROR.
HOW'S GARCIA?
BANGED UP, BUT STILL BREATHING.
WE LOST BEEBONOCK AND HIS GREAT-GRANDDAUGHTER.
IT'S ALL OUR FAULT. WE SHOULD'VE LISTENED TO HIM.
HIS CHOICE WAS TO PROTECT YOU AS WELL...
...INSTEAD OF TAKING THAT THING OUT.
I GUESS HE WAS JUST THINKING WITH HIS HEART. LIKE YOU'RE ALWAYS TELLING ME TO DO.
I'LL SEE YOU GUYS LATER. BACK IN THE GRAY.
I'M GONNA NEED SOME TIME ALONE.
SCUMBAG ALMOST GOT TO ME WITH THAT FATHER CRAP.
I'LL GRAB THAT CAB AND GO STRAIGHT TO THE HOSPITAL...

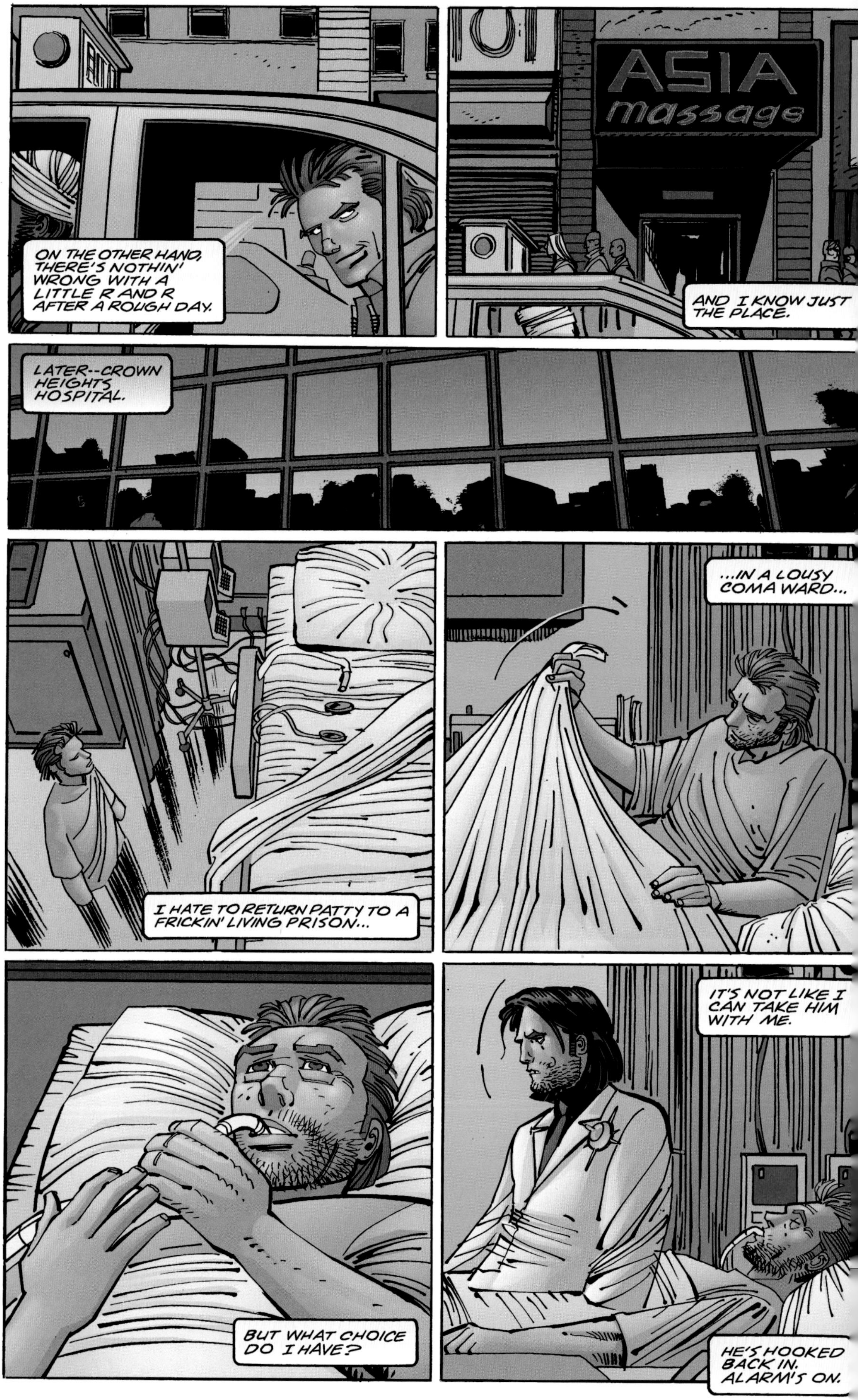
ON THE OTHER HAND, THERE'S NOTHIN' WRONG WITH A LITTLE R AND R AFTER A ROUGH DAY.
ASIA massage
AND I KNOW JUST THE PLACE.
LATER--CROWN HEIGHTS HOSPITAL.
I HATE TO RETURN PATTY TO A FRICKIN' LIVING PRISON...
...IN A LOUSY COMA WARD...
BUT WHAT CHOICE DO I HAVE?
IT'S NOT LIKE I CAN TAKE HIM WITH ME.
HE'S HOOKED BACK IN. ALARM'S ON.

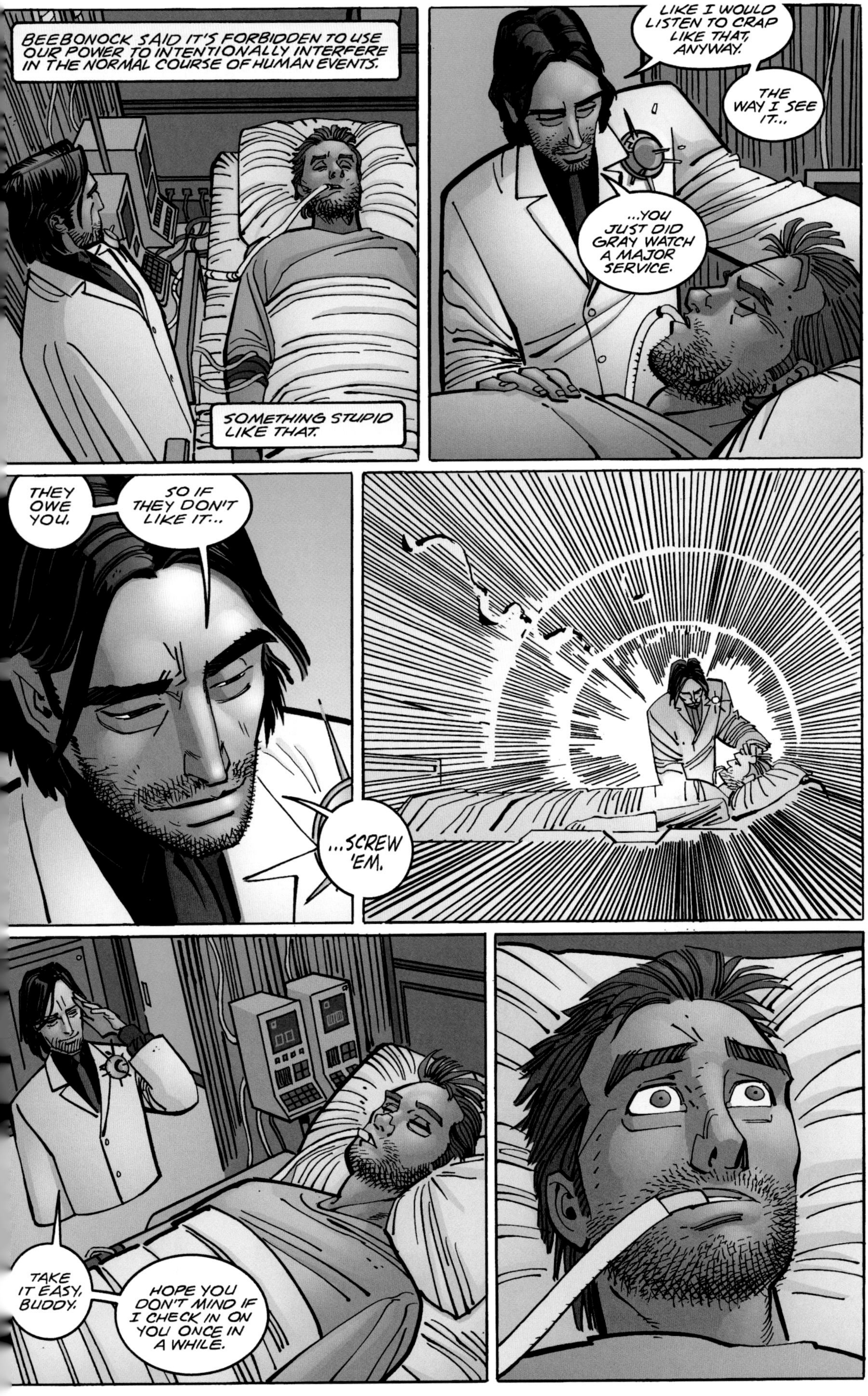
BEEBONOCK SAID IT'S FORBIDDEN TO USE OUR POWER TO INTENTIONALLY INTERFERE IN THE NORMAL COURSE OF HUMAN EVENTS.
SOMETHING STUPID LIKE THAT.
LIKE I WOULD LISTEN TO CRAP LIKE THAT, ANYWAY.
THE WAY I SEE IT...
...YOU JUST DID GRAY WATCH A MAJOR SERVICE.
THEY OWE YOU.
SO IF THEY DON'T LIKE IT...
...SCREW 'EM.
TAKE IT EASY, BUDDY.
HOPE YOU DON'T MIND IF I CHECK IN ON YOU ONCE IN A WHILE.

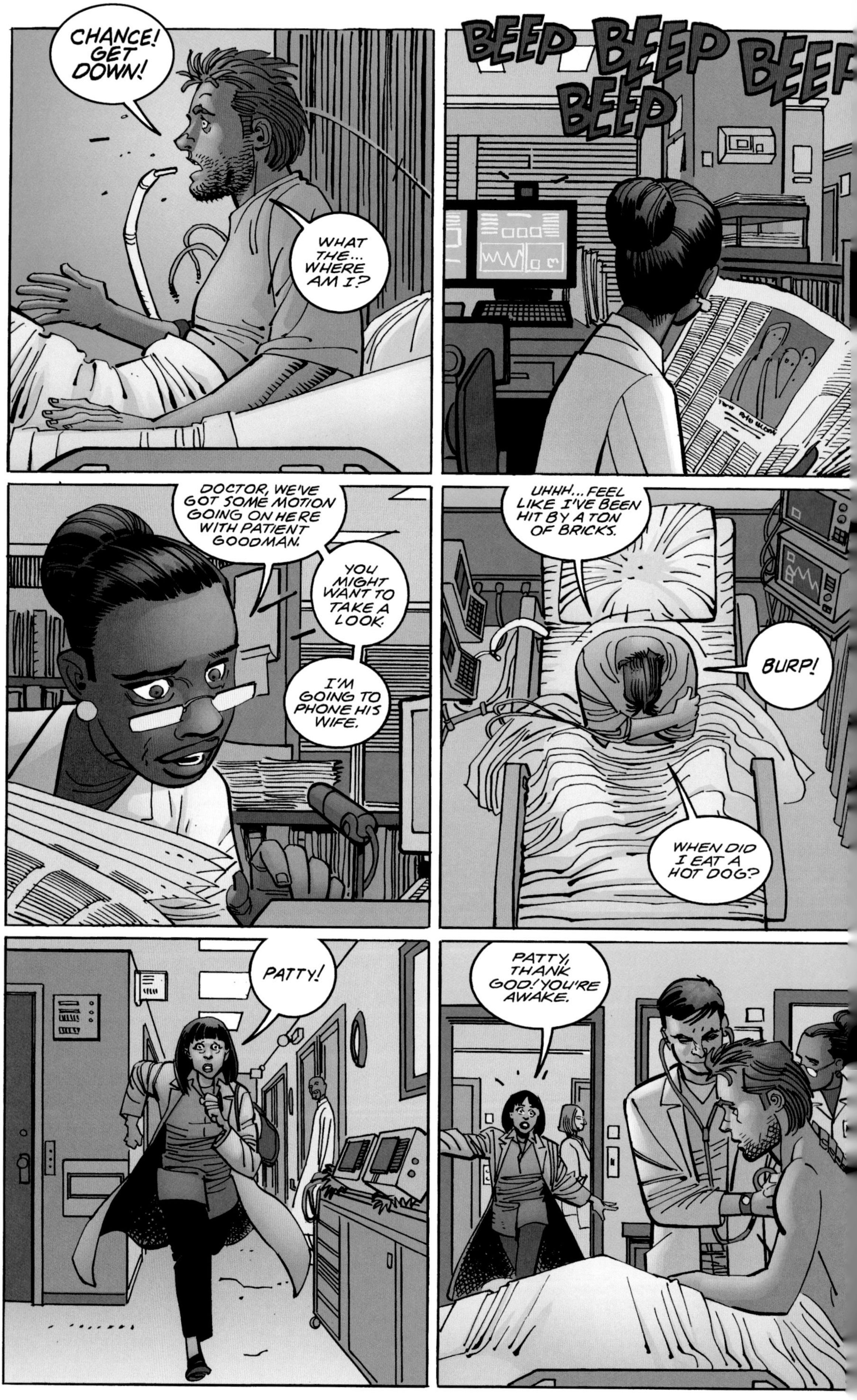
CHANCE! GET DOWN!
WHAT THE... WHERE AM I?
BEEP BEEP BEEP BEEP
DOCTOR, WE'VE GOT SOME MOTION GOING ON HERE WITH PATIENT GOODMAN.
YOU MIGHT WANT TO TAKE A LOOK.
I'M GOING TO PHONE HIS WIFE.
UHHH... FEEL LIKE I'VE BEEN HIT BY A TON OF BRICKS.
BURP!
WHEN DID I EAT A HOT DOG?
PATTY!
PATTY, THANK GOD! YOU'RE AWAKE.

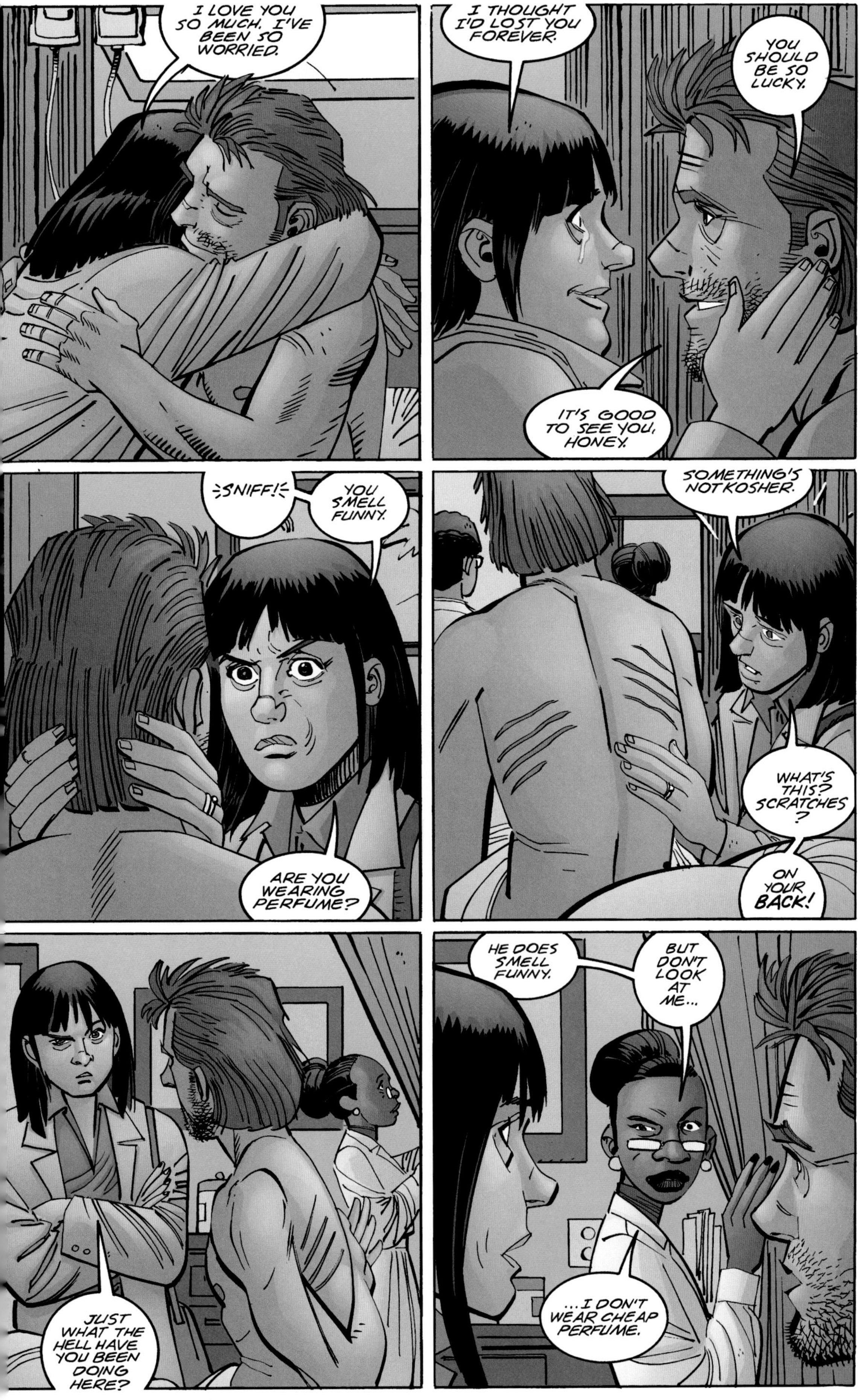
I LOVE YOU SO MUCH. I'VE BEEN SO WORRIED.
I THOUGHT I'D LOST YOU FOREVER.
YOU SHOULD BE SO LUCKY.
IT'S GOOD TO SEE YOU, HONEY.
SNIFF!
YOU SMELL FUNNY.
ARE YOU WEARING PERFUME?
SOMETHING'S NOT KOSHER.
WHAT'S THIS? SCRATCHES?
ON YOUR BACK!
JUST WHAT THE HELL HAVE YOU BEEN DOING HERE?
HE DOES SMELL FUNNY.
BUT DON'T LOOK AT ME...
...I DON'T WEAR CHEAP PERFUME.

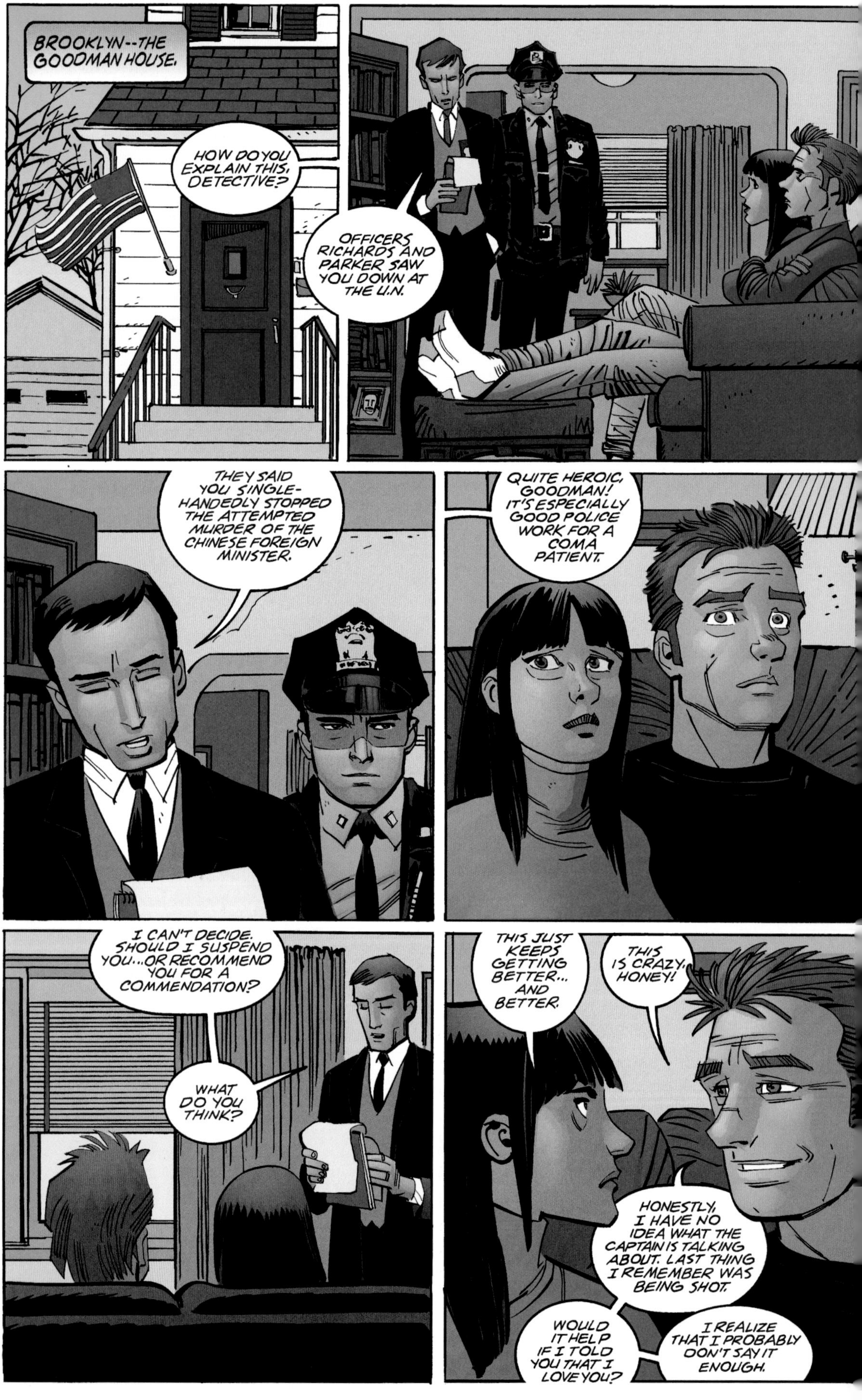
BROOKLYN--THE GOODMAN HOUSE.
HOW DO YOU EXPLAIN THIS, DETECTIVE?
OFFICERS RICHARDS AND PARKER SAW YOU DOWN AT THE U.N.
THEY SAID YOU SINGLE-HANDEDLY STOPPED THE ATTEMPTED MURDER OF THE CHINESE FOREIGN MINISTER.
QUITE HEROIC, GOODMAN! IT'S ESPECIALLY GOOD POLICE WORK FOR A COMA PATIENT.
I CAN'T DECIDE. SHOULD I SUSPEND YOU...OR RECOMMEND YOU FOR A COMMENDATION?
WHAT DO YOU THINK?
THIS JUST KEEPS GETTING BETTER... AND BETTER.
THIS IS CRAZY, HONEY!
HONESTLY, I HAVE NO IDEA WHAT THE CAPTAIN IS TALKING ABOUT. LAST THING I REMEMBER WAS BEING SHOT.
I REALIZE THAT I PROBABLY DON'T SAY IT ENOUGH.
WOULD IT HELP IF I TOLD YOU THAT I LOVE YOU?

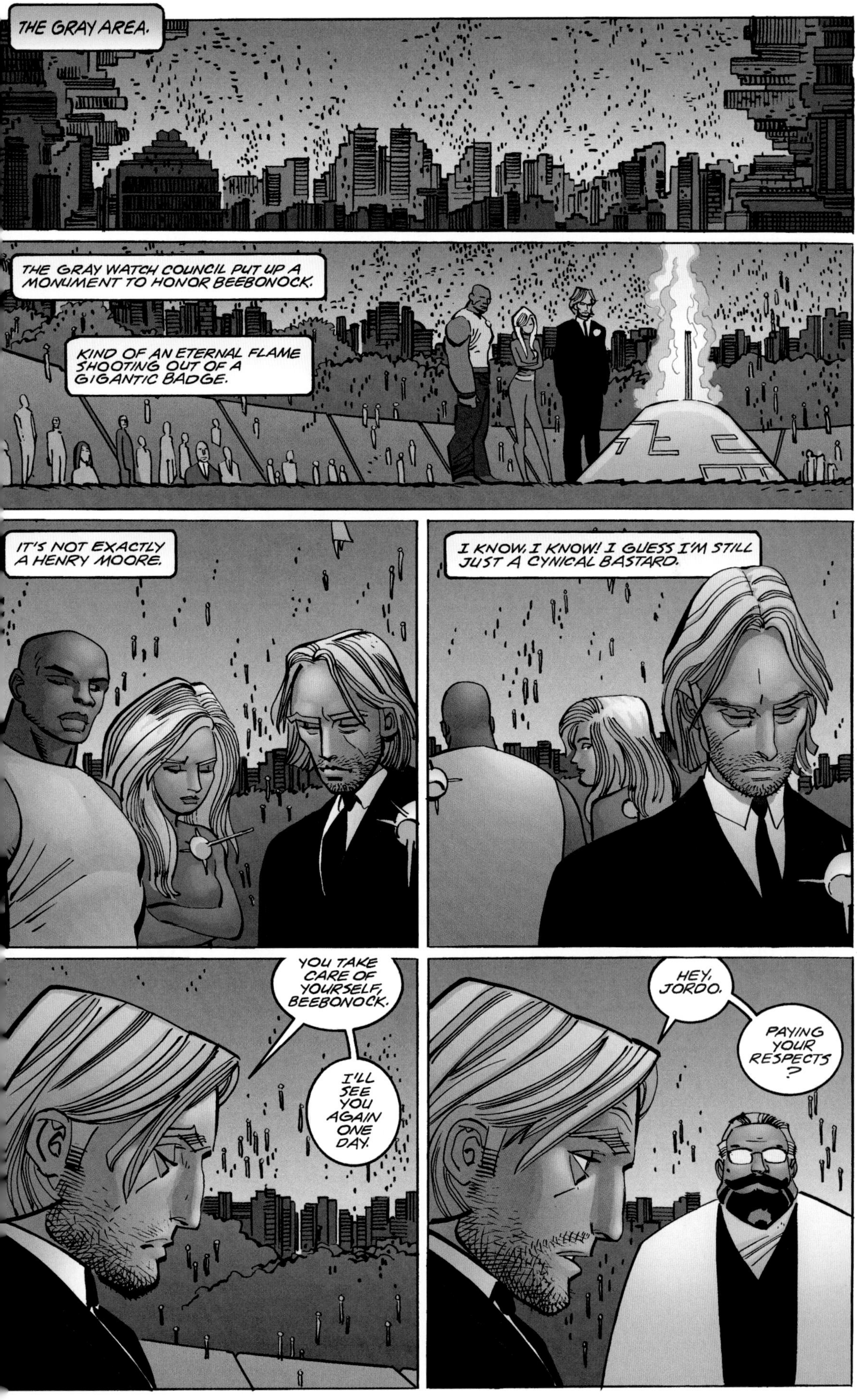
THE GRAY AREA.
THE GRAY WATCH COUNCIL PUT UP A MONUMENT TO HONOR BEEBONOCK.
KIND OF AN ETERNAL FLAME SHOOTING OUT OF A GIGANTIC BADGE.
IT'S NOT EXACTLY A HENRY MOORE.
I KNOW, I KNOW! I GUESS I'M STILL JUST A CYNICAL BASTARD.
YOU TAKE CARE OF YOURSELF, BEEBONOCK.
I'LL SEE YOU AGAIN ONE DAY.
HEY, JORDO.
PAYING YOUR RESPECTS?

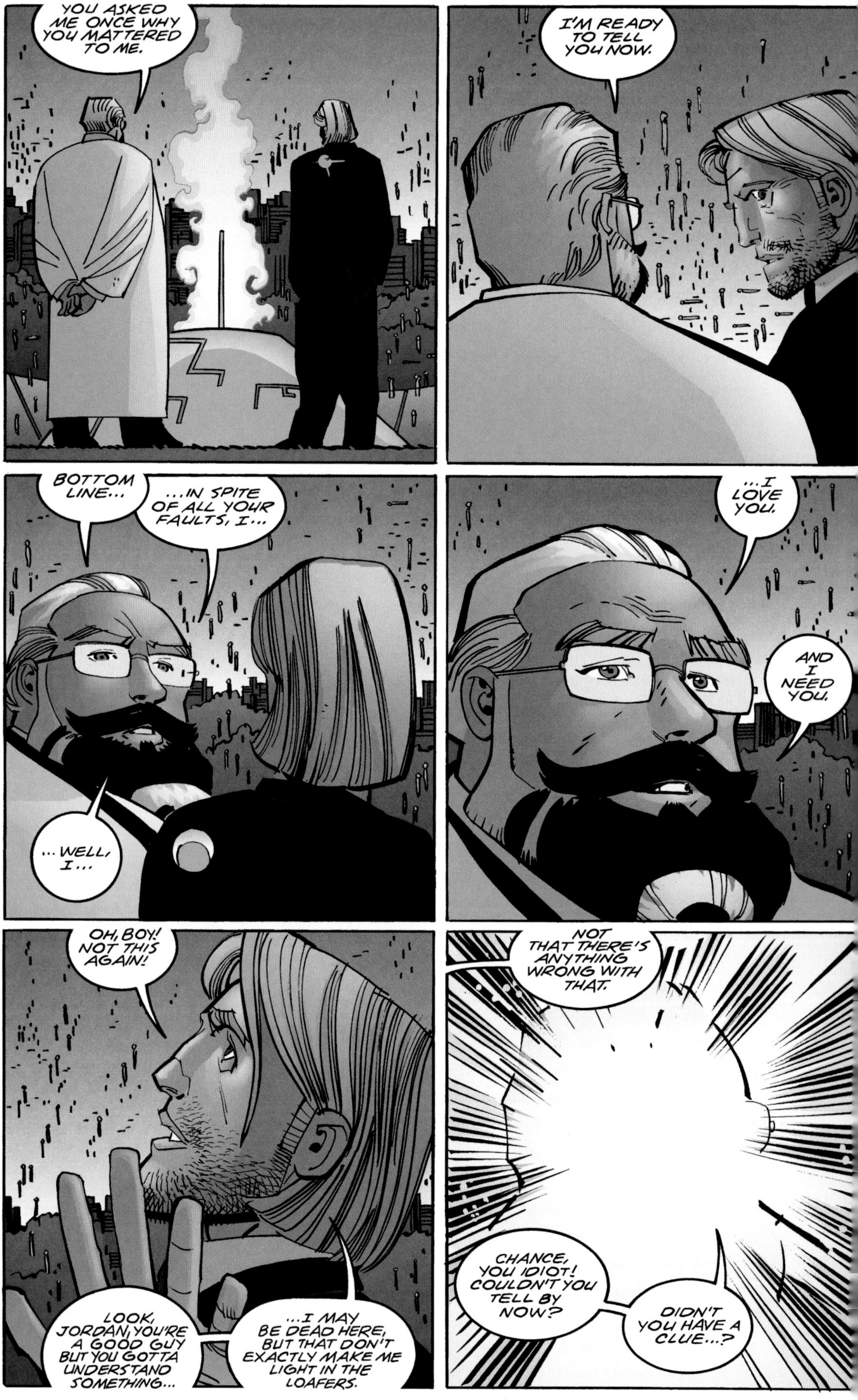
YOU ASKED ME ONCE WHY YOU MATTERED TO ME.
I'M READY TO TELL YOU NOW.
BOTTOM LINE...
...IN SPITE OF ALL YOUR FAULTS, I...
...WELL, I...
...I LOVE YOU.
AND I NEED YOU.
OH, BOY! NOT THIS AGAIN!
LOOK, JORDAN, YOU'RE A GOOD GUY BUT YOU GOTTA UNDERSTAND SOMETHING...
...I MAY BE DEAD HERE, BUT THAT DON'T EXACTLY MAKE ME LIGHT IN THE LOAFERS.
NOT THAT THERE'S ANYTHING WRONG WITH THAT.
CHANCE, YOU IDIOT! COULDN'T YOU TELL BY NOW?
DIDN'T YOU HAVE A CLUE...?

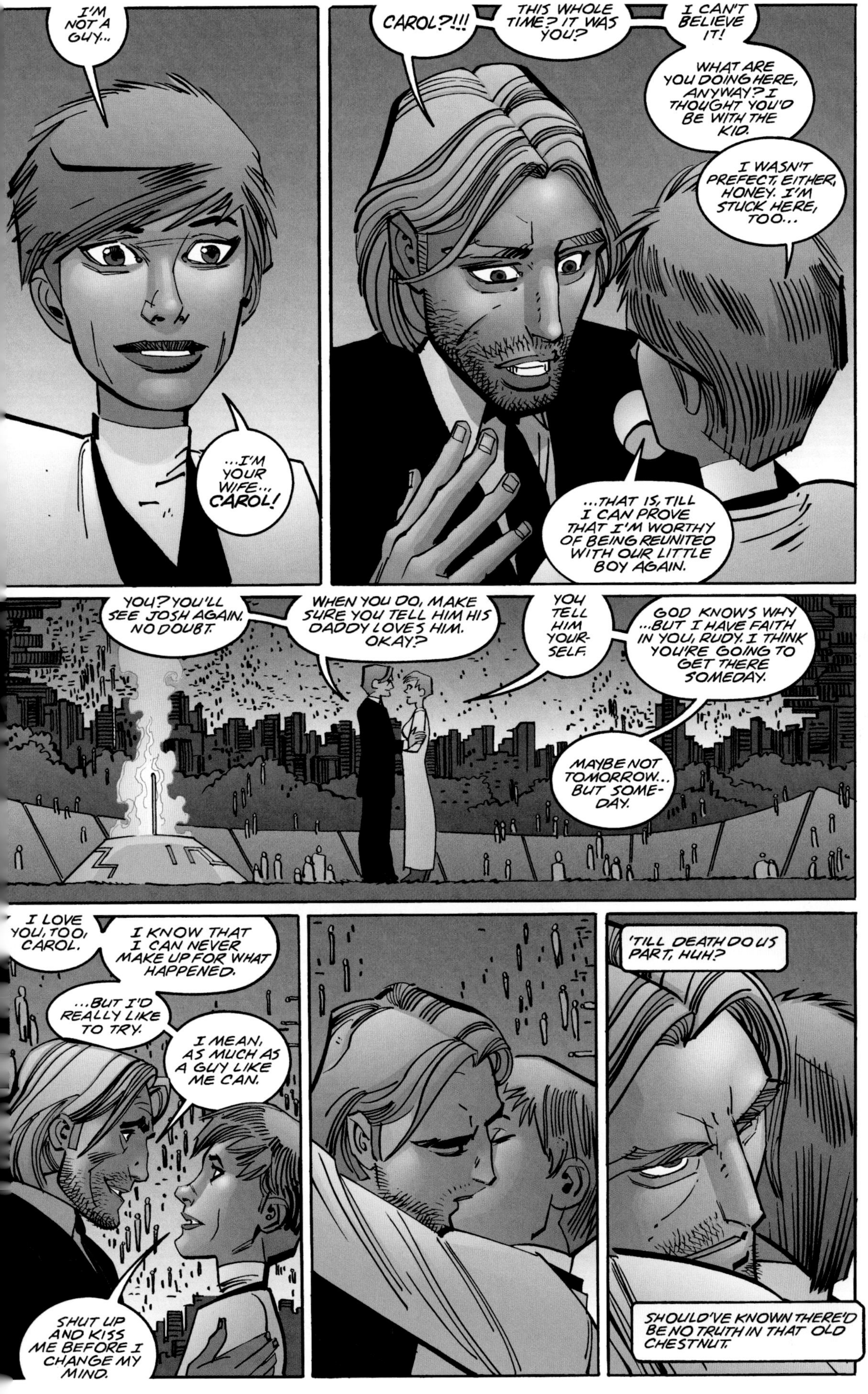
I'M NOT A GUY...
...I'M YOUR WIFE... CAROL!
CAROL?!!!
THIS WHOLE TIME? IT WAS YOU?
I CAN'T BELIEVE IT!
WHAT ARE YOU DOING HERE, ANYWAY? I THOUGHT YOU'D BE WITH THE KID.
I WASN'T PREFECT, EITHER, HONEY. I'M STUCK HERE, TOO...
...THAT IS, TILL I CAN PROVE THAT I'M WORTHY OF BEING REUNITED WITH OUR LITTLE BOY AGAIN.
YOU? YOU'LL SEE JOSH AGAIN. NO DOUBT.
WHEN YOU DO, MAKE SURE YOU TELL HIM HIS DADDY LOVES HIM. OKAY?
YOU TELL HIM YOUR-SELF.
GOD KNOWS WHY ...BUT I HAVE FAITH IN YOU, RUDY. I THINK YOU'RE GOING TO GET THERE SOMEDAY.
MAYBE NOT TOMORROW... BUT SOME-DAY.
I LOVE YOU, TOO, CAROL.
I KNOW THAT I CAN NEVER MAKE UP FOR WHAT HAPPENED.
...BUT I'D REALLY LIKE TO TRY.
I MEAN, AS MUCH AS A GUY LIKE ME CAN.
SHUT UP AND KISS ME BEFORE I CHANGE MY MIND.
'TILL DEATH DO US PART, HUH?
SHOULD'VE KNOWN THERE'D BE NO TRUTH IN THAT OLD CHESTNUT.

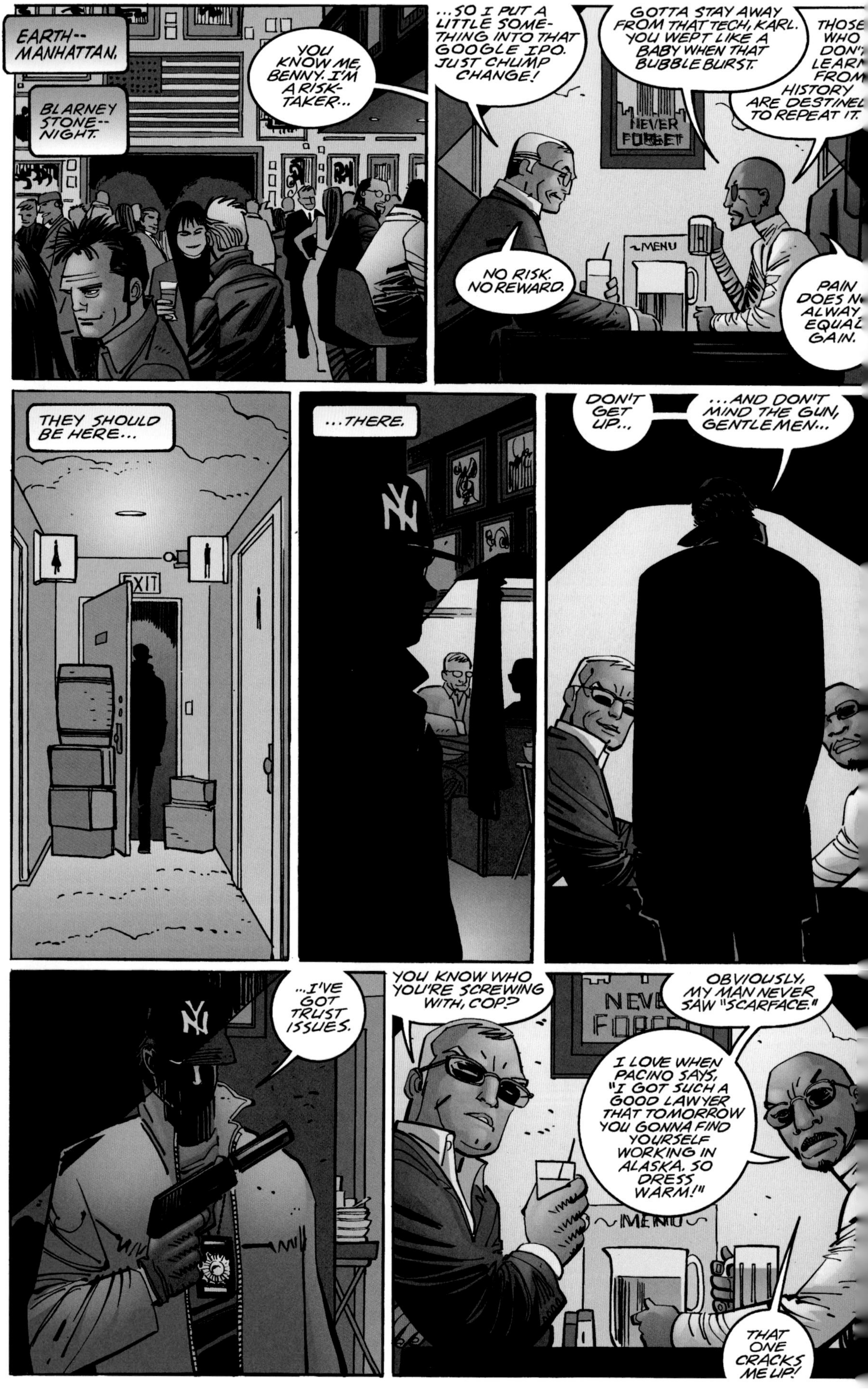
EARTH--
MANHATTAN.
BLARNEY STONE--NIGHT.
YOU KNOW ME, BENNY. I'M A RISK-TAKER...
...SO I PUT A LITTLE SOMETHING INTO THAT GOOGLE IPO. JUST CHUMP CHANGE!
NO RISK. NO REWARD.
GOTTA STAY AWAY FROM THAT TECH, KARL. YOU WEPT LIKE A BABY WHEN THAT BUBBLE BURST.
NEVER FORGET
MENU
THOSE WHO DON'T LEARN FROM HISTORY ARE DESTINED TO REPEAT IT.
PAIN DOES NOT ALWAYS EQUAL GAIN.
THEY SHOULD BE HERE...
EXIT
...THERE.
DON'T GET UP...
...AND DON'T MIND THE GUN, GENTLEMEN...
...I'VE GOT TRUST ISSUES.
YOU KNOW WHO YOU'RE SCREWING WITH, COP?
OBVIOUSLY, MY MAN NEVER SAW "SCARFACE."
I LOVE WHEN PACINO SAYS, "I GOT SUCH A GOOD LAWYER THAT TOMORROW YOU GONNA FIND YOURSELF WORKING IN ALASKA. SO DRESS WARM!"
MENU
THAT ONE CRACKS ME UP!

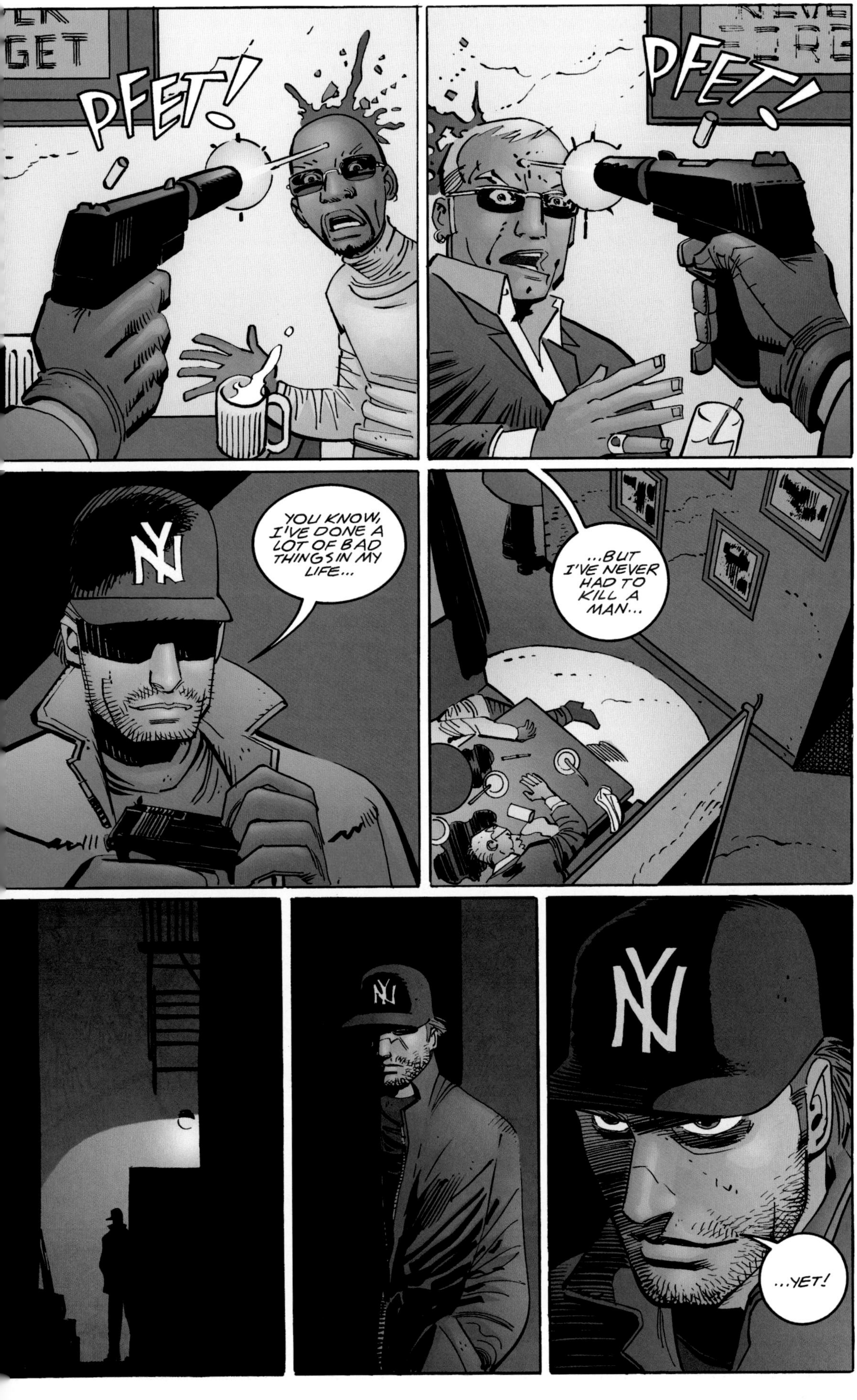
PFFT!
PFFT!
YOU KNOW, I'VE DONE A LOT OF BAD THINGS IN MY LIFE...
...BUT I'VE NEVER HAD TO KILL A MAN...
...YET!

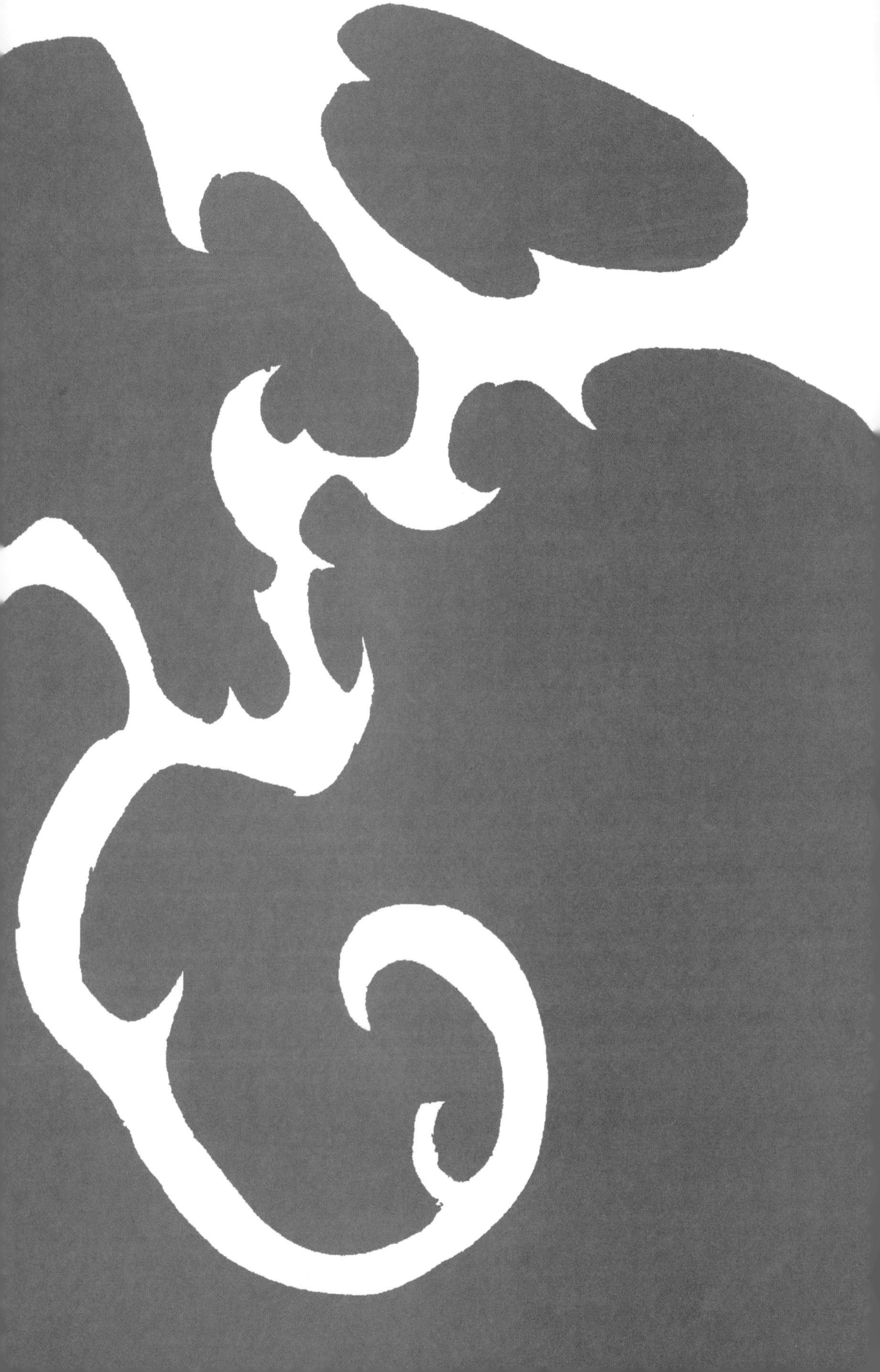

EXTRAS

COVER GALLERY

PIN-UP GALLERY

PENCILS vs. INKS

SKETCHBOOK

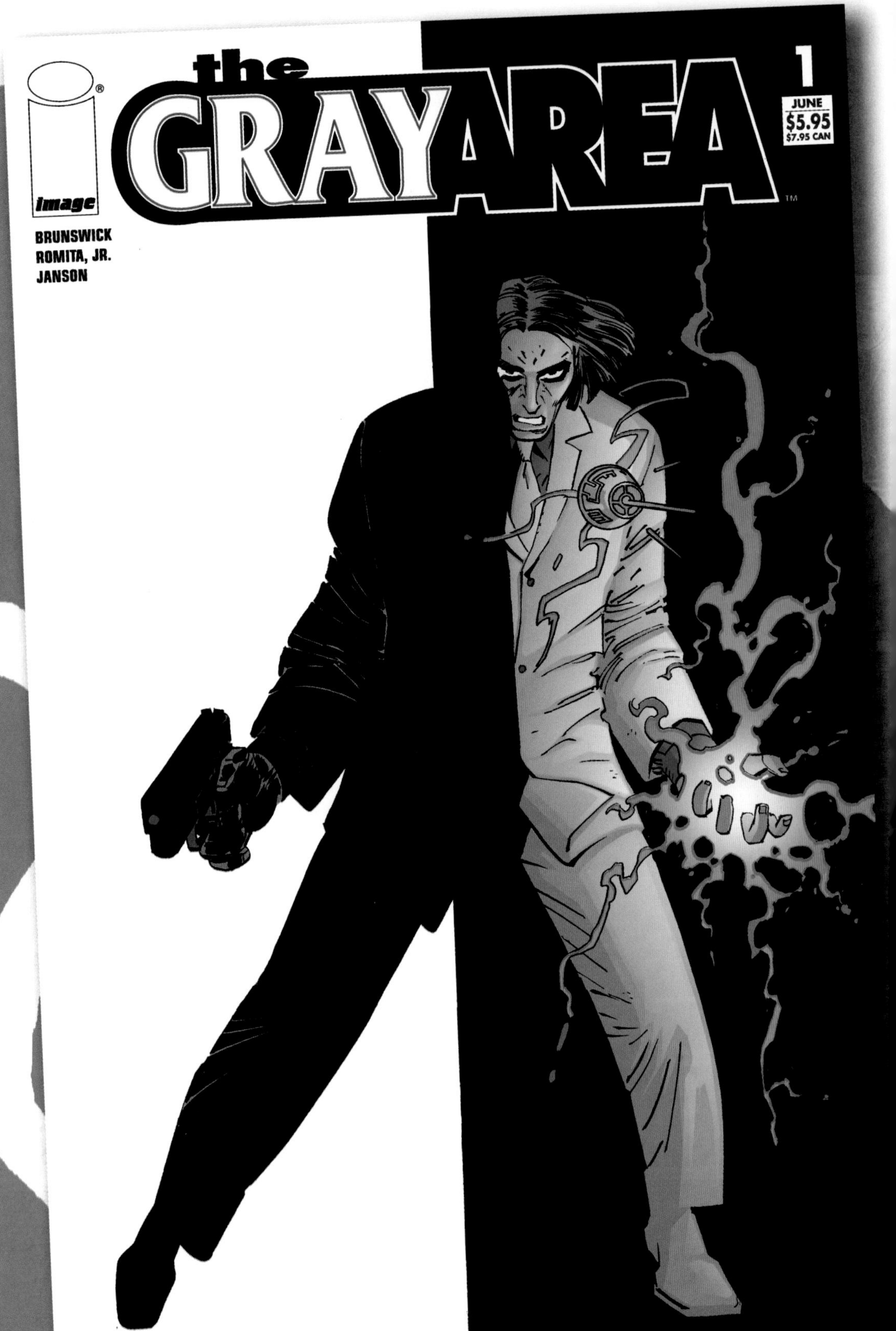

the GRAY AREA
1
JUNE
$5.95
$7.95 CAN
image
BRUNSWICK
ROMITA, JR.
JANSON

ISSUE #1 COVER A

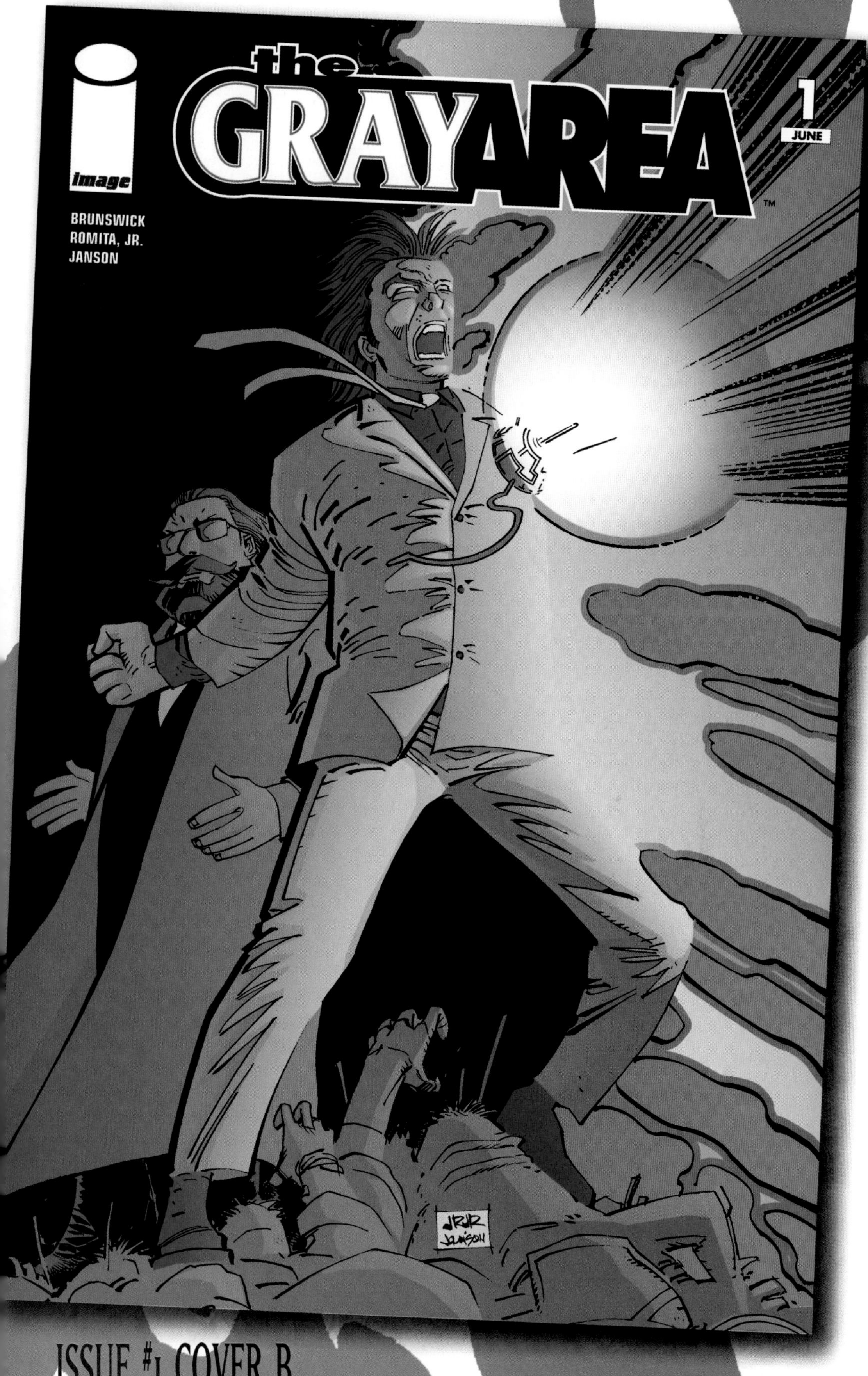
image
the GRAY AREA
1
JUNE
BRUNSWICK
ROMITA, JR.
JANSON

ISSUE #1 COVER B

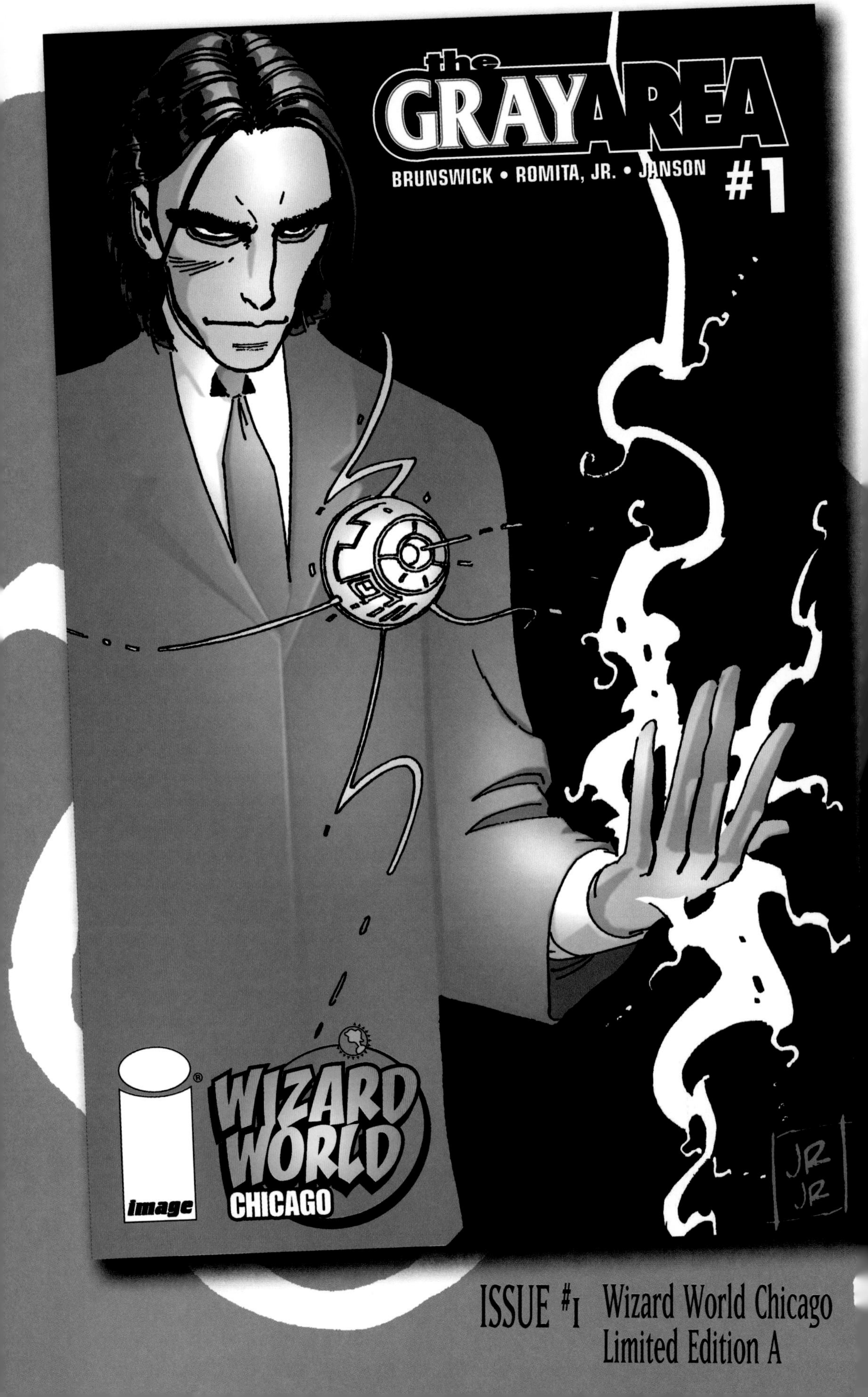
the GRAY AREA
BRUNSWICK • ROMITA, JR. • JANSON
#1
image
WIZARD WORLD CHICAGO
JR JR

ISSUE #I Wizard World Chicago
Limited Edition A

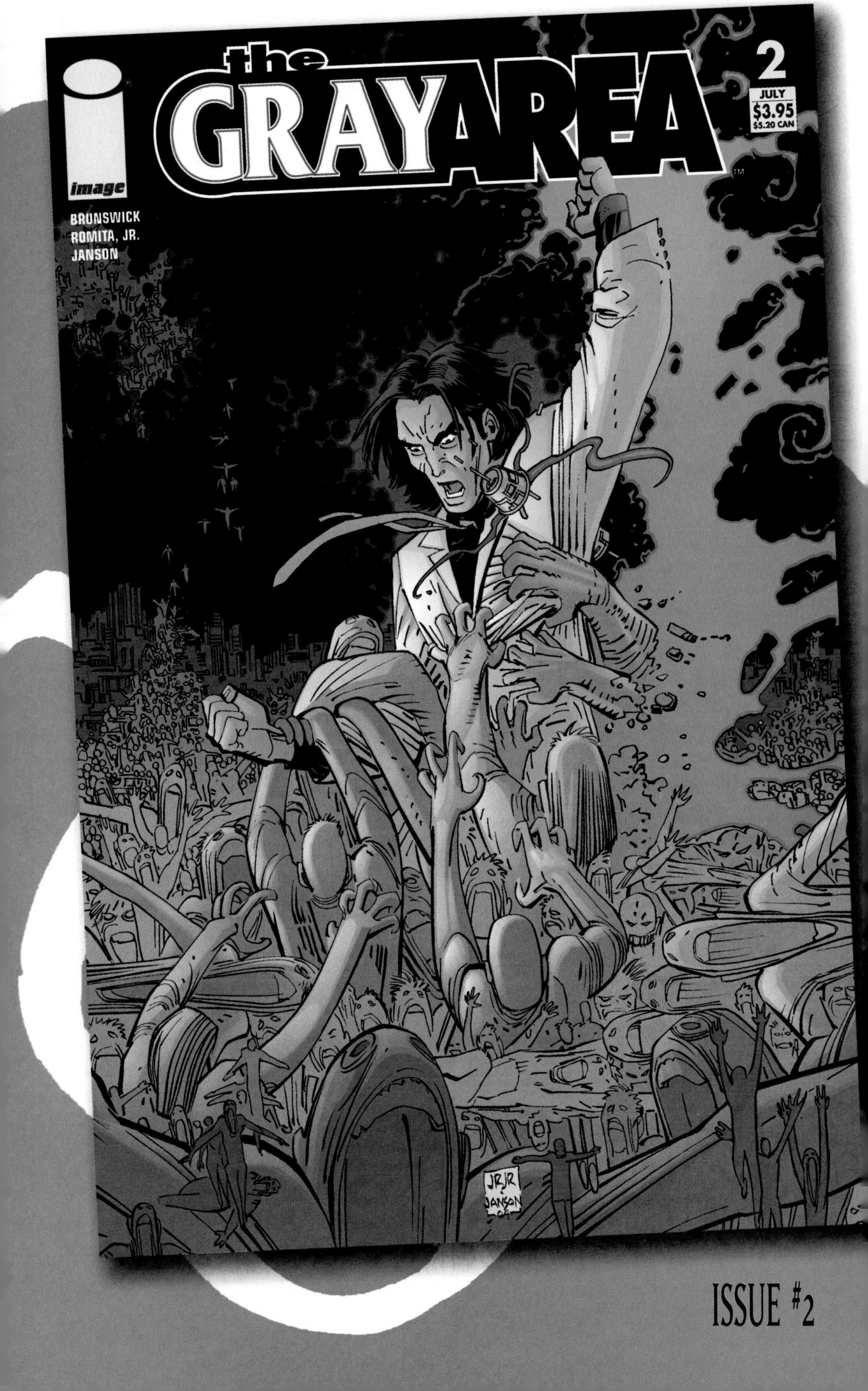
the GRAY AREA
2
JULY
$3.95
$5.20 CAN
image
BRUNSWICK
ROMITA, JR.
JANSON

ISSUE #2

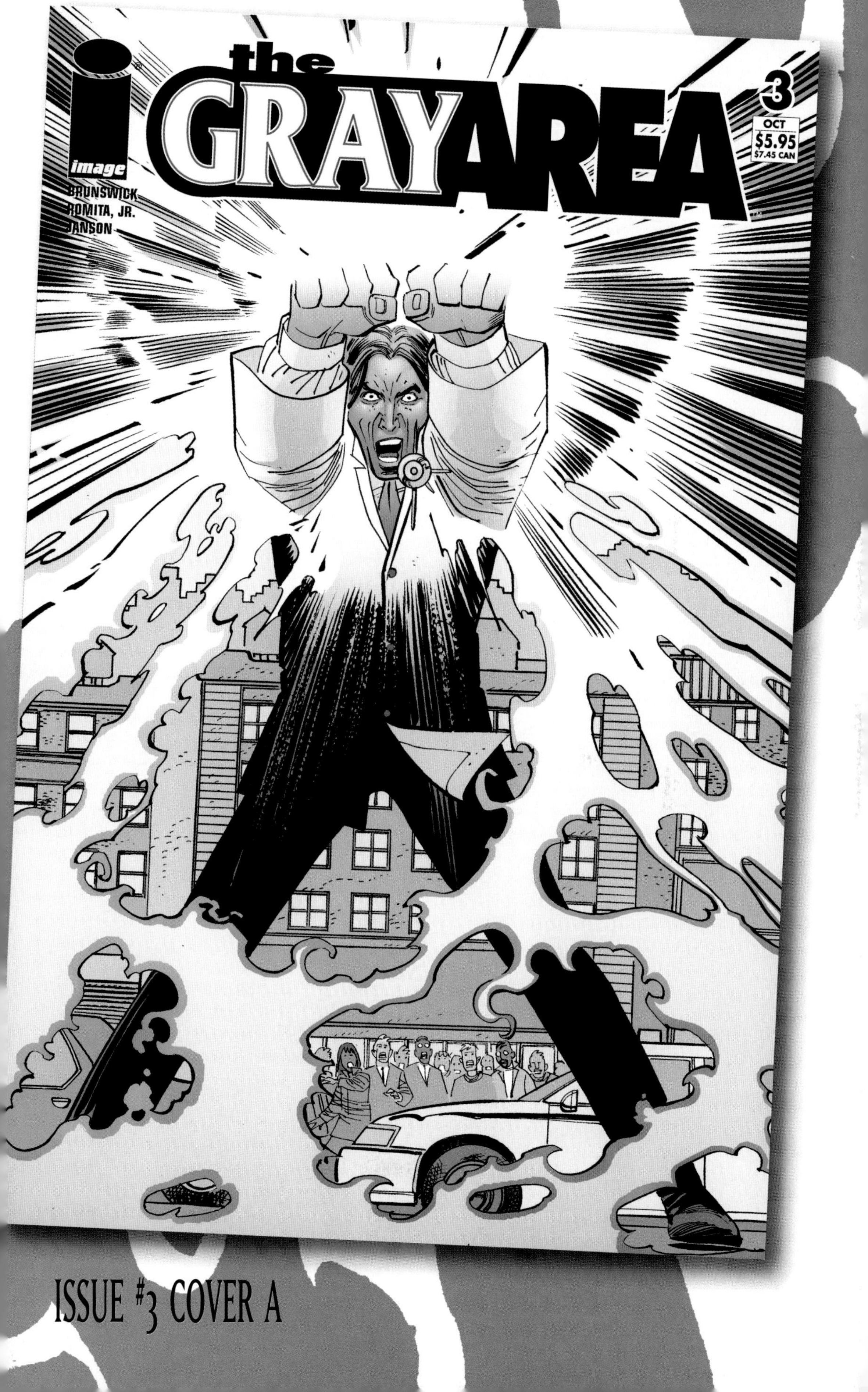
image
the GRAY AREA
3
OCT
$5.95
$7.45 CAN
BRUNSWICK
ROMITA, JR.
JANSON

ISSUE #3 COVER A

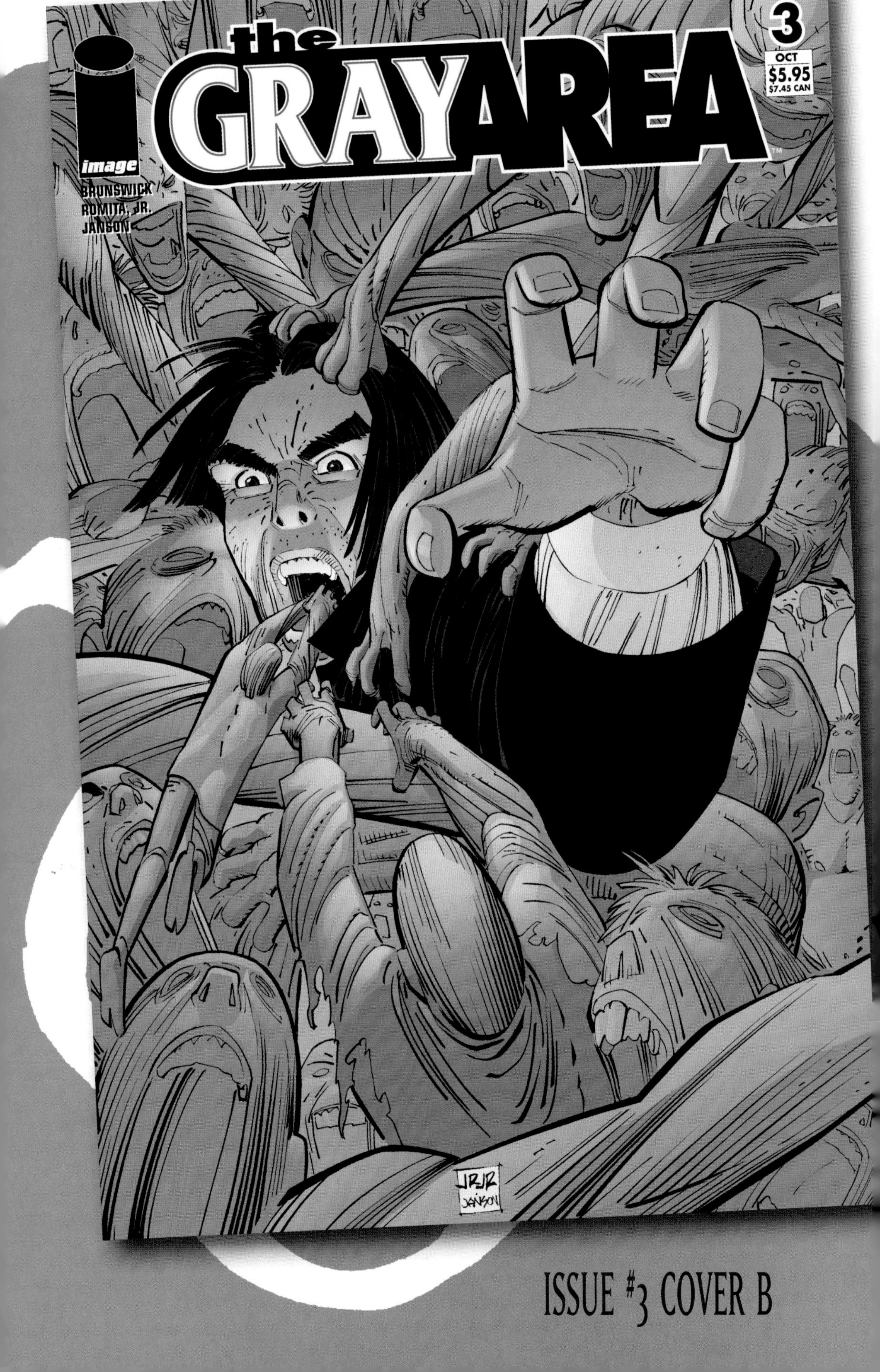
3
the GRAY AREA
OCT
$5.95
$7.45 CAN
image
BRUNSWICK
ROMITA, JR.
JANSON
JRJR
JANSON

ISSUE #3 COVER B

PIN-UP GALLERY

JOHN ROMITA, SR. · COLLEEN DORAN

ERIK LARSEN · BUTCH GUICE

JOHN CASSADAY · MARC SILVESTRI

TERRY AUSTIN · JIM VALENTINO

JIMMY PALMIOTTI · RON FRENZ

JIM LEE

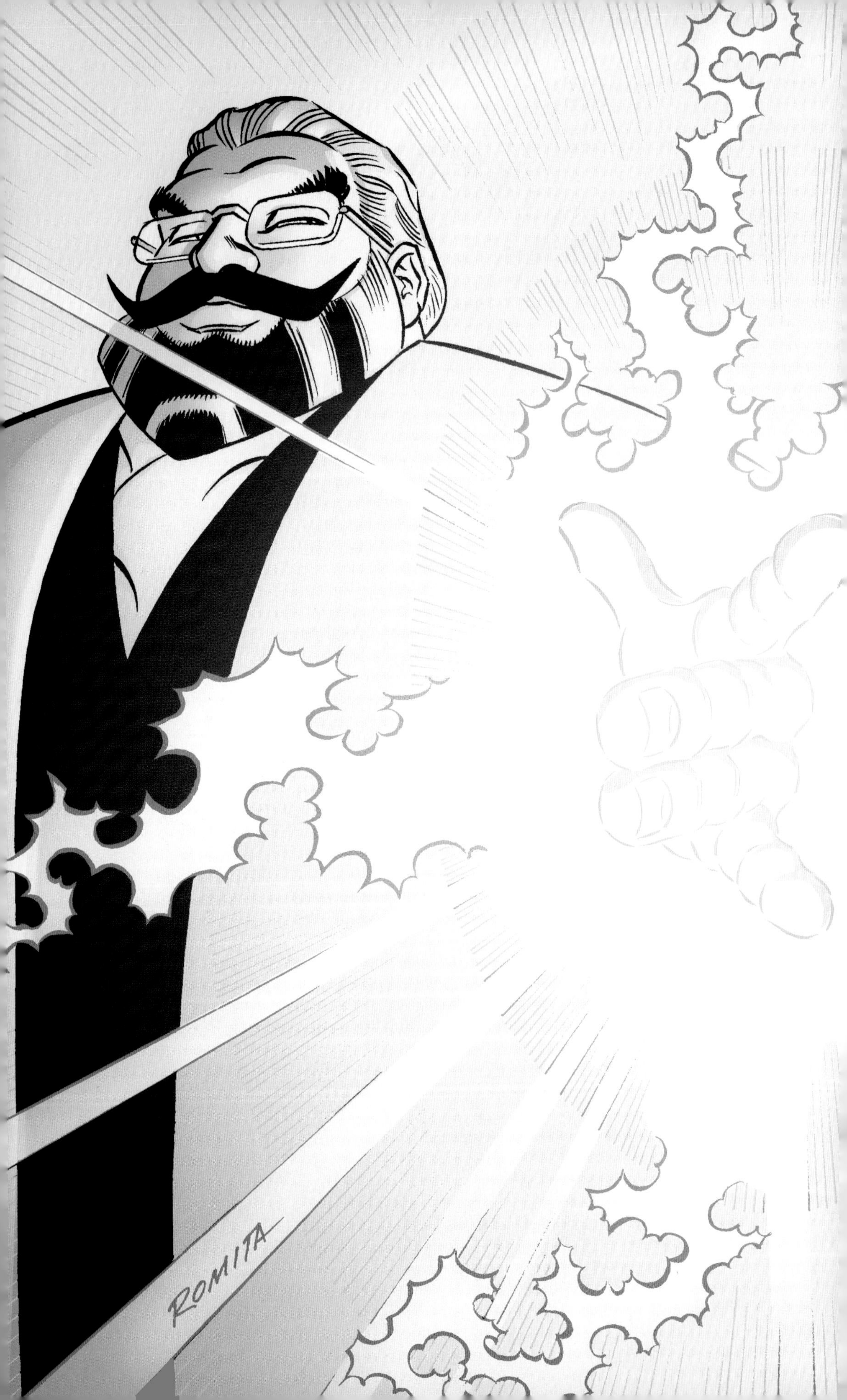
ROMITA

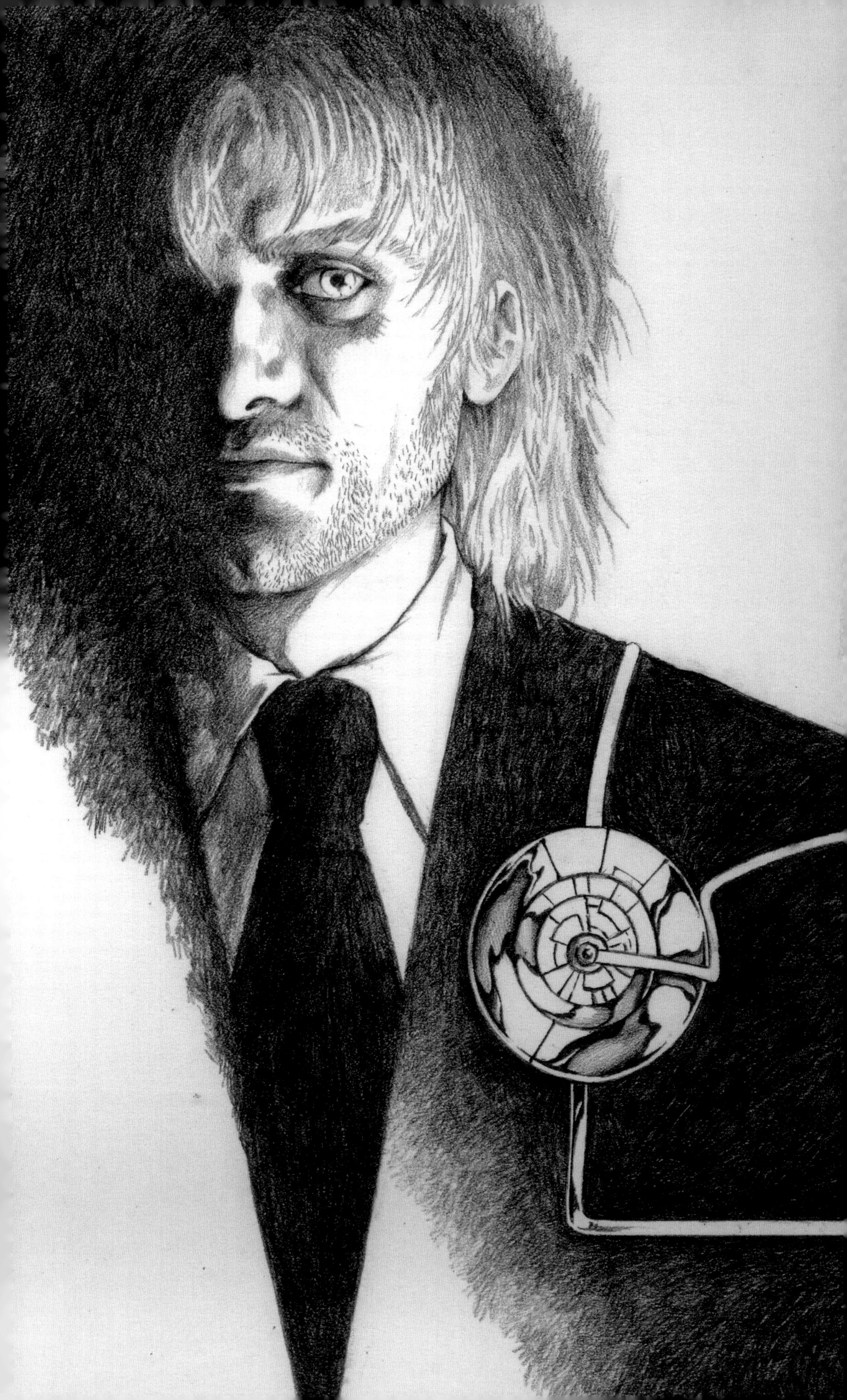

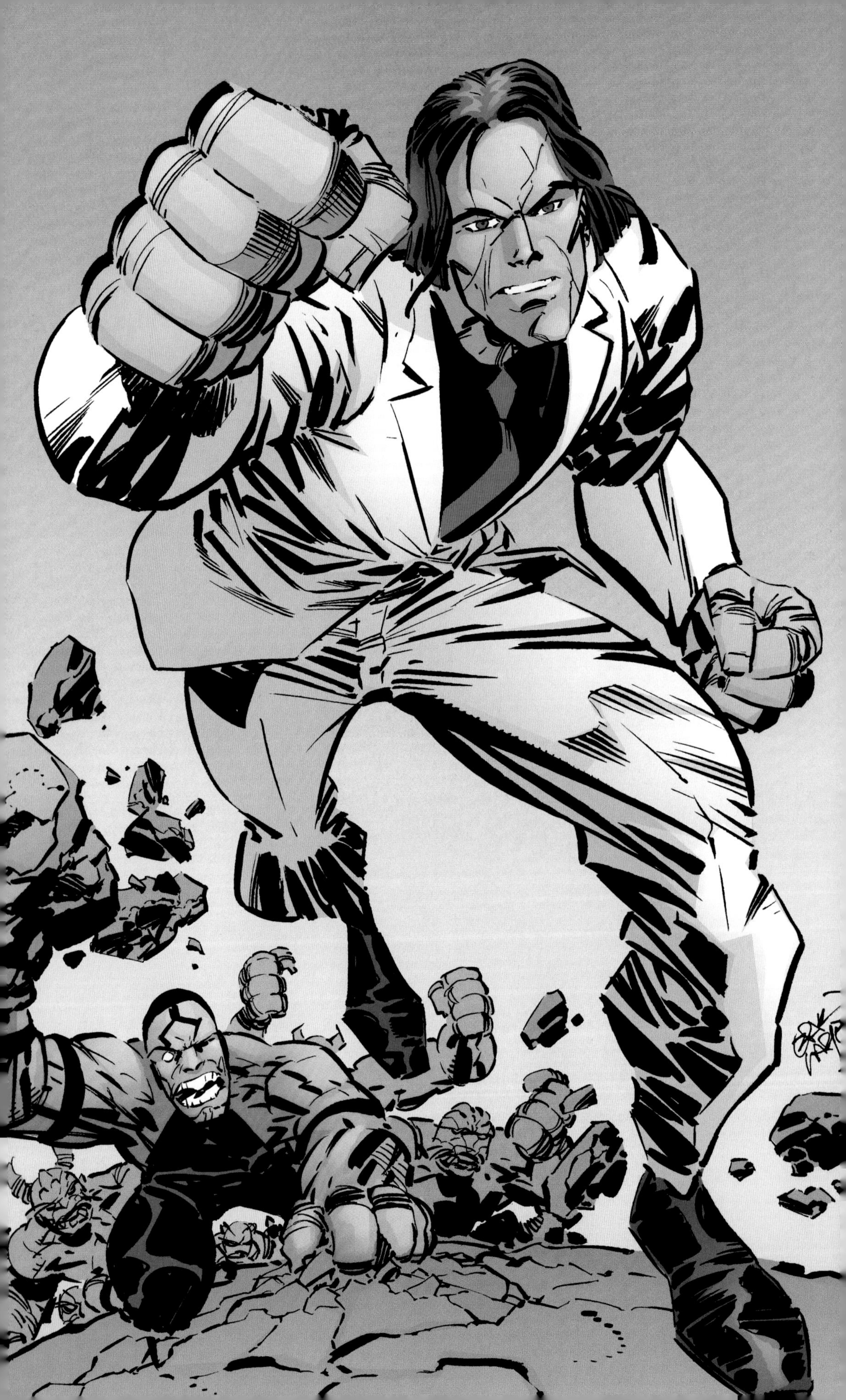

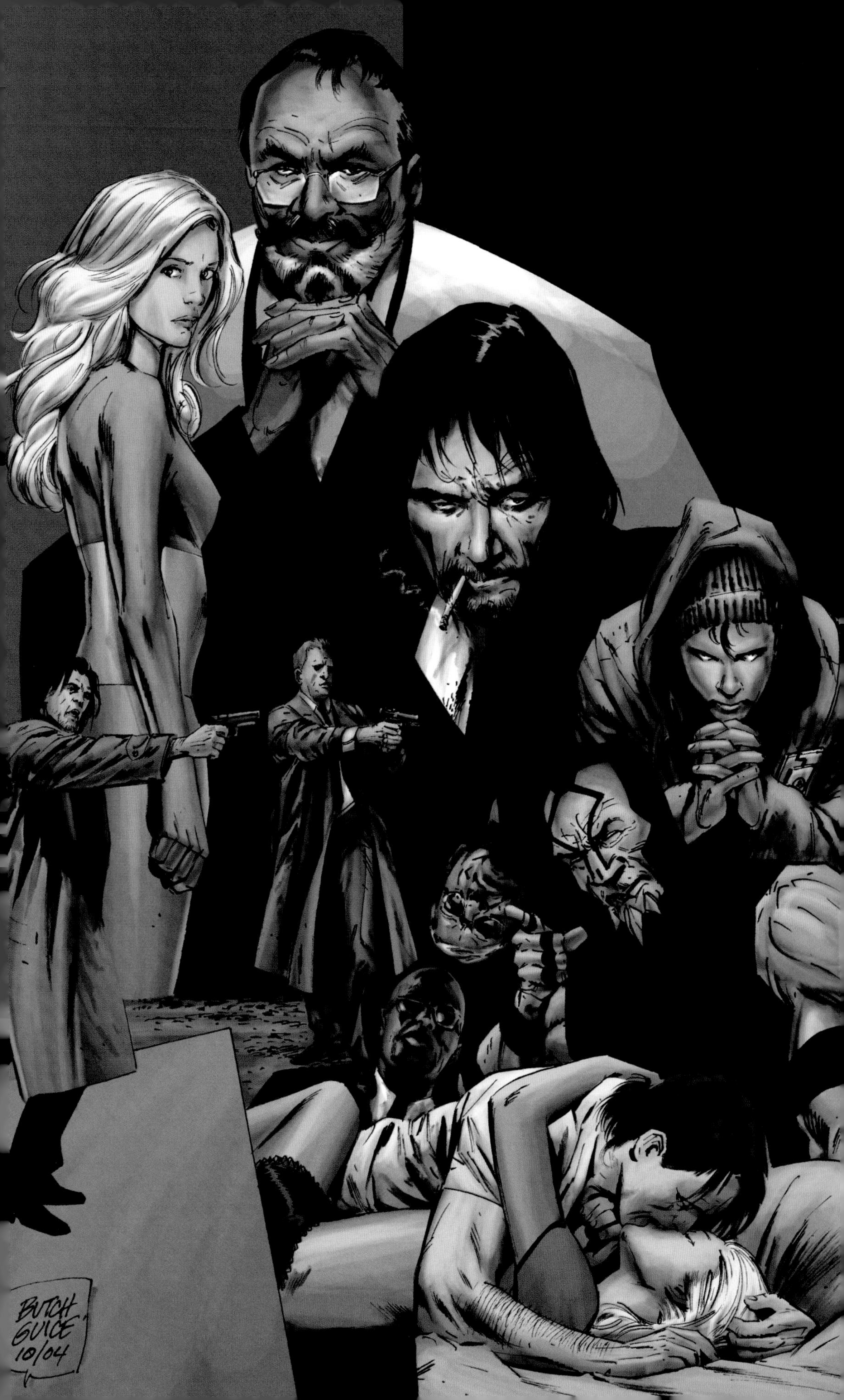
BUTCH GUICE
10/04

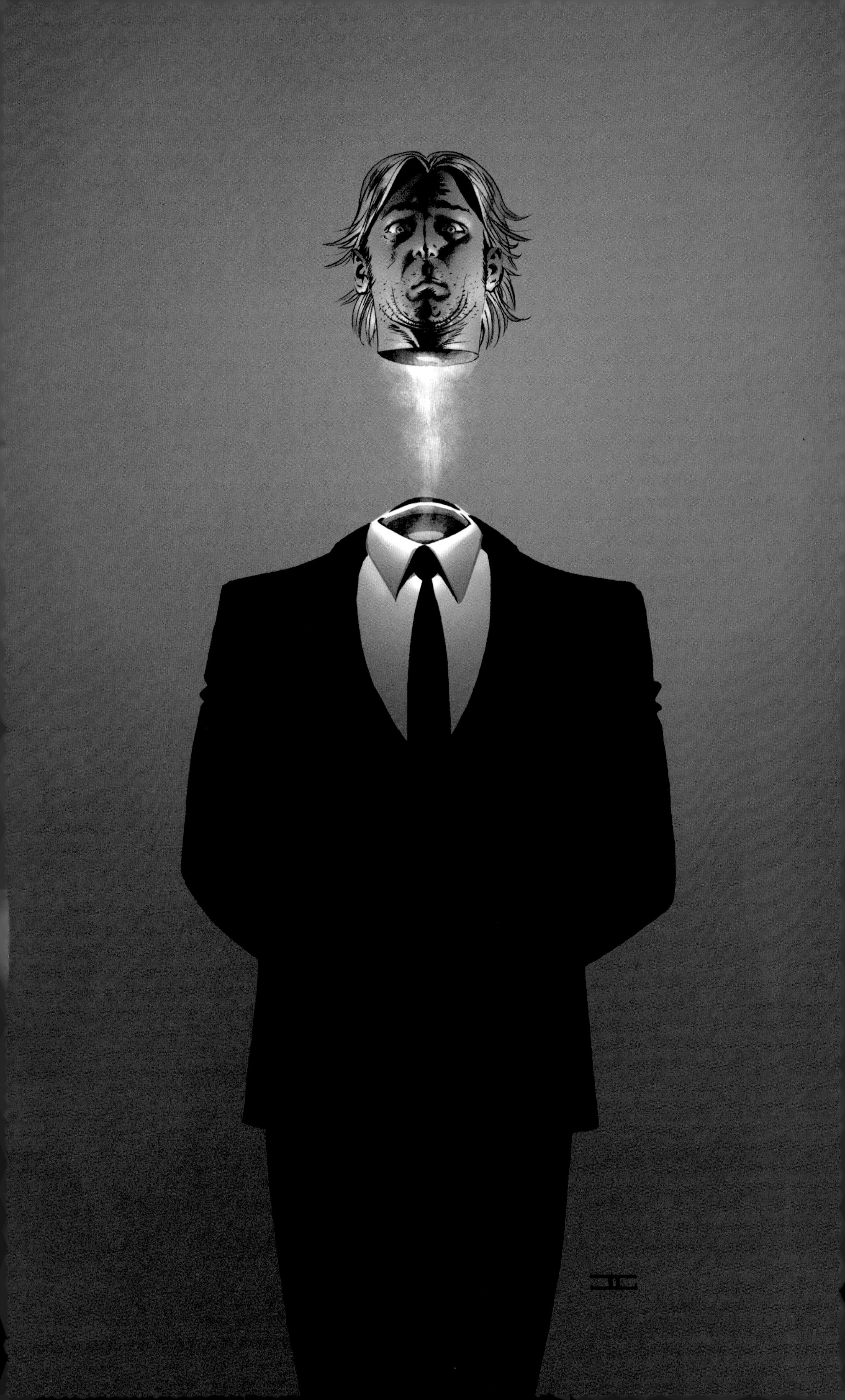

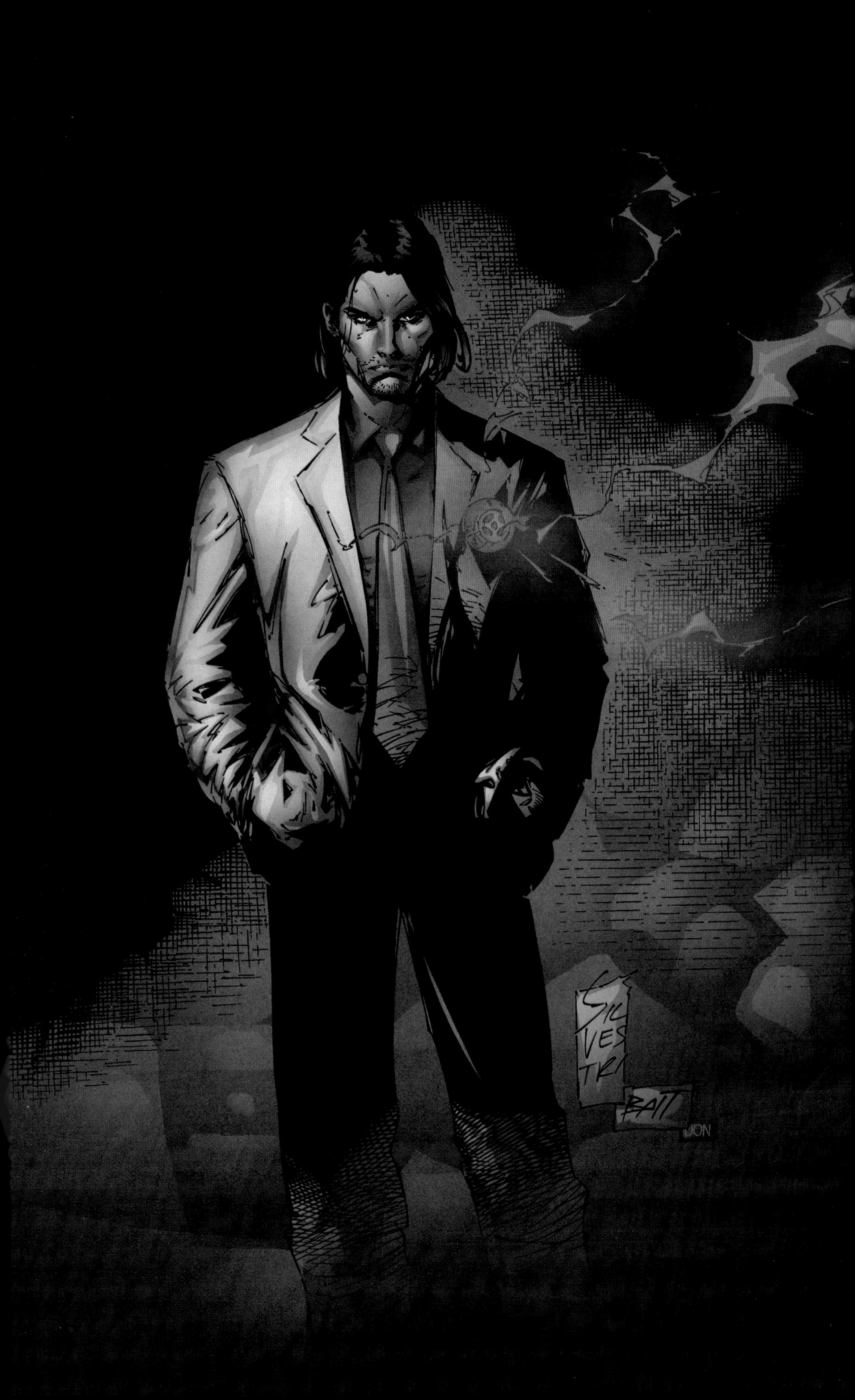

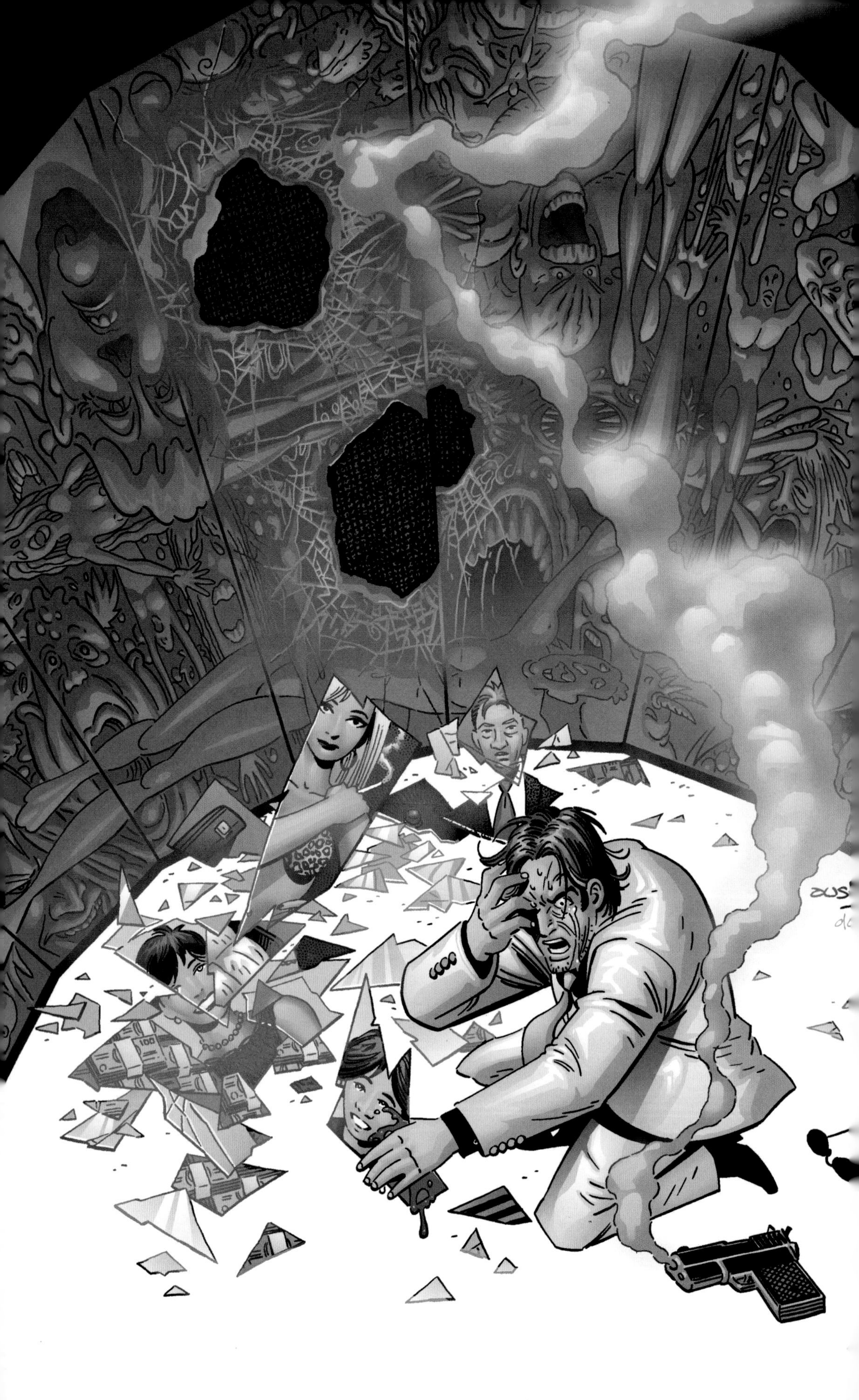

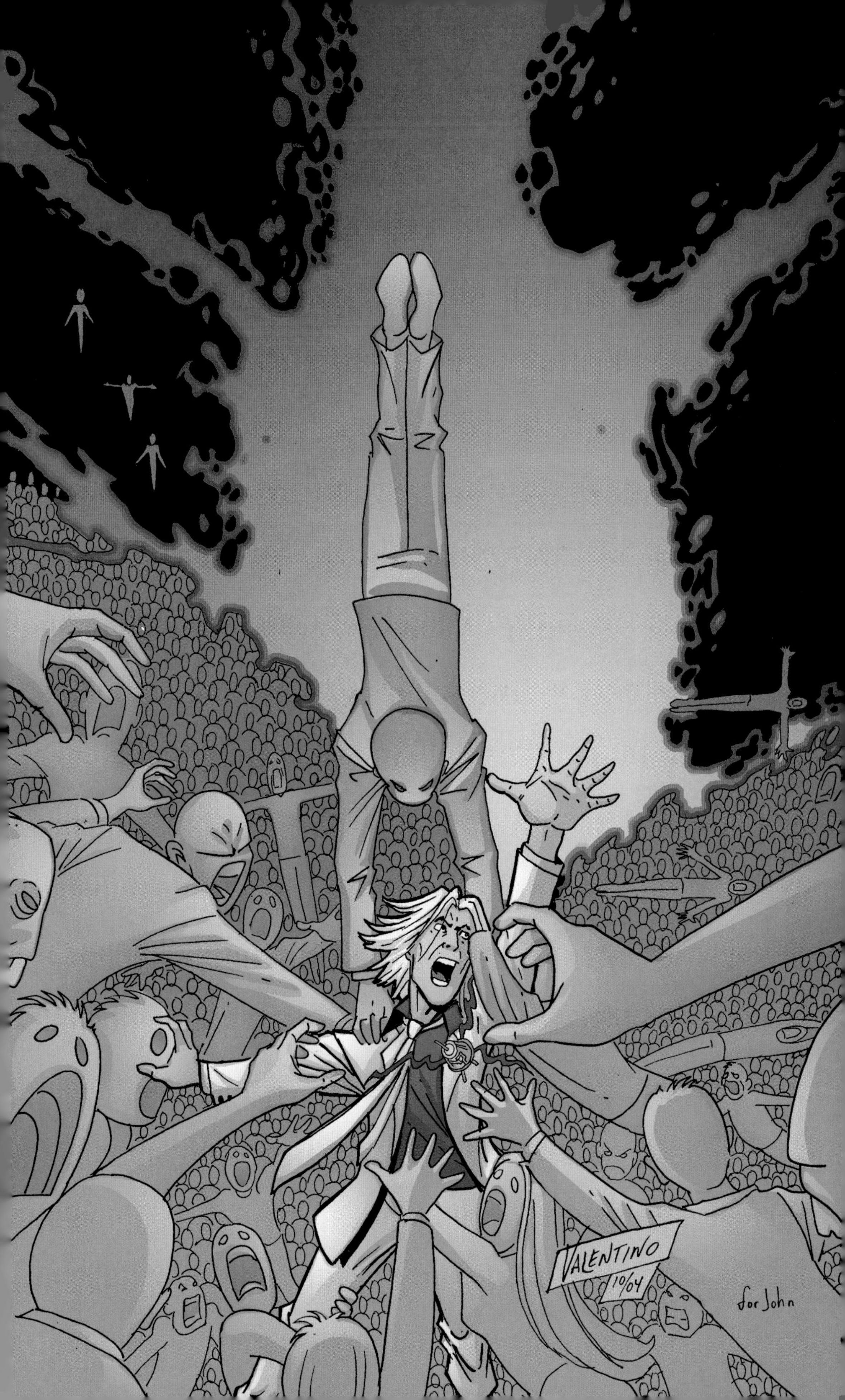
VALENTINO
10/04
for John

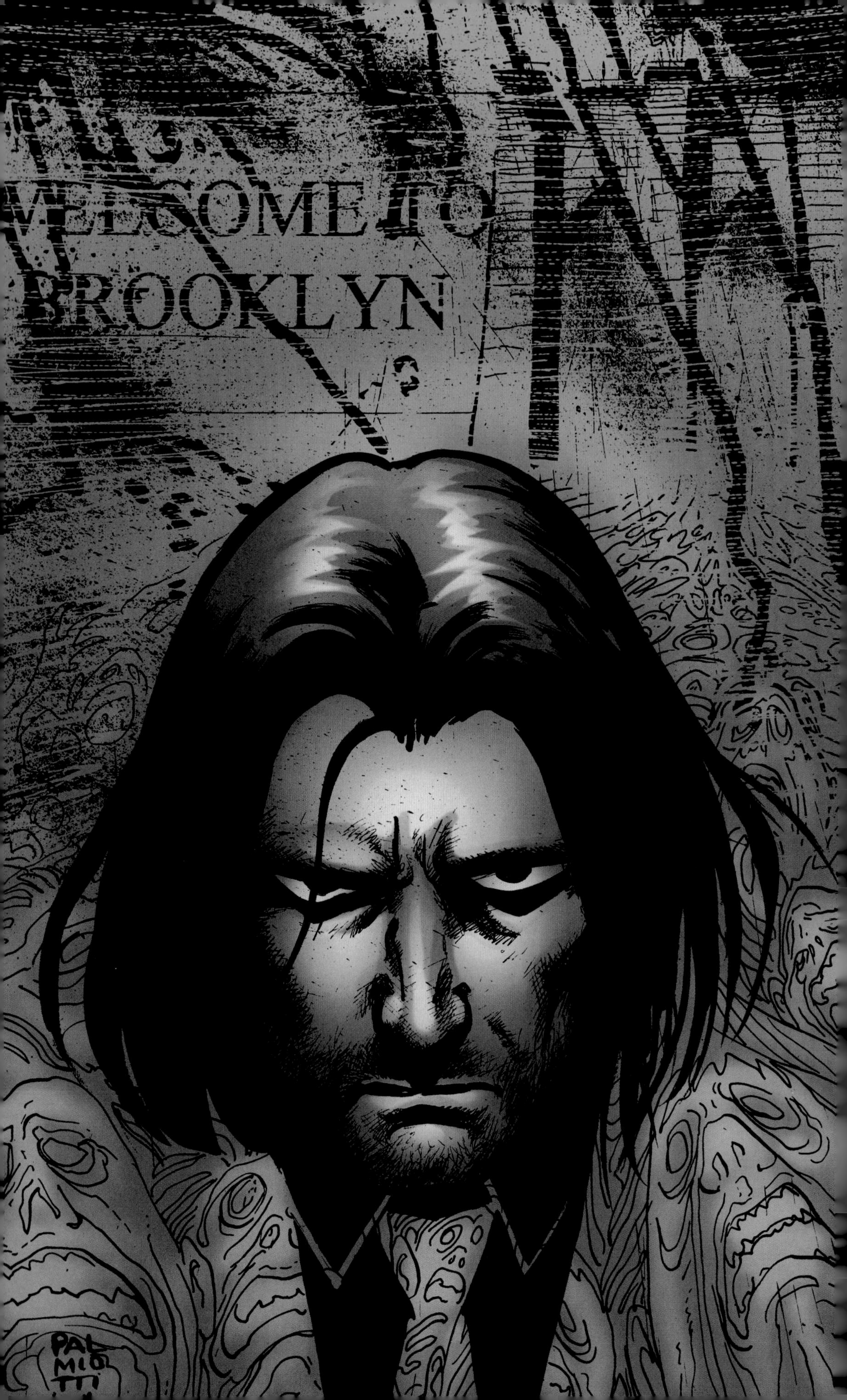

WELCOME TO
BROOKLYN
PAL
MIO
TTI

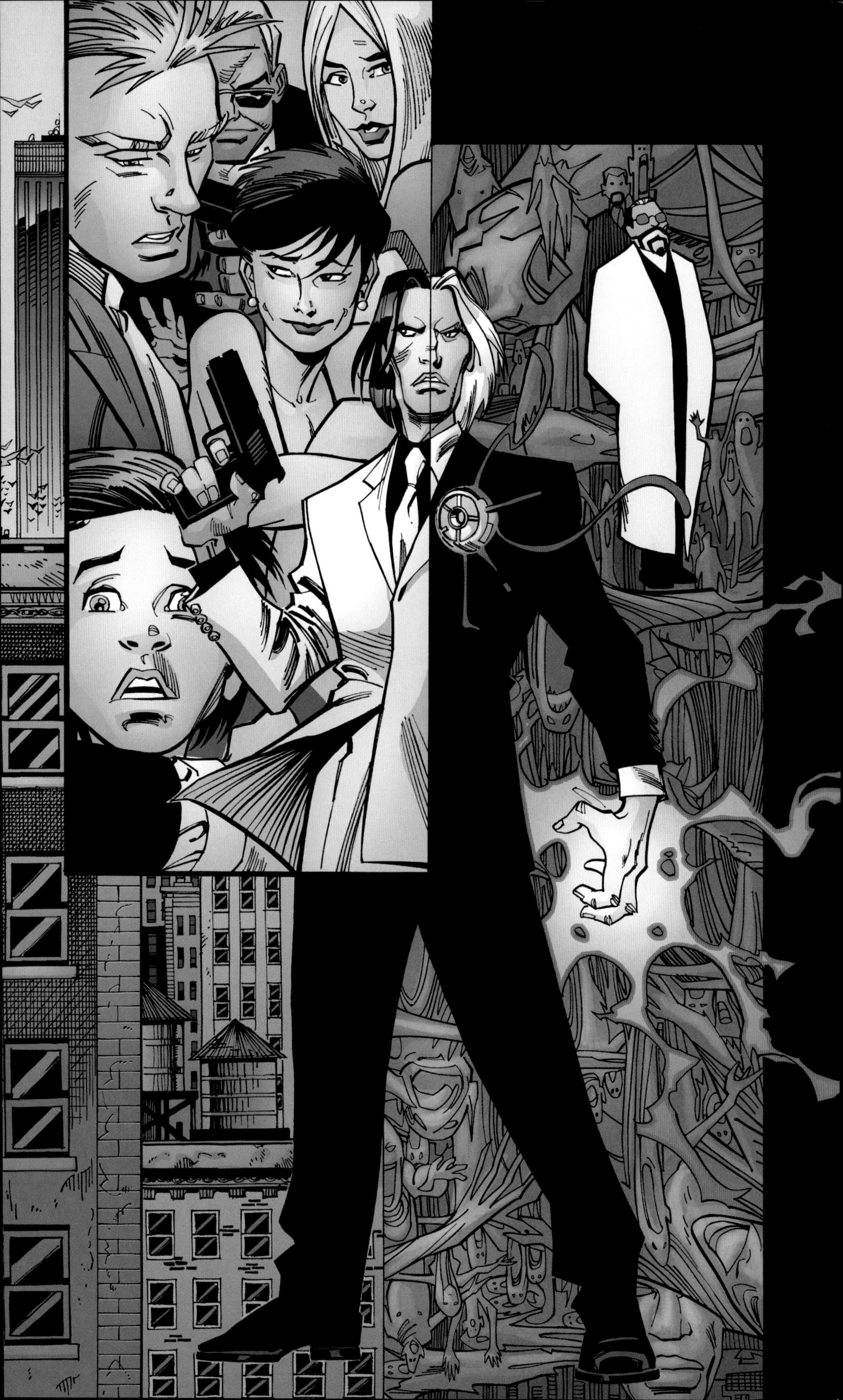

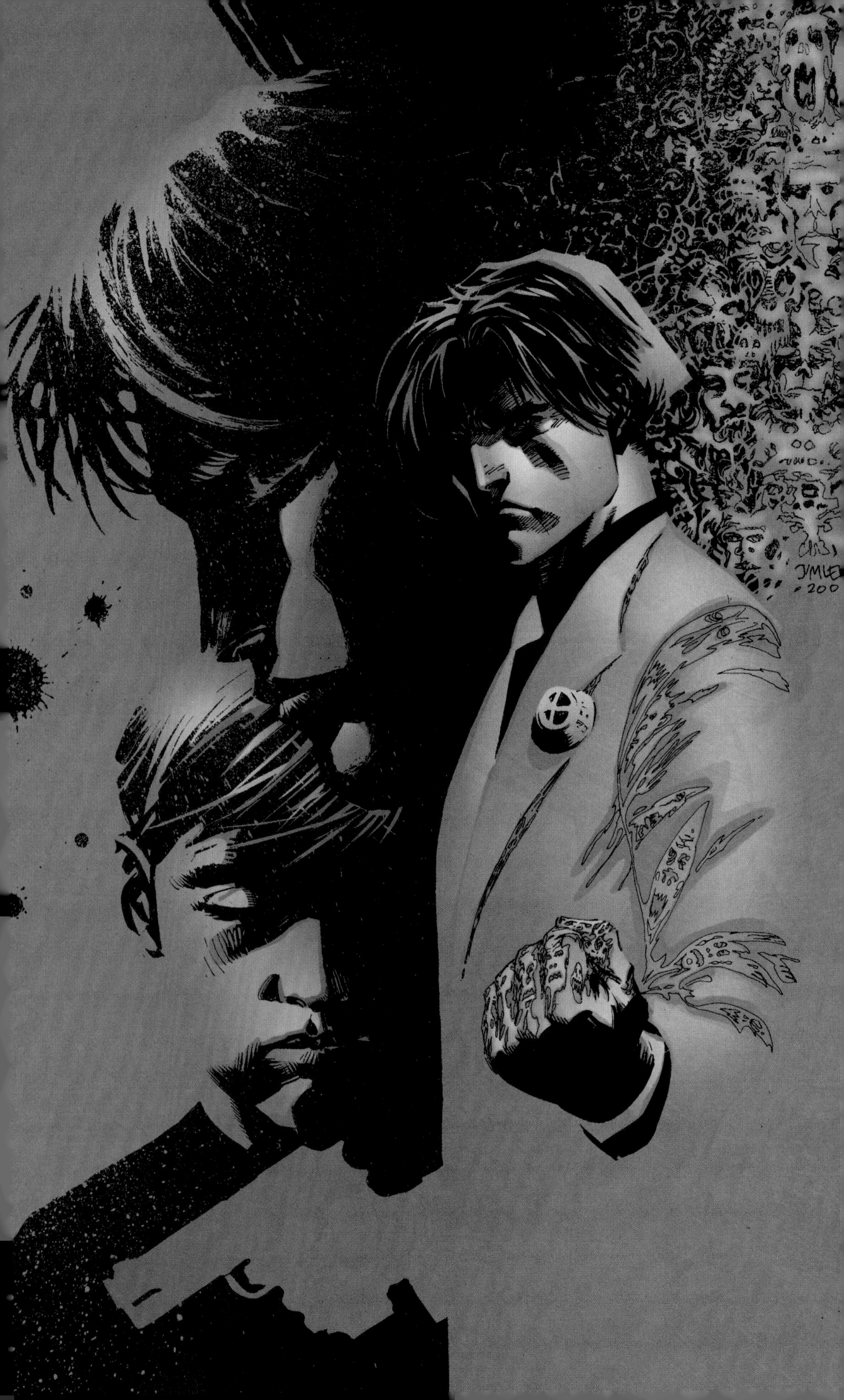

PENCILS VS. INKS

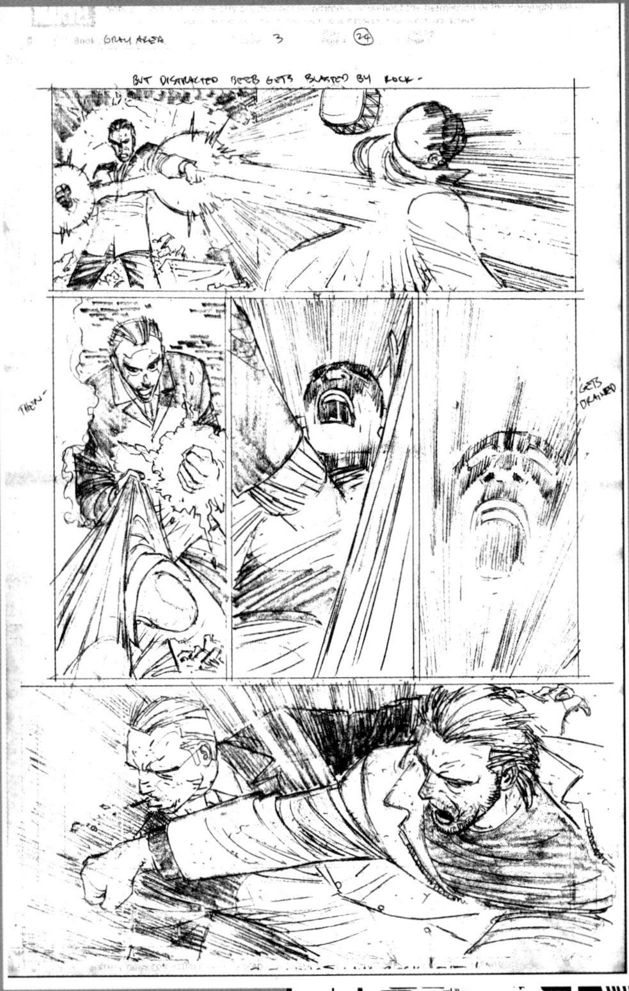
BUT DISTRACTED BEEB GETS BLASTED BY ROCK -

I'm biased. I love JRjr's pencils regardless of who inks him. On the other hand, I must admit that Klaus Janson not only makes John's art shine brighter, but he brings his own special quality to the drawing as well. What could illustrate this point better than a side by side comparison of these two amazing talents?

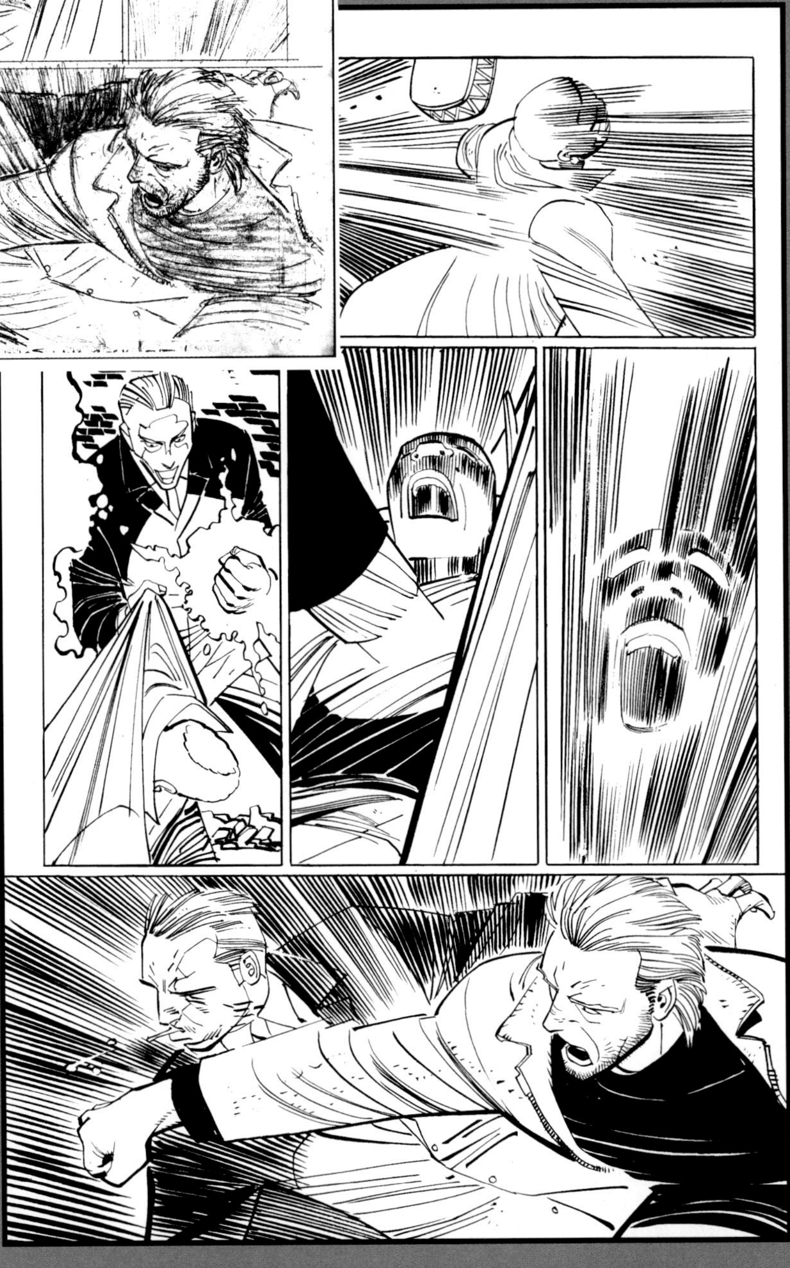

PENCILS VS. INKS

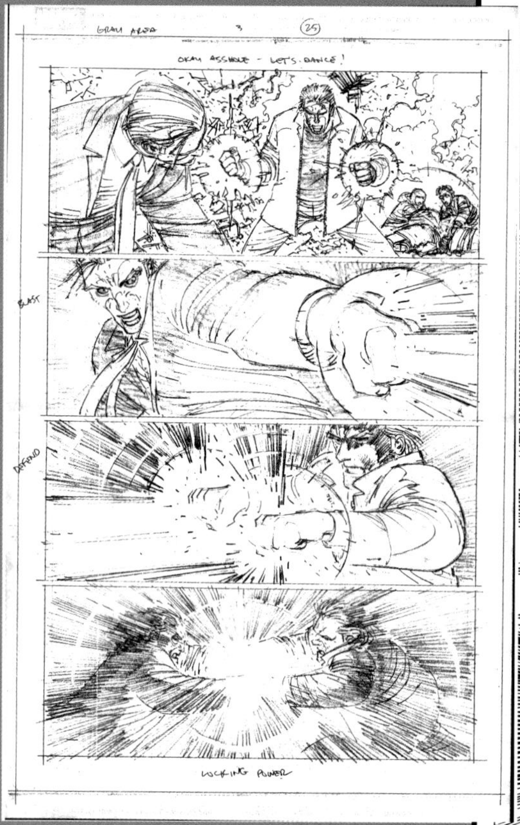
GRAY AREA 3 25
OKAY ASSHOLE - LET'S DANCE!
BLAST
DEFEND
LOCKING POWER

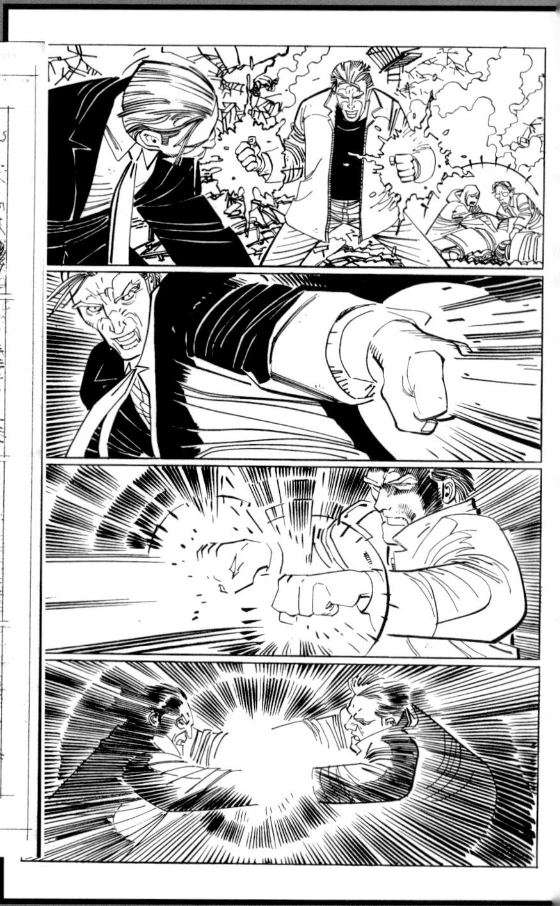

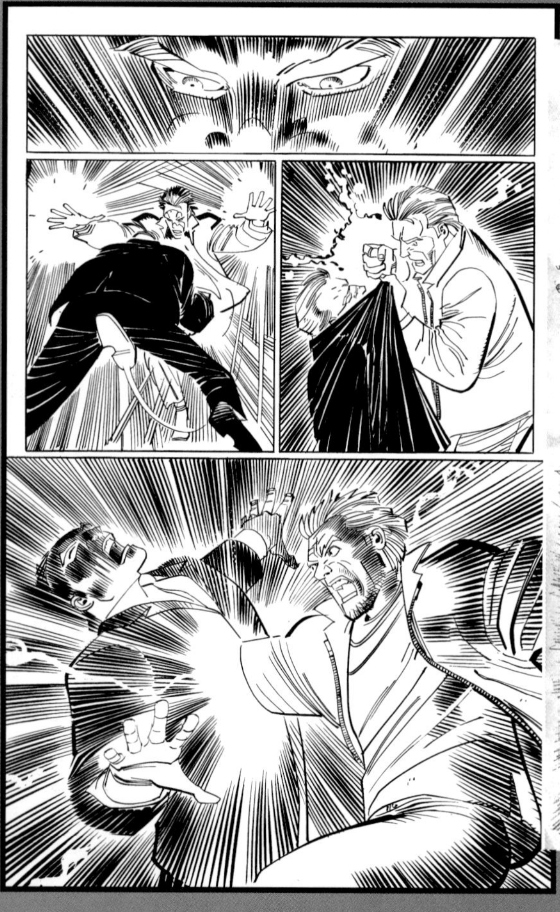

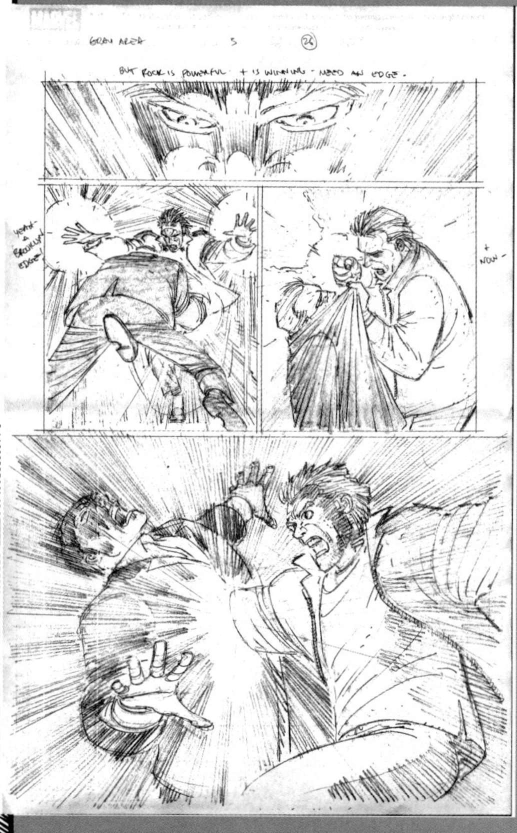
GRAY AREA 3 26
BUT ROCK IS POWERFUL + IS WINNING - NEED AN EDGE.
YEAH - A BROOKLYN EDGE!
+ NOW -

THE ROUGH CUT

It's hard to believe that it's been two and a half years since I first met John Romita, Jr. Since I'm first and foremost a comic book fan, I have long admired John's genius in his incredible artwork. Now I am a huge admirer of John Romita, Jr. the man, as well. Working with John has been an absolute dream come true for me. I am humbled and honored that he was willing to trust in me to co-create and shepherd this truly cool, original idea. And I consider myself quite lucky to be able to call John my good friend now, as well.

After hearing John's pitch, I wrote a treatment based on our combined ideas that we took to Joe Quesada at Marvel. Joe gave us the thumbs up and some terrific support. Before we knew it, we had a deal at Marvel's creator-owned imprint, Epic Comics. Then Marvel decided to put the Epic line on hold. Marvel was kind enough to let John do the book elsewhere. Joe even suggested that we seek out the fine folks at Image Comics. And, as it turned out, we couldn't be happier here. Eric Stephenson, Brett Evans and the entire Image crew have worked tirelessly on our behalf and we can't thank them enough for all of their efforts.

But, getting back to the creative process... After finishing the treatment I thought my job was done. I figured John had the heavy lifting now in illustrating the book. I was unprepared for how cool John's pencils would look. If my writing was even going to come close to measuring up to his artwork, I had some serious rewriting to do. We both worked intensely hard to create something that we view as quite special. We thought it might be fun to pull back the curtain on our collaboration and present some of John's original pencils and a few notes on the production.

Thanks,
Glen Brunswick

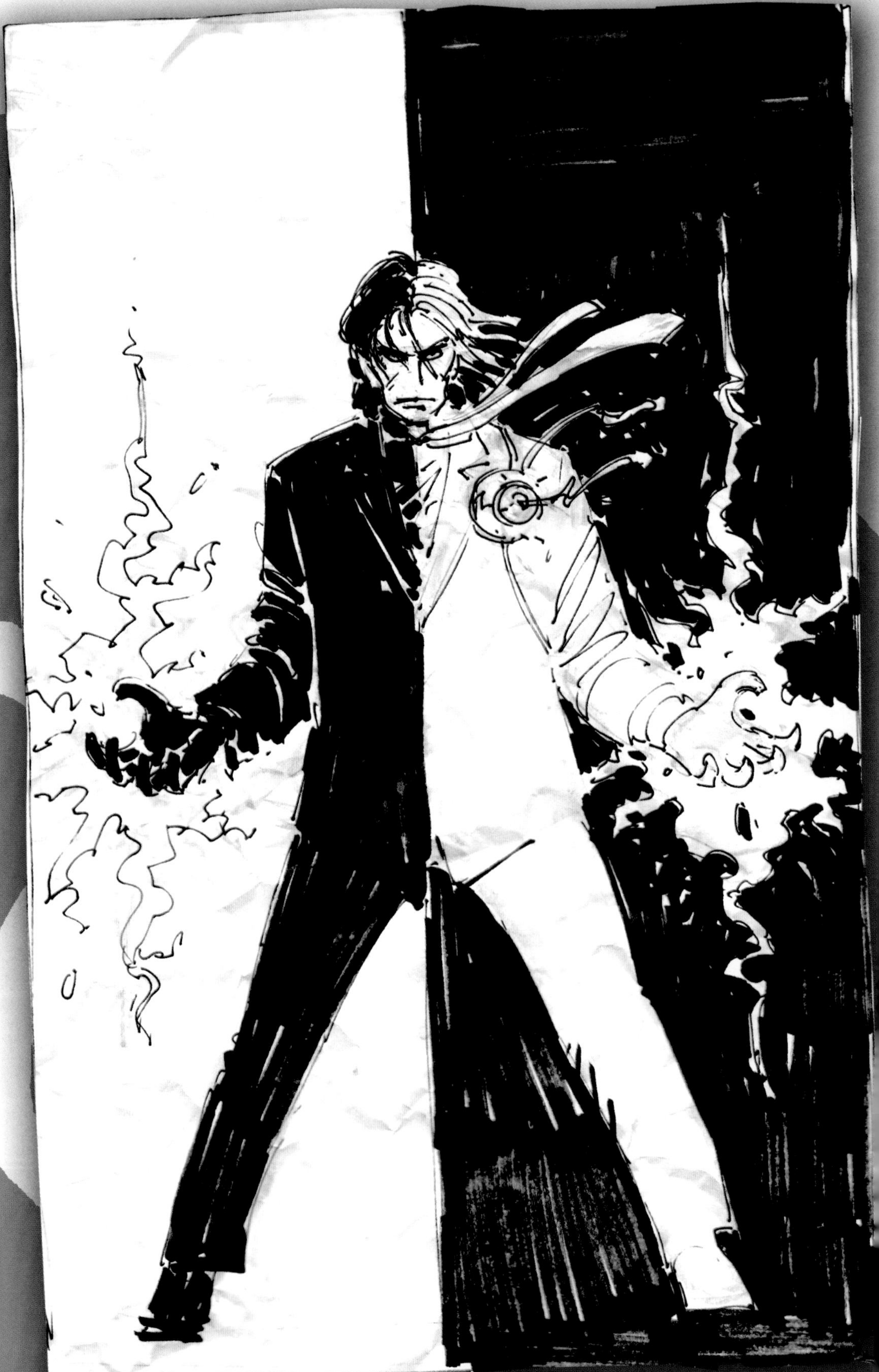

John's first preliminary sketch for the cover. With a nod to the film, *Scarface*, John created a black and white design to represent the good and evil within Chance.

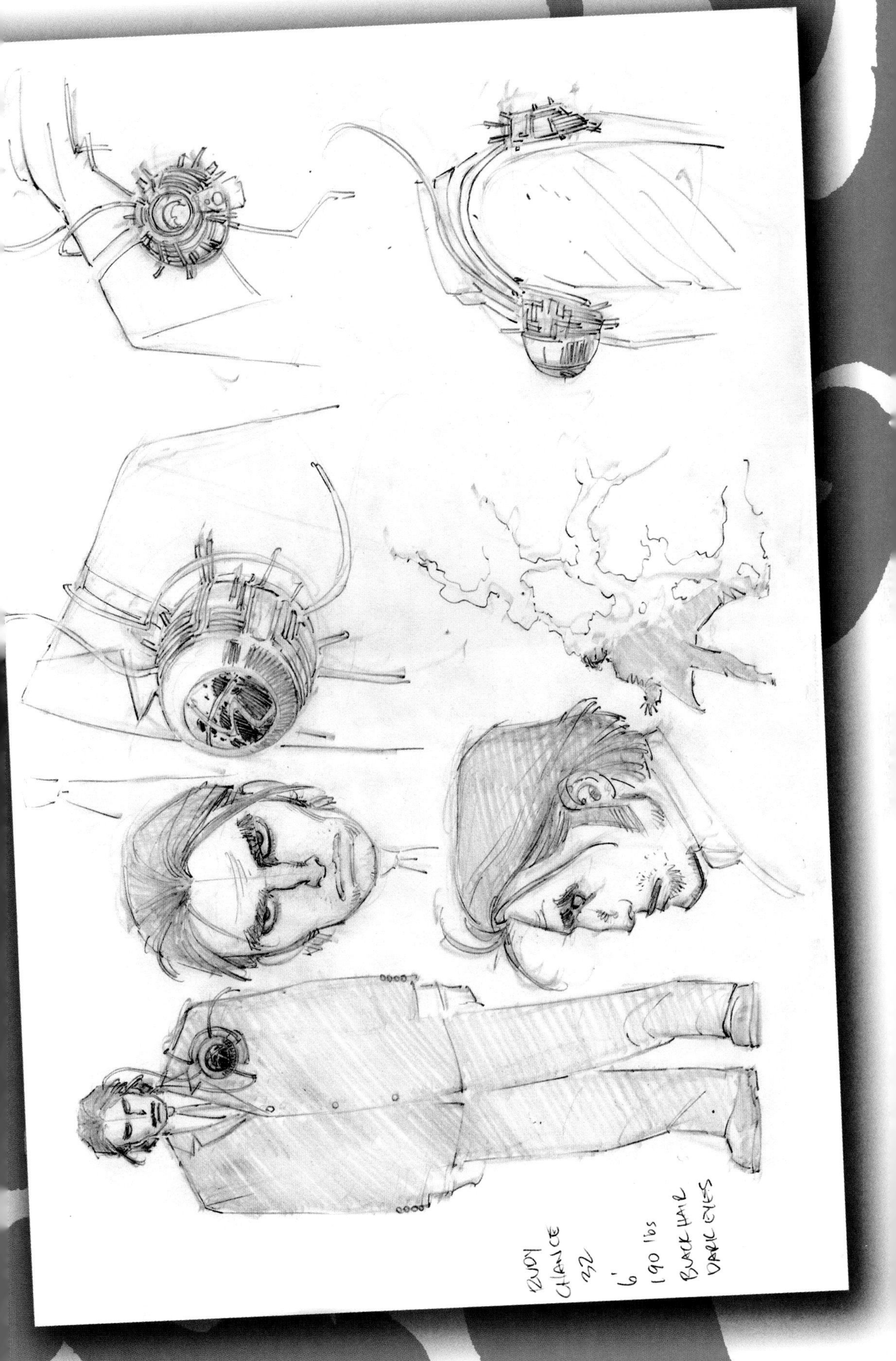
RUDY
CHANCE
32
6'
190 lbs
BLACK HAIR
DARK EYES

Model sheet for Rudy Chance and his power harness

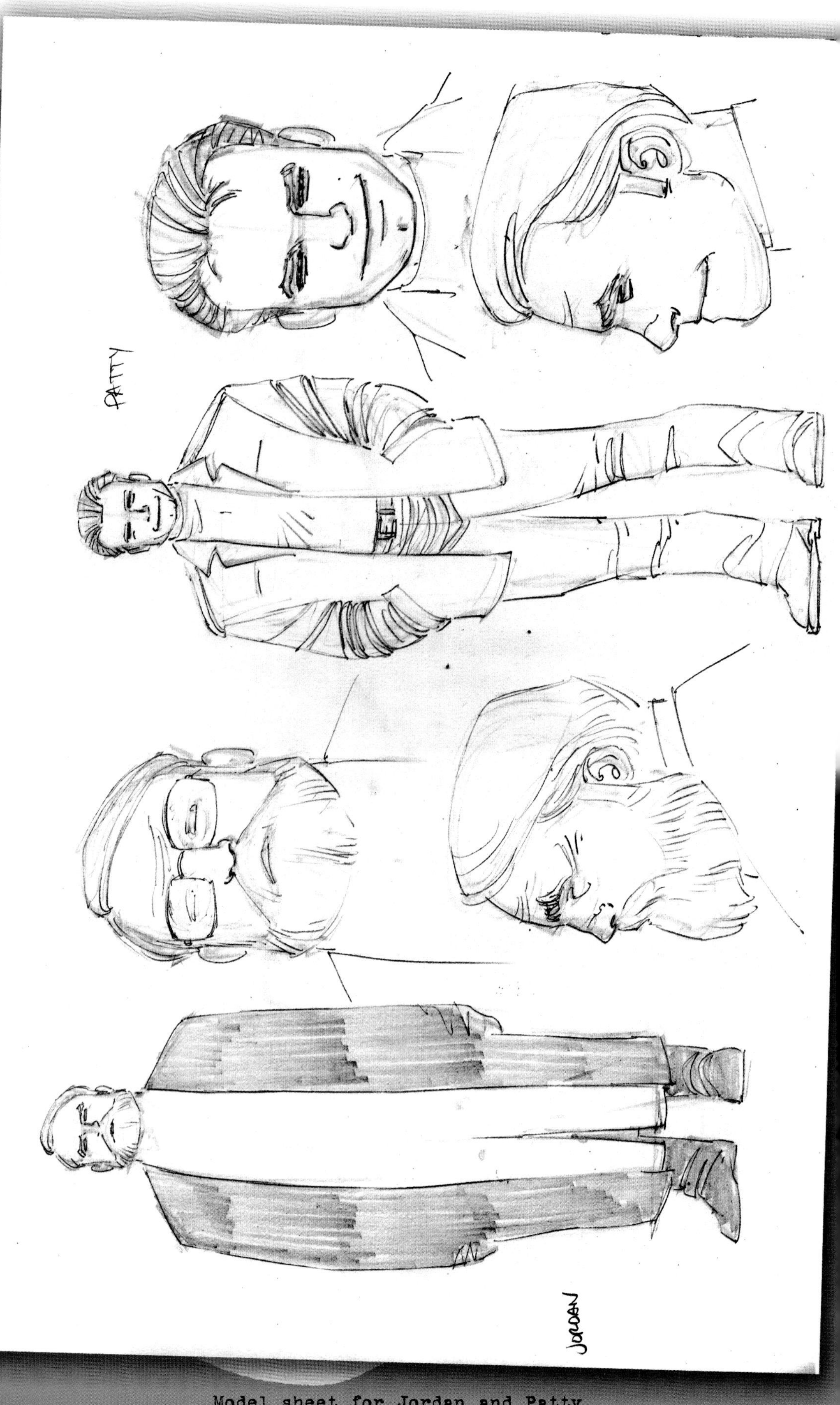
PATTY
JORDAN

Model sheet for Jordan and Patty.

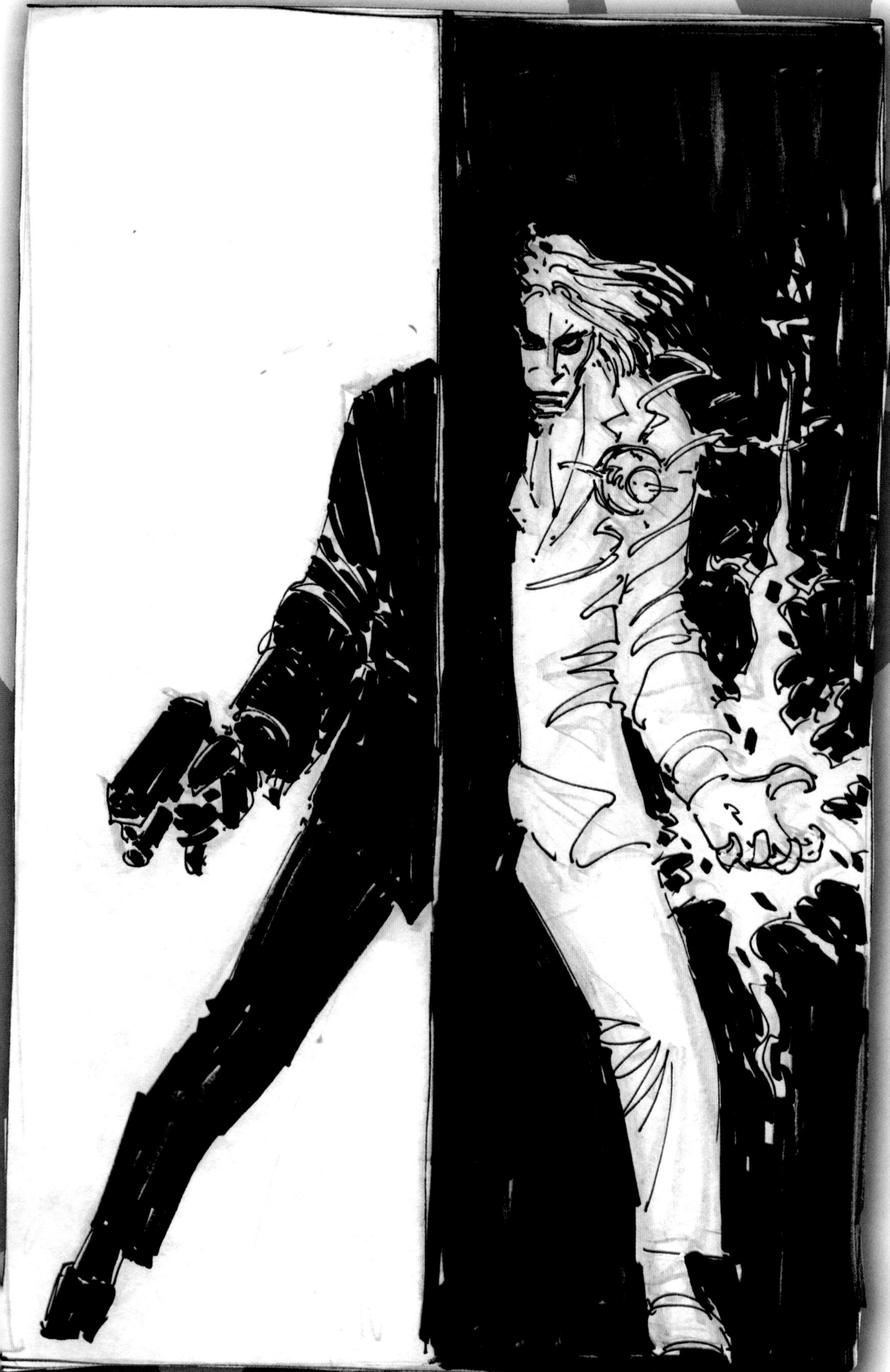

John's final cover sketch. keeping the black and white design, John moved the figure slightly off center. Now, in addition to good and evil, the figure appears to be passing into the afterlife world of the Gray Area as well.

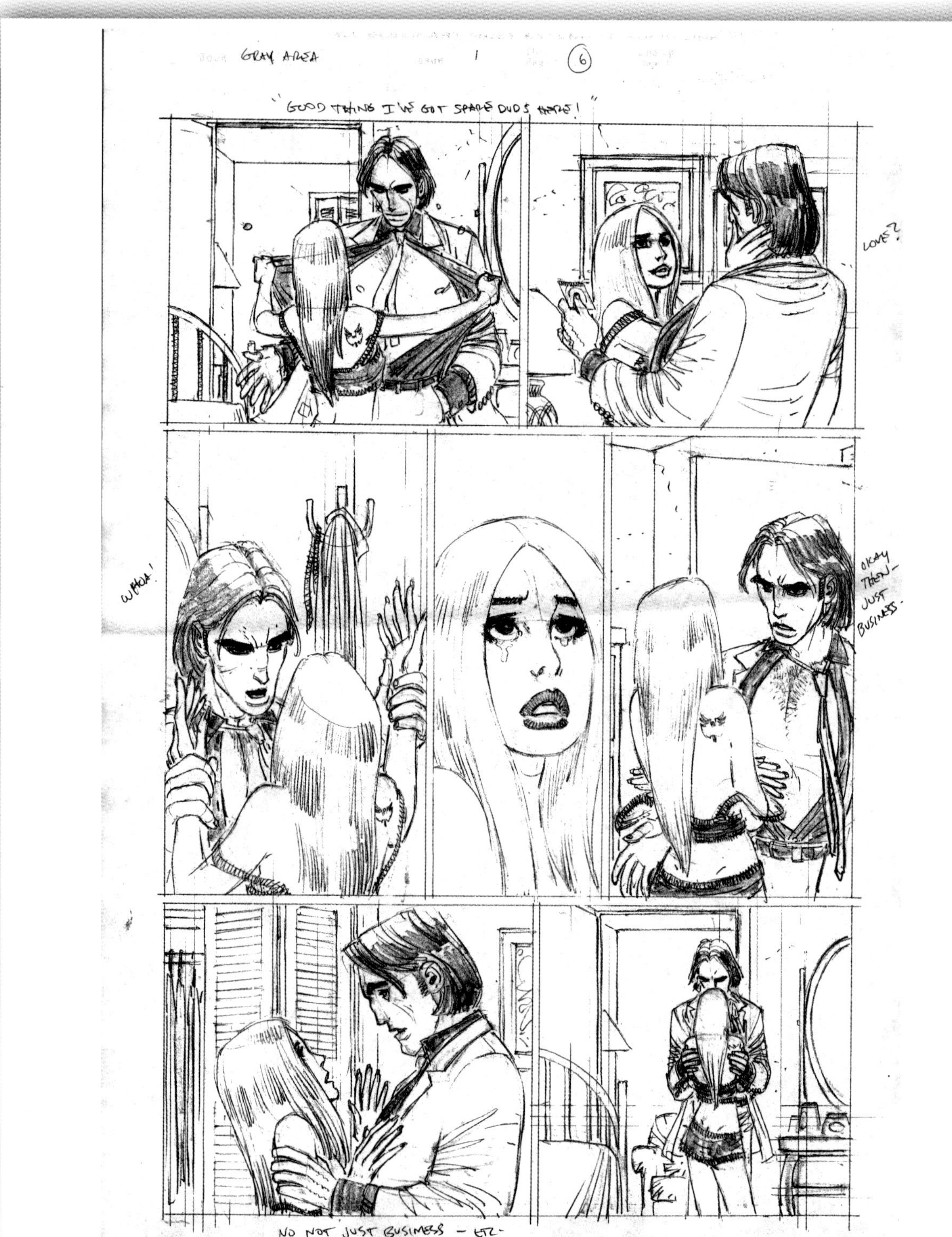
GRAY AREA
1
6
"GOOD THING I'VE GOT SPARE DUDS HERE!"
LOVE?
WHOA!
OKAY THEN— JUST BUSINESS.
NO NOT JUST BUSINESS — ETC.

I think this page is pretty hot. In the original treatment I had Emma kneeling down in front of Chance while unbuttoning his pants. John thought it was a little racy and opted for Emma just undoing her straps instead.

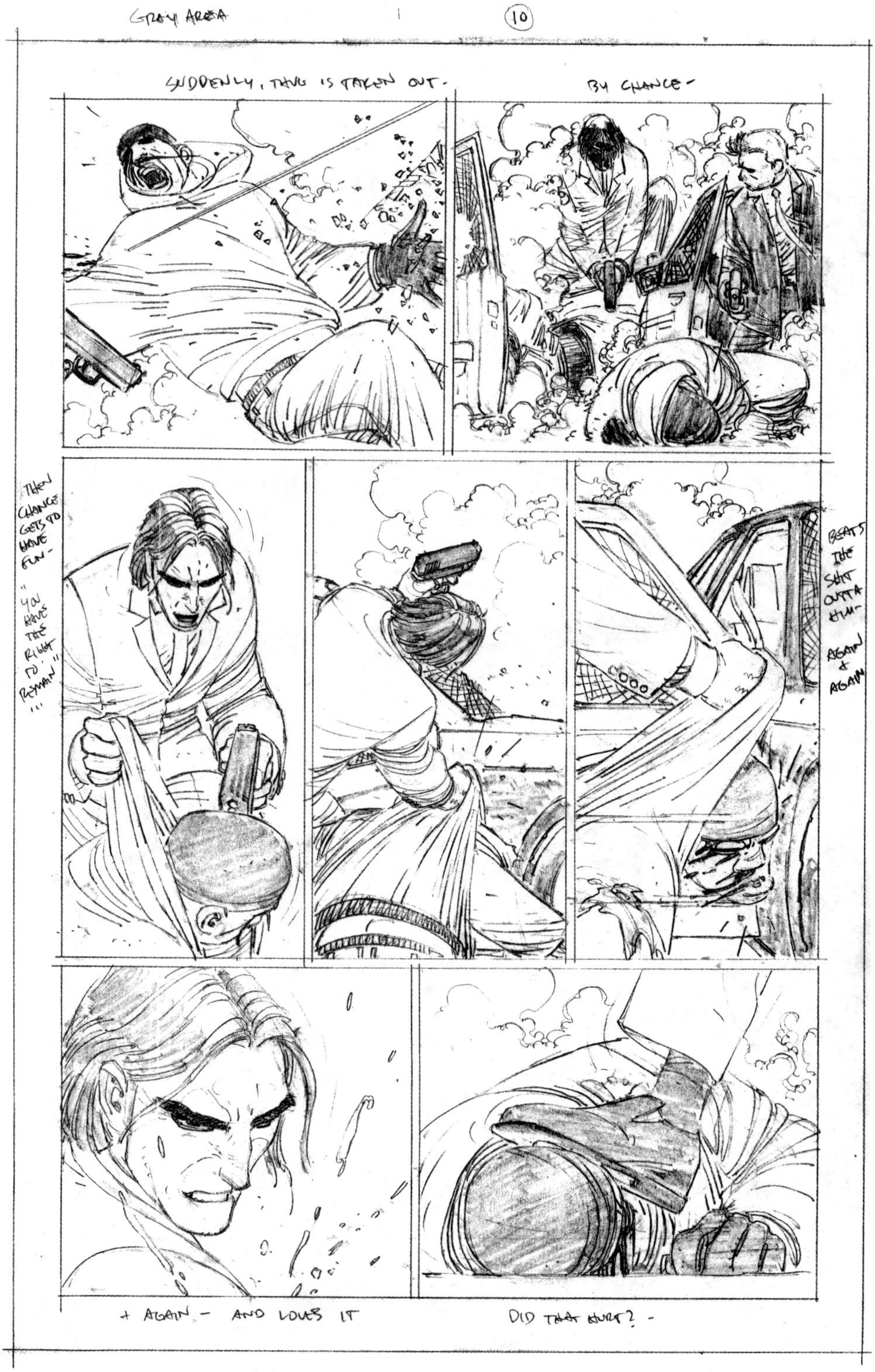
GRAY AREA
10
SUDDENLY, THUG IS TAKEN OUT -
BY CHANCE -
THEN CHANCE GETS TO HAVE FUN -
"YOU HAVE THE RIGHT TO REMAIN"...
BEATS THE SHIT OUTTA HIM - AGAIN + AGAIN
+ AGAIN - AND LOVES IT
DID THAT HURT? -

This page is one of my favorites. It's the first time we get to see Chance as a brutal enforcer. I hadn't written anything on this page before John drew it. it was simply an action page with no dialogue. John added the note that had Chance reading the perp his rights and that just did it for me. I decided to riff on that theme in a way unique to Chance's brutality.

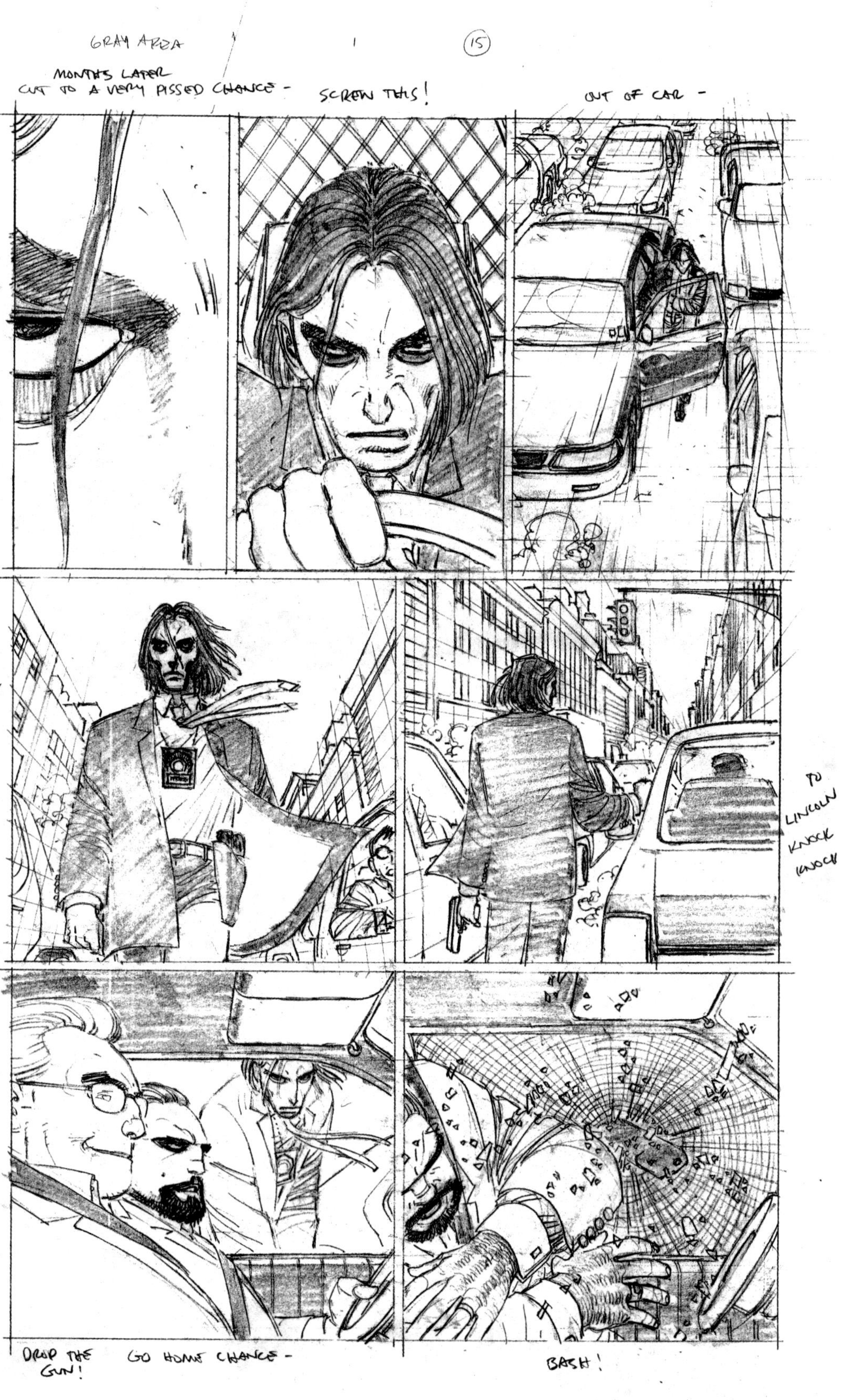
GRAY AREA
15
MONTHS LATER
CUT TO A VERY PISSED CHANCE -
SCREW THIS!
OUT OF CAR -
WALKS-
HORNS
HONK
ETC
TO
LINCOLN
KNOCK
KNOCK
DROP THE GUN!
GO HOME CHANCE -
BASH!

Originally I had planned for Chance to curse at the guy stuck in traffic. I wanted Chance to flip him off and then show him his badge. At first we thought of this book as R rated but we decided to scale it back to more of a PG instead. I love the way John illustrates Chance here. he conveys a real sense of the walking death that Chance feels with the loss of his family.

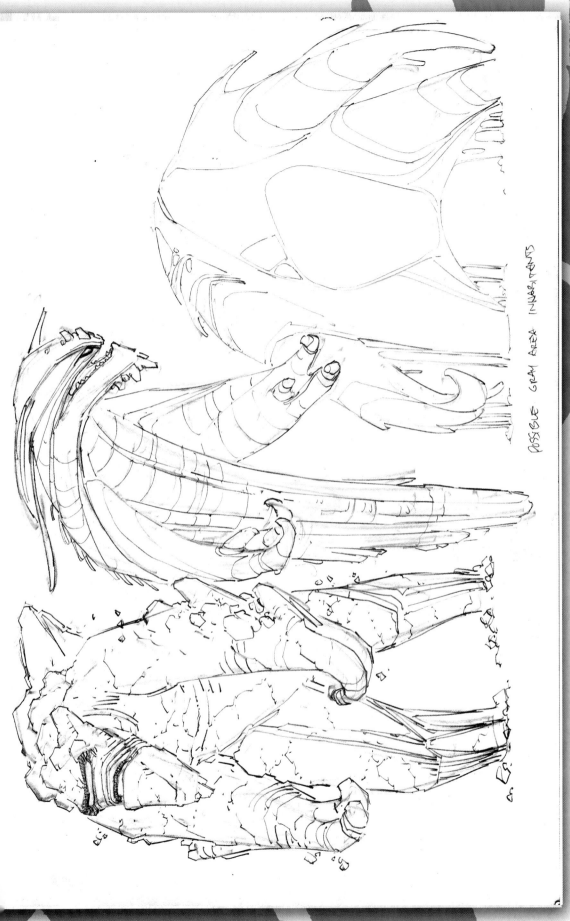

POSSIBLE GRAY AREA INHABITANTS

Originally we were going to have aliens populate the Gray Area as well. Ultimately we decided it would overcomplicate the story. We kept the name of Beebonock and just made him human instead.

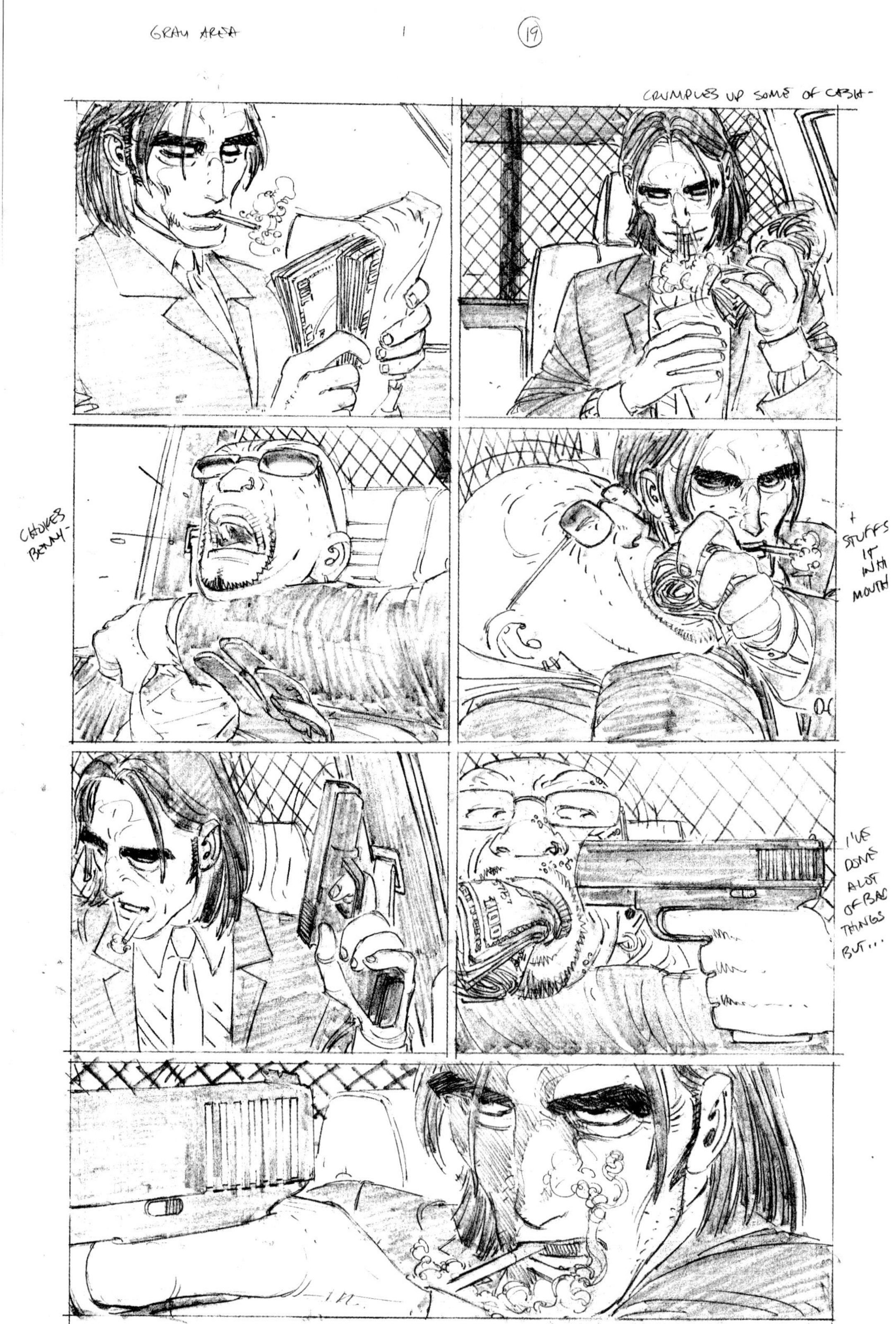
GRAY AREA
1
19
CRUMPLES UP SOME OF CASH -
CHOKES BENNY -
+ STUFFS IT IN HIS MOUTH
I'VE DONE A LOT OF BAD THINGS BUT...
... NEVER KILLED A MAN --- . TELL ME WHERE KARL IS ... AND YOU'LL LIVE!

When I saw this page I was floored. I had written this page in advance as deadly serious moment. But when I saw the third panel I just couldn't leave it alone. I had to throw in the "Say Ahhh!" joke that Chance makes while choking Benny.

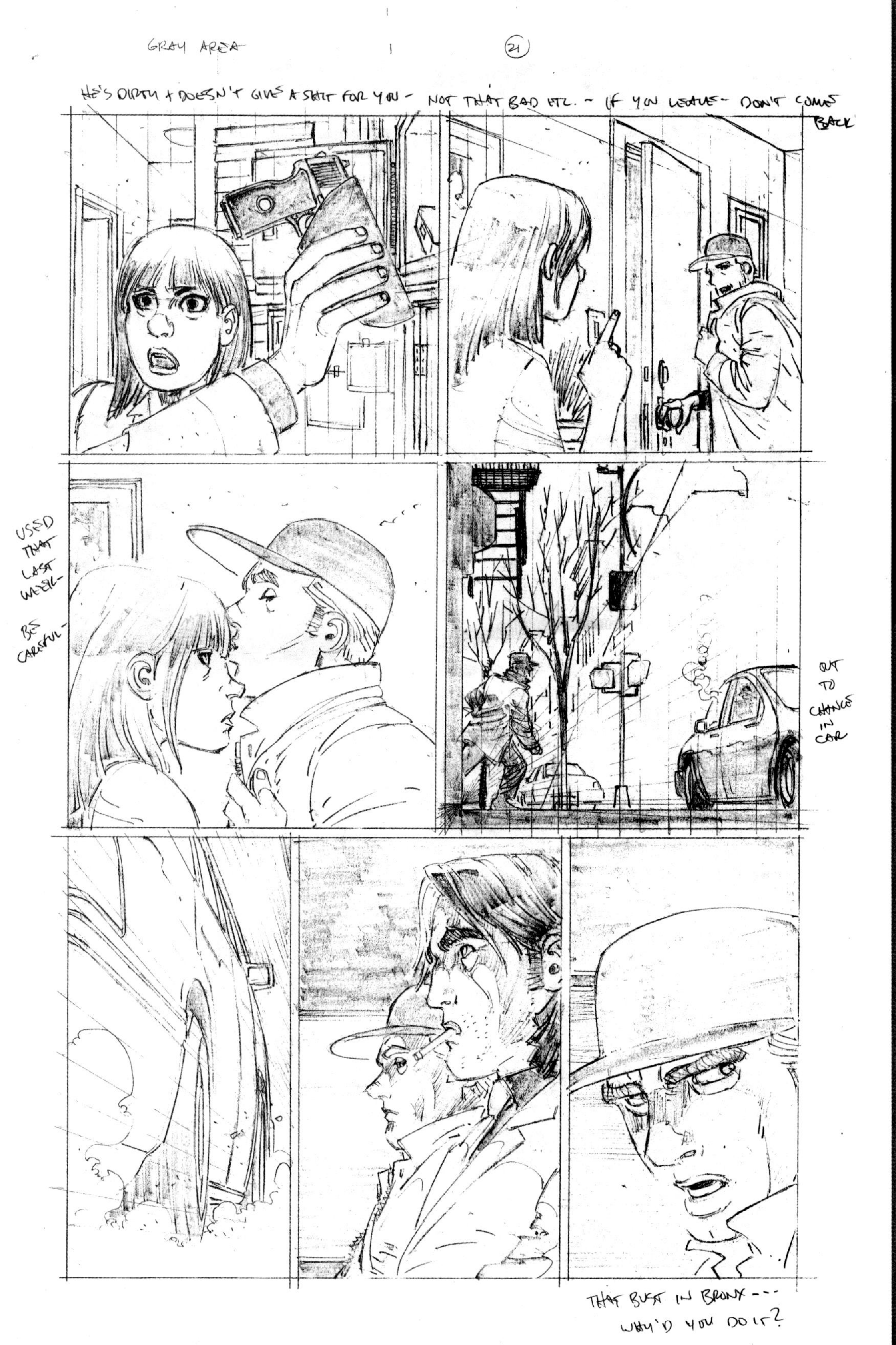
GRAY AREA
1
21
HE'S DIRTY + DOESN'T GIVE A SHIT FOR YOU - NOT THAT BAD ETC. - IF YOU LEAVE - DON'T COME BACK
USED THAT LAST WEEK - BE CAREFUL -
OUT TO CHANCE IN CAR
THAT BUST IN BRONX --- WHY'D YOU DO IT?

ooking at this page I just had to get inside Patty's head. Although Chance arrates most of the book I felt I had an opportunity here to explore Patty better. Throughout the story Patty has been fiercely loyal to Chance even hough he knows what a scumbag he is. I thought it would be interesting to show Patty second-guessing his decision to help Chance.

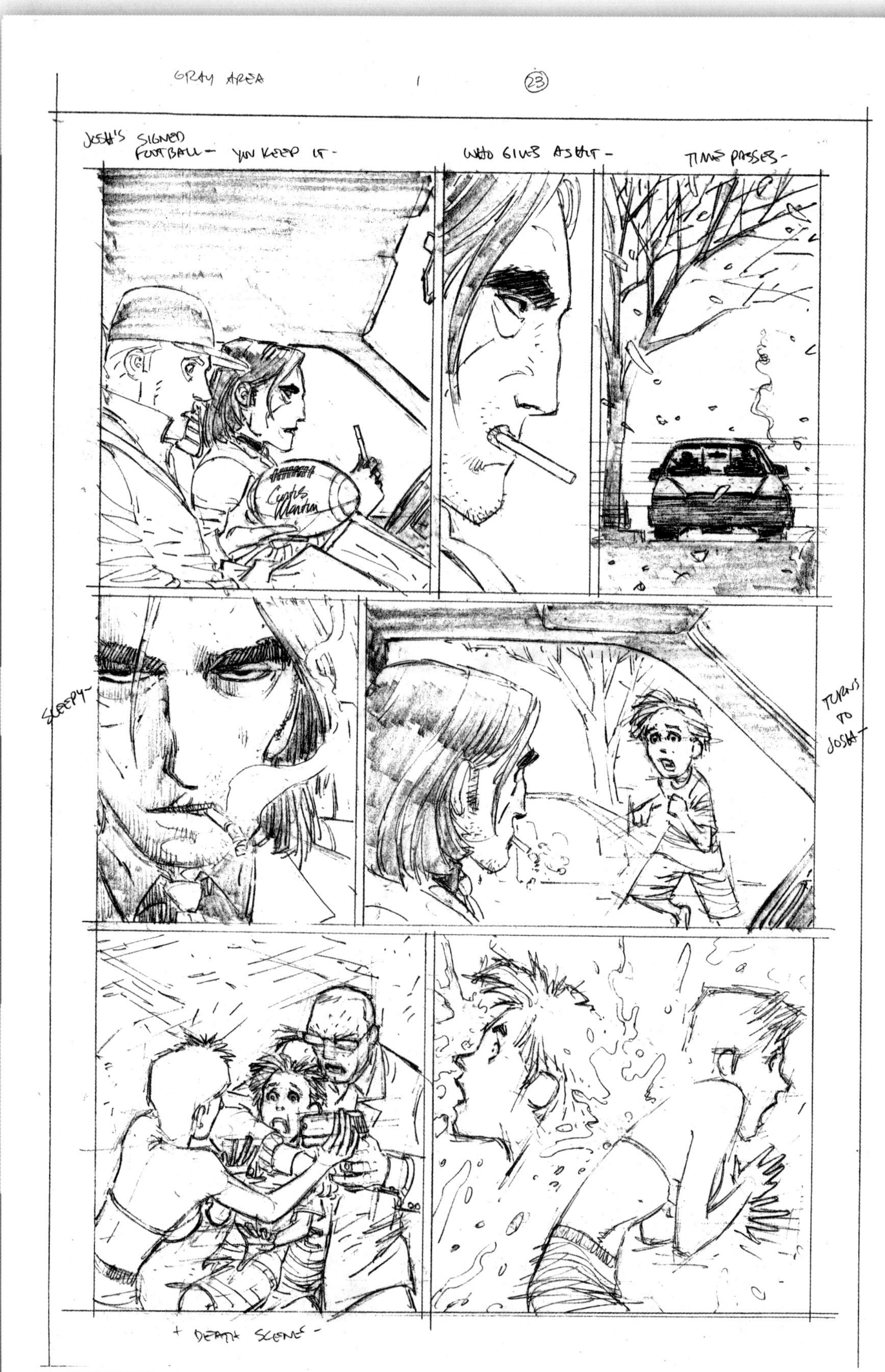
GRAY AREA
1
23
JOSH'S SIGNED FOOTBALL - YOU KEEP IT -
WHO GIVES A SHIT -
TIME PASSES -
SLEEPY -
TURNS TO JOSH -
+ DEATH SCENE -

My original idea for this page was to break away from Chance's narration. I thought third-person narration could offer a more poetic feel for the scene. Eric Stephenson pointed out that it felt jarring to abruptly switch from Chance's narration, so I switched back. Ultimately, I feel the printed version is more effective but I still miss the early words I wrote for this page. Sometimes you've got to kill your little darlings for the overall good of the story. The original narration is on the next page.

PAGE 23

PANEL ONE

> CHANCE
> You keep it.

> PATTY
> No! This was for the kid's
> birthday, huh?

PANEL TWO

> CHANCE
> Who gives a crap.

PANEL THREE

CAPTION

Another hour passes...

PANEL FOUR

CAPTION

Sleep takes hold of Chance.

PANEL FIVE

CAPTION

But no rest is dispensed. Just that reoccurring nightmare...

PANEL SIX

CAPTION

Where seconds and inches mean the difference between a life.

PANEL SEVEN

CAPTION

And a life shattered.

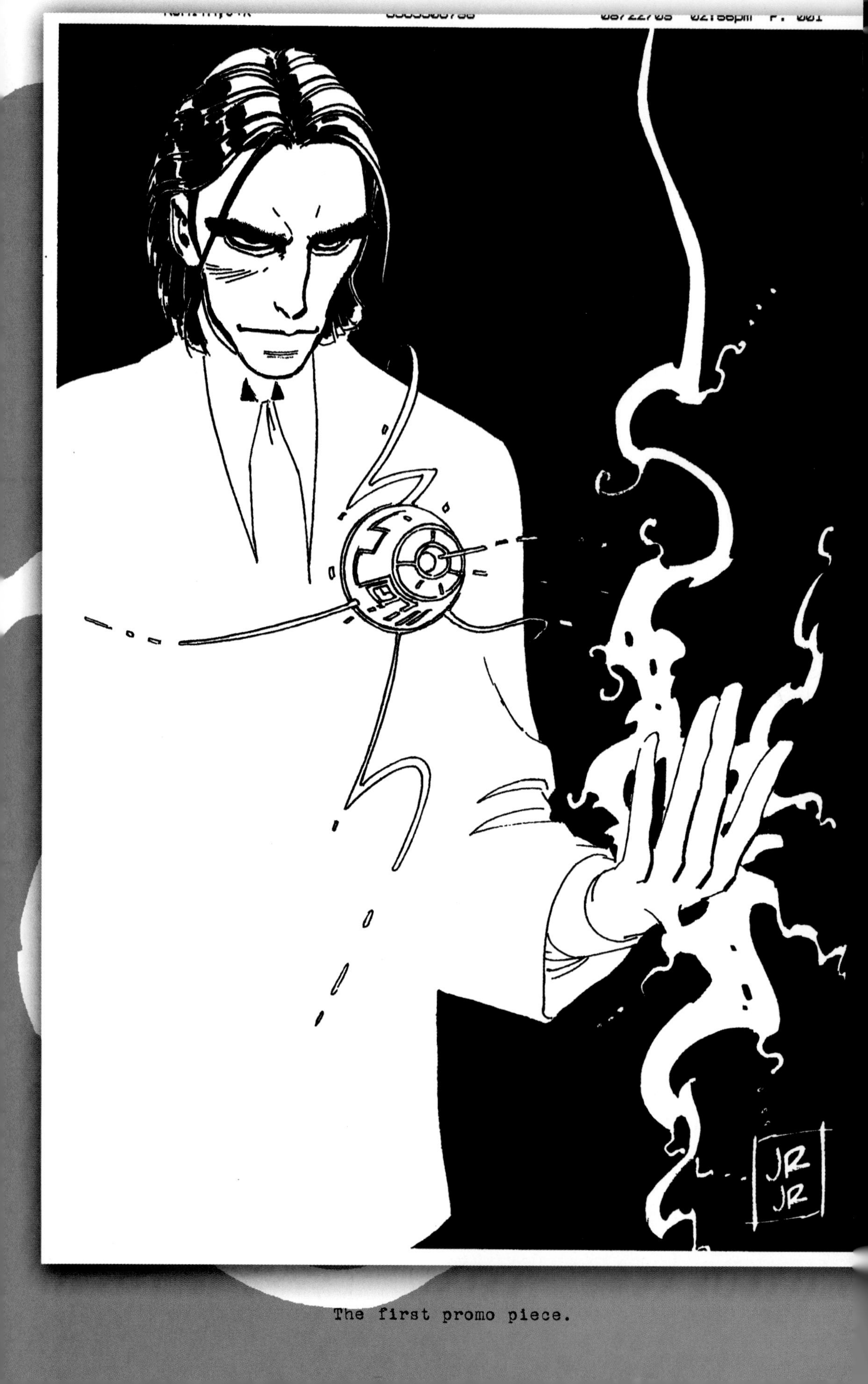
JR
JR

The first promo piece.

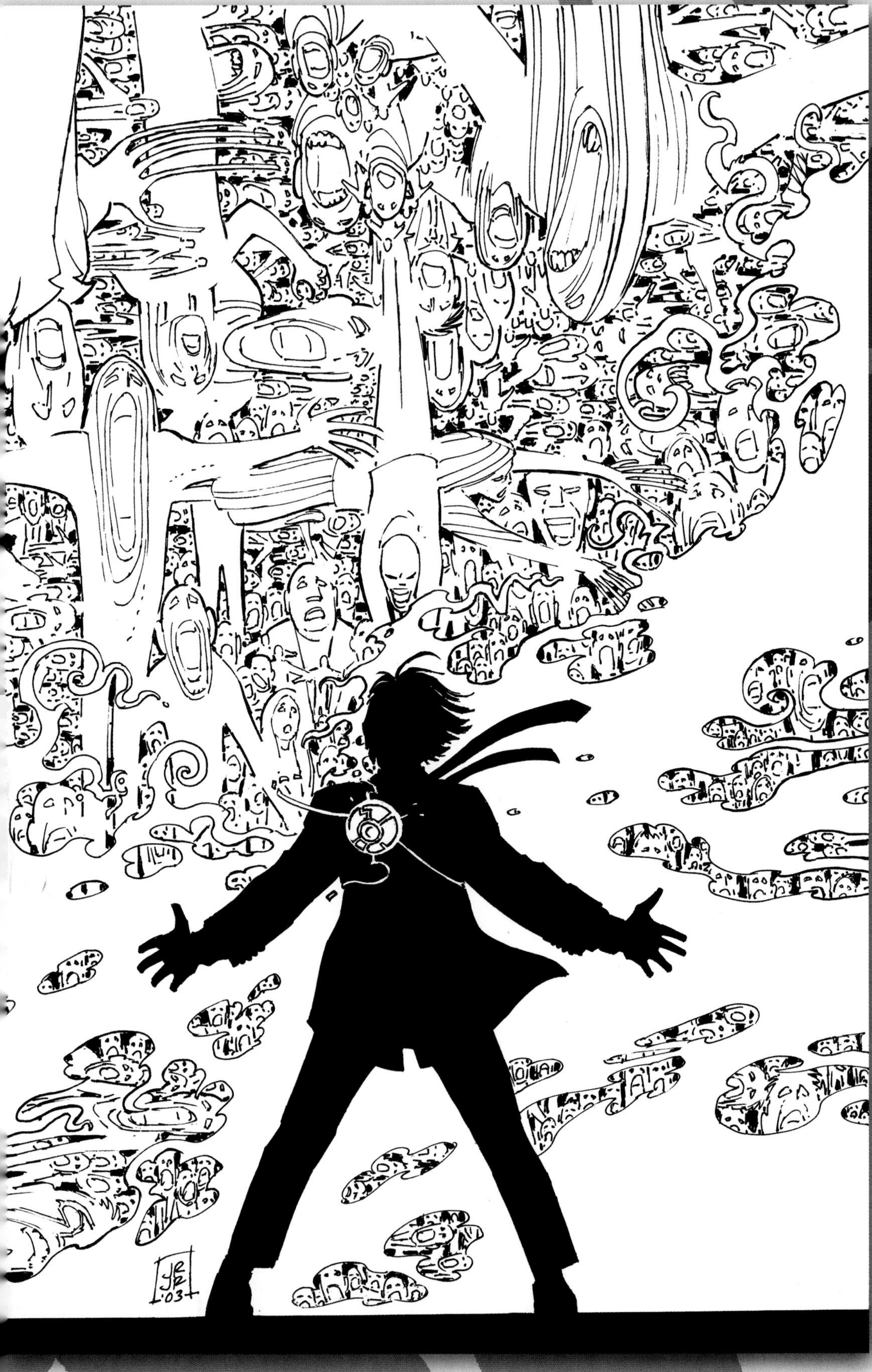

The second promo piece.

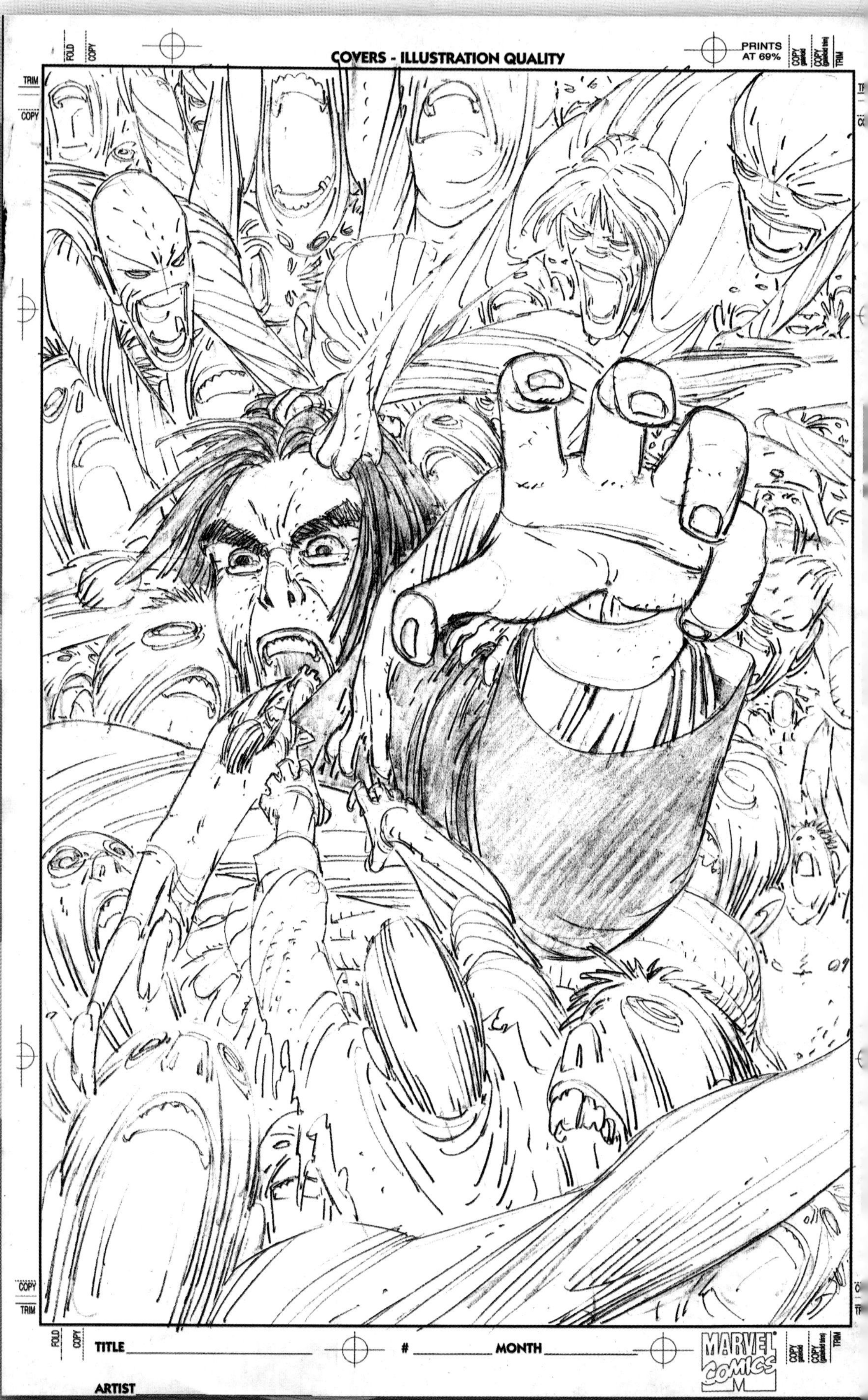
COVERS - ILLUSTRATION QUALITY
PRINTS AT 69%
TRIM
COPY
FOLD
TITLE
#
MONTH
ARTIST
MARVEL COMICS

John's initial cover illustration for issue two.